Profiles of Infamous Psycho Killers

Shah Rukh

Published by Shah Rukh, 2024.

While every precaution has been taken in the preparation of this book, the publisher assumes no responsibility for errors or omissions, or for damages resulting from the use of the information contained herein.

PROFILES OF INFAMOUS PSYCHO KILLERS

First edition. May 13, 2024.

ISBN: 979-8224758265

Written by Shah Rukh.

Table of Contents

Prologue

In the darkest corners of human history, where the boundaries between sanity and madness blur, there exist individuals whose names are etched into the annals of infamy. These are the men and women whose crimes defy comprehension, whose actions challenge our understanding of morality, and whose legacies are marked by terror, fascination, and endless debate. They are the psycho killers—monsters who walked among us, their malevolent desires hidden behind masks of normalcy.

This book, *Profiles of Infamous Psycho Killers*, delves into the chilling lives and minds of the most notorious serial killers and mass murderers to have ever existed. Each chapter offers a glimpse into the twisted psyche of these individuals, exploring the factors that may have driven them to commit such heinous acts and the lasting impact their crimes have had on society.

What compels a person to commit murder? Is it nature or nurture, a byproduct of environment or an inherent darkness within? While these questions may never have definitive answers, the stories within this book serve as a grim reminder of the capacity for evil that lurks within the human soul. From Jeffrey Dahmer's gruesome cannibalism to Jack the Ripper's unsolved killings, these profiles are not just about the crimes—they are about the killers themselves, their backgrounds, their methods, and the psychology that fueled their brutal acts.

But this book is more than just a collection of horror stories. It is an exploration of the macabre, an examination of the human condition when pushed to its most extreme limits. By studying these infamous figures, we seek to understand not just who they were, but what they reveal about the world we live in—a world where the line between sanity and madness is often perilously thin.

As you turn these pages, prepare to enter a realm where reality is more horrifying than fiction. This is not a journey for the faint of heart, but for those who dare to confront the darkness, it offers a chilling glimpse into the minds of those who have become legends of evil.

Welcome to the world of the infamous psycho killers.

Chapter 1: Jeffrey Dahmer

Jeffrey Lionel Dahmer was born on May 21, 1960, in Milwaukee, Wisconsin, to Lionel and Joyce Dahmer. His childhood was marked by a sense of alienation and disconnection. Dahmer's father, a research chemist, was often absorbed in his work, while his mother suffered from a series of mental health issues, including depression and anxiety. These family dynamics contributed to a tumultuous home environment, leaving young Jeffrey feeling increasingly isolated.

From a young age, Dahmer exhibited signs of abnormal behavior. He was fascinated by dead animals, often collecting roadkill and dissecting them in the woods near his home. This morbid curiosity was an early indicator of the darker tendencies that would later define his life. His parents' eventual divorce when he was 18 further exacerbated his feelings of abandonment and loneliness.

First Murder and Escalation

Dahmer's first murder occurred shortly after his high school graduation in 1978, when he was just 18 years old. His first victim was Steven Hicks, a hitchhiker whom Dahmer picked up on the side of the road. Dahmer lured Hicks to his home with the promise of drinking and listening to music. Once there, Dahmer bludgeoned Hicks with a dumbbell before strangling him to death. After killing Hicks, Dahmer dismembered the body and dissolved the flesh in acid, an act that would become a grim hallmark of his later murders.

Despite the horror of this first killing, Dahmer managed to suppress his violent urges for nearly a decade. He attempted to lead a relatively normal life, enrolling in college, joining the U.S. Army, and holding down various jobs. However, his struggles with alcohol and his inability to form meaningful relationships led to a downward spiral. By the late 1980s, Dahmer's homicidal impulses resurfaced with a vengeance.

The Milwaukee Murders

In 1987, Dahmer began a killing spree that would last until his arrest in 1991. During this time, he lured young men, often of African-American or Asian descent, to his apartment under the guise of offering money for photographs or companionship. Once inside, Dahmer would drug his victims, rendering them unconscious before proceeding to sexually assault and murder them. His methods were chillingly methodical; he dismembered the bodies, often keeping certain parts—such as the skulls or genitalia—as macabre trophies.

One of the most disturbing aspects of Dahmer's crimes was his practice of necrophilia and cannibalism. He confessed to eating the flesh of some of his victims, a grotesque act that earned him the nickname "The Milwaukee Cannibal." Dahmer also attempted to create "zombies" by drilling holes into the skulls of his victims and injecting hydrochloric acid or boiling water into their brains. His goal was to create a compliant, submissive partner who would never leave him—a reflection of his deep-seated fear of abandonment.

The Capture and Trial

Dahmer's reign of terror came to an end on July 22, 1991, when Tracy Edwards, a would-be victim, managed to escape from Dahmer's apartment and flagged down two police officers. Edwards led the officers back to Dahmer's apartment, where they discovered photographs of dismembered bodies and a decomposing human head in the refrigerator. The subsequent search revealed a veritable house of horrors, with severed body parts stored in various containers throughout the apartment.

Dahmer was arrested and quickly confessed to the murders, providing investigators with a detailed account of his gruesome activities. His trial began in January 1992 and was closely followed by the media and the public, who were both horrified and fascinated by the revelations of his crimes. Dahmer pleaded guilty but insane to 15 counts of murder, but the jury rejected his insanity plea, finding him legally sane and responsible for his actions.

In February 1992, Dahmer was sentenced to 15 consecutive life terms in prison, amounting to 957 years. Although he expressed remorse for his actions, many were skeptical of his sincerity, given the extreme brutality of his crimes.

Life in Prison and Death

Dahmer's time in prison was marked by a strange mix of notoriety and isolation. Despite his heinous crimes, he reportedly found religion and was baptized by a prison minister. Dahmer also corresponded with a number of individuals outside the prison, some of whom were oddly fascinated by him.

However, his notoriety made him a target within the prison population. On November 28, 1994, Dahmer was attacked and killed by a fellow inmate, Christopher Scarver, while cleaning a bathroom in the Columbia Correctional Institution in Portage, Wisconsin. Scarver later claimed that he was motivated by a combination of anger over Dahmer's crimes and a belief that Dahmer was unrepentant.

The Psychological Profile

Jeffrey Dahmer's crimes have been the subject of extensive psychological analysis. Many experts believe that Dahmer's actions were driven by a complex interplay of factors, including his feelings of alienation, his fascination with death, and his desire for control and dominance over others. Dahmer himself admitted that his need for companionship and fear of abandonment were central to his motivations. He sought to possess his victims completely, to the extent that he was willing to kill them to prevent them from leaving.

Some psychologists have speculated that Dahmer may have suffered from a paraphilic disorder, which is characterized by intense sexual arousal from atypical or extreme activities. In Dahmer's case, his paraphilias included necrophilia, cannibalism, and the desire to create living "zombies" out of his victims. These extreme fantasies likely developed as a way for Dahmer to cope with his deep-seated feelings of inadequacy and isolation.

Impact on Society and Popular Culture

The Jeffrey Dahmer case had a profound impact on American society, both in terms of the criminal justice system and the public's understanding of serial killers. The sheer brutality of his crimes, coupled with the fact that many of his victims were marginalized individuals—young men of color, often from lower socioeconomic backgrounds—raised serious questions about how the police and society at large handle cases involving vulnerable populations.

Dahmer's crimes also highlighted the shortcomings in the mental health system, particularly in its ability to identify and treat individuals with severe psychological disturbances. Dahmer had several encounters with the law before his final arrest, including a 1989 conviction for sexual assault, but these incidents did not prevent him from continuing his killing spree. This failure to intervene earlier has been a point of significant criticism.

In popular culture, Dahmer's story has been the subject of numerous books, documentaries, and films. These portrayals have ranged from attempts to understand the psychological complexities of his character to sensationalized accounts that focus on the more lurid aspects of his crimes. The fascination with Dahmer and other notorious serial killers speaks to a broader societal interest in the darkest aspects of human nature.

Ethical Considerations and Victim Remembrance

While the public's fascination with Jeffrey Dahmer is understandable, it is important to remember the ethical considerations involved in discussing and portraying his crimes. The focus on Dahmer as a criminal mastermind or a "celebrity" serial killer can sometimes overshadow the real tragedy of the lives lost and the pain endured by the victims' families. It is crucial to approach the subject with sensitivity, acknowledging the suffering caused by Dahmer's actions.

In recent years, there has been a growing movement to shift the narrative away from the killers themselves and toward the victims. Efforts have been made to memorialize the young men who lost their lives at Dahmer's hands, ensuring that they are remembered not just as victims of a horrific crime, but as individuals with their own stories, dreams, and aspirations.

Chapter 2: Richard Ramirez

Ricardo Leyva Muñoz Ramírez, known to the world as Richard Ramirez, was born on February 29, 1960, in El Paso, Texas. His early life was marred by violence, neglect, and a chaotic family environment, all of which played a significant role in shaping his later behavior. Ramirez was the youngest of five children born to Julian and Mercedes Ramirez, both of whom were immigrants from Mexico. His father, a former policeman who later worked on the Santa Fe Railroad, was a strict disciplinarian prone to violent outbursts. Ramirez's mother worked in a boot factory, where she was exposed to toxic chemicals that some speculate may have contributed to the birth defects and medical issues suffered by some of her children.

From a young age, Ramirez was exposed to graphic and disturbing imagery. His older cousin, Miguel "Mike" Ramirez, was a Vietnam War veteran who boasted about the atrocities he committed during the war, including rape and murder. Mike frequently shared photos of his crimes with Richard, including pictures of Vietnamese women he had sexually assaulted and murdered. This exposure to violence had a profound impact on the young Ramirez, who began to exhibit troubling behaviors such as bedwetting, a common early indicator of potential psychopathy.

In addition to the influence of his cousin, Ramirez was subjected to frequent physical abuse by his father. To escape the violence at home, he often spent nights in a local cemetery, where he began experimenting with drugs, including marijuana and LSD. The combination of familial violence, exposure to war crimes, and drug use contributed to a growing detachment from reality and a fascination with death and violence.

Teenage Years and First Brushes with the Law

As a teenager, Ramirez's behavior became increasingly erratic and criminal. He was frequently in trouble with the law for petty theft and burglary, crimes that would later escalate into much more serious offenses. He dropped out of high school in the ninth grade and began to drift aimlessly, often staying with relatives or living on the streets.

During this time, Ramirez became deeply interested in Satanism and the occult. He started to believe that he was under the protection of Satan, which further fueled his sense of invincibility and detachment from societal norms. He also developed a fascination with horror films, particularly those that depicted brutal violence and sadism. These influences coalesced into a warped worldview that would guide his actions in the years to come.

In 1973, Ramirez witnessed his cousin Mike murder his wife, Jessie, during a domestic dispute. The incident, which occurred right in front of Ramirez's eyes, left an indelible mark on him. Despite this, he continued to look up to Mike as a mentor and role model, further solidifying his belief in the power of violence.

By the age of 22, Ramirez had moved to California, where he began his descent into a life of crime that would soon escalate into one of the most terrifying crime sprees in American history.

The Night Stalker Emerges: Early Murders

Ramirez's reign of terror began in earnest in June 1984 when he committed his first known murder. His victim was a 79-year-old woman named Jennie Vincow, whom he sexually assaulted and brutally murdered in her Los Angeles apartment. The crime was particularly gruesome; Ramirez stabbed Vincow multiple times and slashed her throat so deeply that she was nearly decapitated. This murder set the tone for the brutal and sadistic nature of the crimes that would follow.

For the next year, Ramirez embarked on a killing spree that would earn him the nickname "The Night Stalker." He terrorized the residents of Los Angeles and later San Francisco with a series of home invasions, sexual assaults, and murders. Ramirez had no clear pattern in choosing his victims; they ranged in age from as young as nine to as old as 83, and they came from different ethnic backgrounds. His only consistent motive seemed to be the thrill of inflicting terror and suffering.

Ramirez's modus operandi was terrifyingly unpredictable. He would break into homes in the dead of night, often through an unlocked window or door, and attack his victims as they slept. His crimes were characterized by extreme brutality—he would bludgeon his victims with a hammer, shoot them with a handgun, or stab them with a knife. In many cases, he sexually assaulted his female victims before killing them. He often left satanic symbols, such as pentagrams, at the crime scenes, further heightening the sense of fear and mystique surrounding his actions.

The Psychological Profile of a Sadistic Killer

Richard Ramirez's psychological profile is complex and deeply disturbing. He exhibited many of the traits associated with psychopathy, including a lack of empathy, superficial charm, and a propensity for manipulation. However, what set Ramirez apart from other serial killers was his deep-seated belief in Satanism and his use of it as a justification for his crimes. He often claimed that Satan protected him and that he was acting on the devil's behalf.

Ramirez's childhood experiences, particularly the influence of his cousin Mike and the violent environment in which he was raised, likely played a significant role in shaping his sadistic tendencies. His early exposure to extreme violence desensitized him to the suffering of others, and his fascination with death and the occult provided a framework for understanding and rationalizing his actions.

Ramirez's drug use also contributed to his erratic and violent behavior. He frequently used cocaine, which heightened his aggression and paranoia, making him even more dangerous. His use of drugs, combined with his belief in Satanism, created a lethal combination that fueled his desire to commit increasingly brutal and sadistic crimes.

The Media Frenzy and Public Fear

As Ramirez's killing spree continued, the media dubbed him "The Night Stalker," a name that struck fear into the hearts of Californians. The press played a significant role in shaping the public's perception of Ramirez, portraying him as a shadowy, almost mythical figure who could strike at any moment. The randomness of his attacks and the brutality of his crimes led to widespread panic, with many residents taking extreme measures to protect themselves, such as installing new locks, adding security systems, and even sleeping with firearms.

The police were under immense pressure to catch Ramirez, but the investigation was hampered by the seemingly random nature of his crimes and his ability to evade capture. Despite this, investigators began to piece together clues that pointed to Ramirez as the suspect. His distinctive shoe print, left at multiple crime scenes, was one of the key pieces of evidence that linked him to the murders.

In August 1985, Ramirez's luck began to run out. He was identified by several witnesses who had seen him fleeing the scene of one of his attacks. A composite sketch was released to the public, and it wasn't long before Ramirez's face was plastered on the front pages of newspapers across the country.

The Capture and Trial

Richard Ramirez was finally apprehended on August 31, 1985, after being recognized by residents in East Los Angeles. After a failed carjacking attempt, Ramirez was chased down and subdued by a group of citizens who held him until the police arrived. His capture marked the end of a reign of terror that had left 14 people dead and many more injured.

Ramirez's trial was one of the most sensationalized in American history, drawing widespread media attention and public interest. During the proceedings, Ramirez showed little remorse for his actions, often smiling or making obscene gestures in court. His defiance and lack of remorse only served to reinforce his image as a cold-blooded killer.

The trial was also notable for Ramirez's bizarre behavior, which included frequent outbursts, threats against the judge, and his declaration of allegiance to Satan. At one point, he drew a pentagram on his palm and flashed it to the courtroom, further cementing his reputation as a man driven by dark, demonic forces.

In September 1989, Ramirez was convicted on 13 counts of murder, five counts of attempted murder, 11 counts of sexual assault, and 14 counts of burglary. He was sentenced to death and sent to San Quentin State Prison to await execution. However, due to the lengthy appeals process in California, Ramirez remained on death row for over two decades.

Ramirez's Life on Death Row and Death

While on death row, Richard Ramirez became something of a cult figure, attracting a number of followers and admirers, particularly women who were fascinated by his dark persona and the mystique surrounding his crimes. Ramirez received numerous letters from admirers, some of whom sent him money or gifts. In 1996, he even married one of his admirers, Doreen Lioy, a freelance magazine editor who believed in his innocence despite the overwhelming evidence against him.

Ramirez's time on death row was marked by a series of appeals, but none were successful in overturning his conviction. He remained defiant until the end, never expressing any genuine remorse for his crimes. On June 7, 2013, Ramirez died of complications related to B-cell lymphoma at the age of 53. His death brought a grim end to the life of one of America's most notorious serial killers.

The Legacy of the Night Stalker

The legacy of Richard Ramirez, the Night Stalker, is one of horror, fear, and the enduring fascination with the darkest aspects of human nature. His crimes have been the subject of numerous books, documentaries, and television shows, each attempting to unravel the mysteries of his psyche and the motives behind his brutal actions.

Ramirez's case also highlighted the vulnerabilities in society that allowed him to commit such heinous crimes for so long. The random nature of his attacks, coupled with the fear he instilled in the public, served as a stark reminder of the potential for evil that exists in the world. His ability to evade capture for over a year despite the efforts of law enforcement underscored the challenges faced by those tasked with protecting the public from individuals like Ramirez.

In the years since his death, Richard Ramirez has remained a figure of morbid fascination, his story serving as a chilling example of the depths of human depravity. While his crimes continue to haunt the memories of those who lived through his reign of terror, they also serve as a grim reminder of the importance of vigilance and the need to understand the psychological and social factors that contribute to the making of a serial killer.

Chapter 3: John Wayne Gacy

John Wayne Gacy, one of the most infamous serial killers in American history, was born on March 17, 1942, in Chicago, Illinois. His early life was marked by a tumultuous family environment, which played a significant role in shaping the person he would become. Gacy was the second of three children born to John Stanley Gacy and Marion Elaine Robinson. His father, a World War I veteran and machinist, was a strict disciplinarian with a violent temper. Gacy's father was also an alcoholic, prone to verbally and physically abusing his wife and children, particularly John, whom he often ridiculed as being weak and effeminate.

From a young age, Gacy struggled with his identity and self-worth. His father's relentless abuse left deep emotional scars, and Gacy spent much of his childhood seeking his father's approval, which he never received. This desire for acceptance and fear of rejection became central themes in Gacy's life, driving many of his later actions.

Despite the difficulties at home, Gacy was known as a bright and affable child. He had a natural charm and was well-liked by his peers. However, his school life was marred by health problems that frequently kept him out of class. He suffered from a congenital heart condition, which caused him to experience blackouts and seizures. These health issues further alienated him from his peers and exacerbated his feelings of inadequacy and isolation.

Gacy's troubled childhood also included instances of sexual abuse. At the age of seven, he was molested by a family friend, an incident he kept secret for years. The abuse added another layer of trauma to Gacy's already turbulent life and likely contributed to the development of his later deviant behavior.

Adulthood and the Formation of a Double Life

As Gacy entered adulthood, he began to create a façade of normalcy that masked his darker impulses. He attended Northwestern Business College, where he studied management and marketing. After graduation, he took a job as a manager in a shoe company, where his charm and work ethic quickly earned him promotions. In 1964, Gacy married Marlynn Myers, the daughter of a wealthy businessman, and moved to Waterloo, Iowa, where he took over the management of his father-in-law's chain of KFC restaurants.

On the surface, Gacy appeared to be living the American Dream. He was a successful businessman, a loving husband, and the father of two children. He was also an active member of his community, involved in various charitable organizations and even becoming a member of the local Jaycees, a leadership and civic organization. Gacy's public persona was one of a model citizen and family man, but behind closed doors, he was leading a very different life.

Gacy's marriage to Marlynn Myers was marked by tensions that stemmed from his sexual orientation. Although Gacy tried to maintain the appearance of a heterosexual family man, he struggled with his attraction to young men. His unresolved sexual identity issues, combined with the deep-seated emotional trauma from his childhood, created a dangerous internal conflict. Gacy began to act out his fantasies in secret, engaging in extramarital affairs with men and frequenting gay bars.

In 1968, Gacy's double life began to unravel when he was arrested and charged with sodomy. He had lured a teenage boy into his home, where he assaulted him. Gacy pleaded guilty to the charges and was sentenced to 10 years in prison. This marked a significant turning point in his life, as it was the first time his dark side had been exposed to the public.

While in prison, Gacy maintained his charm and manipulative tendencies. He was considered a model prisoner, earning the respect of the prison staff and even being granted early release after serving only 18 months of his sentence. However, his time in prison did little to rehabilitate him. If anything, it hardened his resolve to continue leading a double life, hiding his true nature from the world.

Return to Chicago and the Birth of the Killer Clown

After his release from prison, Gacy returned to Chicago in 1970. His marriage to Marlynn Myers had ended in divorce during his incarceration, and he was now free to start anew. Gacy quickly reintegrated into society, using his charm and business acumen to rebuild his life. He started his own construction company, PDM Contractors, which became quite successful. Gacy was once again seen as a respected member of his community, and he resumed his involvement in local civic organizations.

One of the most bizarre and chilling aspects of Gacy's life was his creation of the character "Pogo the Clown." Gacy joined the "Jolly Joker" clown club in 1975, where he performed at children's parties, hospitals, and charity events dressed as Pogo, a clown character he had created. Gacy's clown persona became a significant part of his public identity, further cementing his reputation as a friendly and generous man. However, this benign image was a grotesque contrast to the horrifying crimes he was committing in secret.

The Horrific Murders: A Reign of Terror

Between 1972 and 1978, John Wayne Gacy embarked on a killing spree that claimed the lives of at least 33 young men and boys. His victims were typically teenage boys or young men, many of whom were runaways or had been lured to Gacy's home under the pretense of job opportunities, social gatherings, or simply for a ride. Gacy's method of killing was both methodical and brutal. He would often handcuff his victims, telling them it was a magic trick, and then proceed to sexually assault and torture them before ultimately strangling or suffocating them to death.

Gacy was meticulous in his approach to murder. After killing his victims, he would often keep their bodies in his home for several days before burying them in the crawl space beneath his house. The crawl space became a mass grave, where he hid the evidence of his horrific crimes. When the crawl space became too full, Gacy began disposing of bodies in the Des Plaines River.

Despite the sheer number of his crimes, Gacy managed to evade suspicion for several years. He maintained his public image as a hardworking businessman and community leader, all while committing unspeakable atrocities. Gacy's ability to compartmentalize his life allowed him to continue his killing spree without drawing the attention of law enforcement.

The Investigation and Capture

Gacy's downfall began in December 1978, when 15-year-old Robert Piest went missing. Piest was last seen leaving his job at a pharmacy to meet with Gacy about a potential job opportunity. When Piest failed to return home, his parents reported him missing, and the police began to investigate. Gacy was quickly identified as the last person to have seen Piest, and the authorities obtained a search warrant for his home.

During the search of Gacy's home, police discovered evidence that linked him to several missing persons cases, including a receipt that belonged to another of his victims. The investigation intensified, and a second search warrant was issued, allowing the police to dig up the crawl space beneath Gacy's house. What they found was a scene of unimaginable horror: the remains of 29 bodies, all buried in various stages of decomposition. Four more bodies were later found in the Des Plaines River, bringing the total number of Gacy's known victims to 33.

Gacy was arrested on December 21, 1978, and quickly confessed to the murders. However, his confession was full of inconsistencies and contradictions, as he attempted to downplay his role in the killings by blaming others or claiming he was not in his right mind. Despite his attempts to evade responsibility, the overwhelming evidence against him left no doubt about his guilt.

The Trial and Conviction

John Wayne Gacy's trial began on February 6, 1980, in Cook County, Illinois. The trial was a media sensation, drawing national and international attention due to the gruesome nature of the crimes and Gacy's bizarre behavior. Gacy's defense team attempted to argue that he was insane and therefore not responsible for his actions. They claimed that Gacy suffered from multiple personality disorder and that his alter ego, "Jack Hanley," was responsible for the murders.

However, the prosecution successfully countered this argument by presenting evidence that Gacy had planned and executed the murders in a calculated and methodical manner. The prosecution also pointed to Gacy's ability to maintain a normal life and deceive those around him as proof that he was fully aware of his actions.

The jury deliberated for less than two hours before finding Gacy guilty of all 33 murders. On March 13, 1980, he was sentenced to death by lethal injection. Gacy showed little emotion upon hearing the verdict, maintaining his innocence and claiming that he had been set up by others.

Life on Death Row and Psychological Examination

John Wayne Gacy spent 14 years on death row at Menard Correctional Center in Chester, Illinois. During this time, he continued to assert his innocence, often giving interviews in which he blamed others for the murders or claimed that he had been framed. Gacy's time on death row was also marked by his bizarre and manipulative behavior. He became known for his artwork, particularly his paintings of clowns, which he sold to collectors and fans. The macabre fascination with Gacy's artwork only added to his notoriety.

Psychologists and criminologists who studied Gacy's case have offered various theories about his mental state and motivations. Some believe that Gacy suffered from antisocial personality disorder, a condition characterized by a lack of empathy, manipulative behavior, and a disregard for the rights of others. Others have suggested that his actions were driven by deep-seated feelings of inadequacy, stemming from his abusive childhood and unresolved sexual identity conflicts. These psychological factors, combined with Gacy's ability to compartmentalize his life, allowed him to commit his heinous crimes while maintaining a façade of normalcy.

Some experts have speculated that Gacy's persona as "Pogo the Clown" may have been a symbolic expression of his internal conflict. The clown, often seen as a figure of joy and innocence, contrasted sharply with Gacy's dark and violent nature. This duality mirrored the dichotomy in Gacy's life—his public image as a successful, charitable man versus his secret life as a sadistic murderer.

Execution and Legacy

On May 10, 1994, John Wayne Gacy was executed by lethal injection at Stateville Correctional Center in Crest Hill, Illinois. His execution marked the end of one of the most notorious criminal cases in American history. Gacy's final words were reportedly, "Kiss my ass," reflecting his defiant and unrepentant attitude until the very end.

Gacy's legacy is one of horror and infamy. He is often cited as one of the most depraved serial killers in history, and his crimes have left an indelible mark on popular culture. His case has been the subject of numerous books, documentaries, and films, and his name is often mentioned in discussions about the psychology of serial killers and the criminal justice system's handling of such individuals.

The investigation into Gacy's crimes also had a lasting impact on law enforcement practices, particularly in how missing persons cases involving young men were handled. The sheer scale of Gacy's murders and the length of time he was able to evade capture prompted changes in how police investigated similar cases, leading to improvements in communication between jurisdictions and the establishment of more comprehensive databases for tracking missing persons.

The Victims: Remembering the Lives Lost

While much of the focus on John Wayne Gacy has been on his crimes and psychological profile, it is important to remember the lives of his victims. The young men and boys who fell prey to Gacy's manipulations were individuals with hopes, dreams, and families who loved them. Many of Gacy's victims were vulnerable, either because they were runaways or seeking employment, which made them easy targets for his predatory tactics.

In the years since Gacy's arrest, efforts have been made to identify all of his victims and provide closure to their families. Some victims remained unidentified for years, their remains discovered in the crawl space of Gacy's home without any clear indication of their identity. Advances in forensic technology, including DNA testing, have helped to identify some of these victims, but others remain unknown.

Memorials have been established to honor the memory of Gacy's victims, ensuring that they are not forgotten in the shadow of their killer's infamy. These memorials serve as a reminder of the human cost of Gacy's crimes and the importance of remembering those who lost their lives to his brutality.

Cultural Impact and Media Representation

John Wayne Gacy's crimes have had a significant impact on popular culture, inspiring countless books, documentaries, and films. His case is often referenced in discussions about serial killers, and his persona as "Pogo the Clown" has become an enduring symbol of the terrifying potential for evil to exist behind a seemingly benign façade.

Gacy's story has been the subject of numerous true crime documentaries, each exploring different aspects of his life and crimes. These documentaries often delve into the psychological factors that drove Gacy to kill, as well as the failures in the criminal justice system that allowed him to continue his killing spree for so long.

In addition to documentaries, Gacy's crimes have also inspired works of fiction, including films and television series that draw on elements of his case. These fictionalized accounts often emphasize the horror of Gacy's actions and the chilling reality that such evil can exist in the most unsuspected places.

Chapter 4: Ted Bundy

Ted Bundy remains one of the most infamous and enigmatic serial killers in American history. His crimes shocked the nation and left an indelible mark on the criminal justice system and popular culture. Unlike many other serial killers, Bundy was not an outcast or someone who fit the traditional profile of a murderer. Instead, he was a charismatic, well-educated, and attractive man who used his charm to lure his victims. The juxtaposition of his outward appearance and his heinous actions has made Ted Bundy a subject of enduring fascination and horror.

Early Life and Background

Theodore Robert Bundy was born on November 24, 1946, in Burlington, Vermont. He was the illegitimate son of Eleanor Louise Cowell, and for the first few years of his life, he was raised by his maternal grandparents, who led him to believe they were his parents and that his mother was his older sister. This deception and the stigma of illegitimacy would later be cited by some as a contributing factor to Bundy's psychological issues.

Bundy's early life appeared relatively normal, but there were hints of the darkness that would later consume him. He exhibited signs of social awkwardness and had difficulty forming relationships with his peers. Despite these early challenges, Bundy was intelligent and excelled academically, eventually attending the University of Puget Sound before transferring to the University of Washington to study psychology.

During his time at the University of Washington, Bundy fell in love with a young woman who fit the type of many of his future victims—attractive, with long dark hair parted in the middle. This relationship ended in heartbreak when the woman ended their relationship, a rejection that reportedly had a profound impact on Bundy. Some speculate that this breakup was a catalyst for his later crimes, as many of his victims bore a striking resemblance to his first love.

The Emergence of a Serial Killer

Bundy's first known attempted abduction occurred in 1969, but it was not until the mid-1970s that he began his killing spree in earnest. His modus operandi involved using his charm and good looks to gain the trust of young women, often feigning an injury or pretending to be an authority figure to lure them into his car. Once they were in his grasp, Bundy would overpower them, sexually assault them, and then murder them. He often revisited the bodies of his victims, engaging in necrophilic acts and sometimes keeping body parts as trophies.

Bundy's killing spree spanned multiple states, including Washington, Oregon, Utah, Colorado, and Florida, making him one of the most elusive and difficult-to-catch serial killers of his time. His ability to blend in with society, coupled with his intelligence and cunning, allowed him to evade capture for years.

Arrest, Escape, and Recapture

Ted Bundy's first arrest occurred on August 16, 1975, in Salt Lake City, Utah, when he was pulled over by police. A search of his vehicle revealed a crowbar, handcuffs, and other suspicious items, leading to his arrest for suspicion of burglary. However, it was not until later those investigators began to connect Bundy to the disappearances of several young women.

In 1976, Bundy was convicted of kidnapping Carol DaRonch, one of the few women who managed to escape his clutches. He was sentenced to 15 years in prison, but this was far from the end of his criminal activities. While awaiting trial for murder in Colorado, Bundy managed to escape from custody twice. The first escape occurred in June 1977, when Bundy jumped from a second-story courthouse window and evaded capture for six days. The second escape, in December of the same year, saw Bundy flee from the Garfield County Jail by sawing through the ceiling of his cell and crawling through a crawl space to freedom.

After his second escape, Bundy made his way to Florida, where he committed some of his most brutal murders. On January 15, 1978, Bundy broke into the Chi Omega sorority house at Florida State University and attacked four women, killing two of them. His final known murder was the abduction and killing of 12-year-old Kimberly Leach, whose body was found weeks later.

Trial and Media Sensation

Ted Bundy's trial was one of the first to be nationally televised, and it became a media sensation. Bundy, who was a former law student, chose to represent himself in court, adding to the spectacle. His courtroom demeanor, combined with his charm and intelligence, captivated the public and created an unsettling dichotomy between his appearance and the heinousness of his crimes.

Bundy's trial also highlighted significant issues within the criminal justice system, particularly regarding how serial killers were prosecuted and how media coverage could influence public perception. Despite his efforts to manipulate the legal process, Bundy was found guilty of the Chi Omega murders and sentenced to death in 1979. In 1980, he was also convicted of the murder of Kimberly Leach and received a second death sentence.

Psychological Profile and Motives

Understanding Ted Bundy's psychological profile has been the subject of extensive analysis by criminologists, psychologists, and forensic experts. Bundy himself provided numerous interviews and insights into his mind, though he often contradicted himself and provided misleading information, making it difficult to discern the truth.

Bundy was diagnosed by some experts as a sociopath or psychopath, characterized by his lack of empathy, manipulative behavior, and ability to charm others. He exhibited signs of narcissistic personality disorder, believing himself to be above the law and capable of outsmarting those around him. Bundy's murders were often sexually motivated, and he later admitted that he was addicted to pornography, which he claimed fueled his violent fantasies.

One of the most chilling aspects of Bundy's psychology was his ability to compartmentalize his life. He maintained relationships, held down jobs, and even volunteered for political campaigns while simultaneously engaging in a campaign of terror against young women. This duality made him an especially dangerous individual, as he was able to operate under the radar for so long.

Final Confessions and Execution

In the days leading up to his execution, Ted Bundy finally began to confess to some of his crimes, revealing the full extent of his depravity. He admitted to killing at least 30 women across several states, though some believe the actual number could be much higher. Bundy's confessions were often vague and self-serving, with him sometimes providing information in exchange for delays in his execution.

Bundy's final hours were marked by a flurry of media attention and public debate over the death penalty. On January 24, 1989, Ted

Bundy was executed in the electric chair at Florida State Prison. His execution was witnessed by hundreds of people outside the prison, many of whom celebrated the end of one of the most notorious serial killers in American history.

Impact on Society and Legacy

Ted Bundy's crimes had a profound impact on American society and the criminal justice system. His ability to evade capture for so long highlighted the need for better coordination between law enforcement agencies across state lines. His case also underscored the importance of forensic evidence, particularly in the use of bite mark analysis, which was pivotal in his conviction for the Chi Omega murders.

Bundy's legacy continues to influence how serial killers are portrayed in the media and understood by the public. His case has been the subject of numerous books, documentaries, and films, each attempting to unravel the complexities of his mind and the horrors he inflicted on his victims.

Bundy's story also serves as a cautionary tale about the dangers of underestimating individuals who do not fit the traditional profile of a criminal. His ability to manipulate and charm those around him allowed him to carry out his crimes undetected for years, making him one of the most dangerous serial killers in history.

The Victims: Remembering Those Who Were Lost

While Ted Bundy's name is well-known, it is important to remember the lives of his victims, who were tragically cut short by his actions. The young women who fell prey to Bundy's manipulations were daughters, sisters, and friends, each with their own hopes, dreams, and potential. The impact of their loss continues to be felt by their families and communities.

Efforts have been made to memorialize Bundy's victims, ensuring that they are not forgotten in the shadow of their killer's infamy. Memorials, scholarships, and awareness campaigns have been established in their honor, serving as a reminder of the human cost of Bundy's crimes and the importance of vigilance in protecting others from similar predators.

Cultural Impact and Representation in Media

Ted Bundy's story has permeated popular culture, inspiring countless true crime narratives and fictionalized accounts. His case is often cited in discussions about the psychology of serial killers, the criminal justice system, and the media's role in shaping public perception. Films such as "The Deliberate Stranger" and "Extremely Wicked, Shockingly Evil and Vile" have dramatized Bundy's life and crimes, with actors like Mark Harmon and Zac Efron portraying the killer on screen.

These portrayals have sparked debates about the ethics of depicting real-life criminals in entertainment media, particularly when such depictions risk glamorizing or romanticizing their actions. While some argue that these films and documentaries serve to educate the public and keep the memory of the victims alive, others contend that they risk sensationalizing the crimes and focusing too much on the killer rather than the impact on the victims and their families.

Chapter 5: Charles Manson

Charles Manson is one of the most notorious figures in American criminal history. Known primarily as the mastermind behind the infamous Manson Family murders, Manson's name has become synonymous with evil, manipulation, and the darkest aspects of human nature. His ability to control and manipulate his followers, combined with the brutal nature of the crimes he orchestrated, has made him a subject of morbid fascination for decades. Manson's story is not just one of murder, but of psychological manipulation, the power of charisma, and the social upheaval of the 1960s.

Early Life and Troubled Beginnings

Charles Milles Manson was born on November 12, 1934, in Cincinnati, Ohio, to Kathleen Maddox, a 16-year-old girl who was both unmarried and struggling with alcohol addiction. Manson's early life was marked by instability and neglect. His mother was often absent, leaving young Charles in the care of relatives or in state institutions. Manson's father was a transient laborer who had little to do with him, and his mother was eventually imprisoned for robbery. During her incarceration, Manson was placed in a series of homes, foster care, and reform schools, where he began to develop a deep resentment towards authority figures.

Manson's childhood was marked by delinquency and crime. He committed his first known crime at the age of nine, and by his teenage years, he was already deeply entrenched in a life of petty crime, including theft and burglary. Manson was frequently in and out of juvenile detention centers, where he reportedly suffered from abuse and neglect. This troubled upbringing likely played a significant role in shaping Manson's later behavior and his ability to manipulate others.

The Birth of the Manson Family

In the 1960s, Charles Manson emerged from prison with a new vision of himself as a messianic figure. He was deeply influenced by the counterculture movement of the time, as well as by the music of The Beatles and the teachings of various religious and spiritual leaders. Manson moved to San Francisco during the Summer of Love in 1967, where he began to attract a group of followers, primarily young women, who were drawn to his charisma and his message of love, freedom, and rejection of conventional society.

Manson's followers, who would later be known as the Manson Family, were typically young people who were disillusioned with mainstream society. Many of them were from middle-class backgrounds but had dropped out of society in search of meaning and belonging. Manson provided them with a sense of purpose and community, albeit one built on twisted ideologies and a perverse interpretation of the countercultural ethos.

The Manson Family eventually relocated to the Spahn Ranch, an old movie set in the California desert, where they lived in a commune-like setting. It was here that Manson's influence over his followers deepened. He began to preach about an impending race war, which he called "Helter Skelter," a term he borrowed from The Beatles' song of the same name. Manson believed that this apocalyptic race war would lead to the downfall of society, after which he and his followers would emerge as the new leaders of the world.

Manson's Ideology and the Concept of Helter Skelter

Manson's ideology was a convoluted mixture of apocalyptic beliefs, racial hatred, and twisted interpretations of popular culture. At the heart of his teachings was the idea of "Helter Skelter," a term Manson used to describe an impending race war between whites and African Americans. He believed that this war would be ignited by acts of violence and chaos, which he and his followers would instigate.

Manson's interpretation of The Beatles' "White Album" played a significant role in shaping his beliefs. He believed that the album contained hidden messages that predicted the coming of this race war and that it was his duty to bring about the chaos necessary to trigger it. Manson told his followers that after the race war had devastated society, they would emerge from their hiding place in the desert to take control and lead the surviving population.

This delusional belief system provided the justification for the murders that would soon follow. Manson convinced his followers that they were the chosen ones, destined to carry out his vision and bring about the new order. His charismatic authority and the isolation of the group at the Spahn Ranch allowed him to exert near-total control over his followers, who were willing to commit horrific acts of violence at his command.

The Tate-LaBianca Murders

The most infamous crimes associated with Charles Manson are the Tate-LaBianca murders, which took place in Los Angeles in August 1969. These murders were carried out by Manson's followers under his direction, and they shocked the nation with their brutality and apparent senselessness.

On the night of August 8, 1969, Manson sent several of his followers, including Susan Atkins, Patricia Krenwinkel, and Charles "Tex" Watson, to the home of actress Sharon Tate. Tate, who was eight months pregnant at the time, was married to film director Roman Polanski, who was away in Europe. Also present in the house were Tate's friends, including Jay Sebring, a celebrity hairstylist;

Abigail Folger, the heiress to the Folger coffee fortune; and Wojciech Frykowski, a friend of Polanski's.

Manson's followers were instructed to kill everyone in the house and to make the murders as gruesome as possible. The killers brutally murdered all five victims, writing the word "PIG" on the front door of the house in Tate's blood. The brutality of the murders and the fact that the victims were seemingly chosen at random created a sense of fear and panic in Los Angeles and across the country.

The following night, on August 9, 1969, Manson himself joined his followers in selecting the next victims. They drove to the home of Leno and Rosemary LaBianca, a wealthy couple who lived in the Los Feliz neighborhood of Los Angeles. Manson entered the house with his followers and tied up the couple before leaving the actual murders to his followers. The LaBiancas were brutally stabbed to death, and the killers left messages written in the victims' blood at the scene, including "Rise" and "Death to Pigs."

Capture and Trial

The Tate-LaBianca murders were among the most sensationalized crimes in American history, and they led to one of the most high-profile trials ever seen. Manson and several of his followers were arrested in the months following the murders, initially for unrelated crimes. It was not until Susan Atkins, one of the participants in the murders, boasted about the killings while in jail that the authorities began to piece together the full extent of the Manson Family's crimes.

The trial of Charles Manson and his followers began in July 1970 and quickly became a media circus. Manson, ever the showman, used the trial as a platform to promote his twisted ideology and to manipulate public opinion. He carved an "X" into his forehead, which he later turned into a swastika, and his followers mimicked his actions. Manson frequently disrupted the proceedings with outbursts and threats, while his followers outside the courthouse engaged in bizarre behavior to demonstrate their loyalty to him.

The trial lasted for several months, and the prosecution, led by Vincent Bugliosi, successfully argued that Manson had orchestrated the murders, even if he had not personally participated in the killings. The prosecution's case was bolstered by the testimony of Linda Kasabian, a former member of the Manson Family who had been present at the Tate murders but did not participate. Kasabian's testimony provided crucial details about Manson's role in planning and directing the murders.

In January 1971, Charles Manson, along with his followers Susan Atkins, Patricia Krenwinkel, and Leslie Van Houten, was convicted of first-degree murder and conspiracy to commit murder. Manson was sentenced to death, but his sentence was later commuted to life imprisonment when the California Supreme Court invalidated the state's death penalty statutes in 1972.

Psychological Profile and Influence

Charles Manson's ability to manipulate and control his followers has been the subject of extensive analysis by psychologists and criminologists. Manson exhibited many of the traits associated with psychopathy, including a lack of empathy, a grandiose sense of self, and a propensity for manipulative and antisocial behavior. However, what set Manson apart from other criminals was his ability to exert an almost hypnotic influence over his followers.

Manson's charismatic authority allowed him to attract vulnerable individuals who were searching for meaning and belonging. He used a combination of psychological manipulation, mind-altering drugs, and social isolation to break down his followers' sense of individuality and reshape their identities in accordance with his own delusional beliefs. Manson's followers were often young, impressionable, and disconnected from their families, making them particularly susceptible to his influence.

Manson's ability to exploit the social and cultural upheavals of the 1960s also played a significant role in his success as a cult leader. The era was marked by widespread disillusionment with traditional values, and many young people were seeking alternative ways of living and thinking. Manson's message of love, freedom, and rejection of conventional society resonated with his followers, even as he twisted these ideals into something dark and destructive.

Cultural Impact and Legacy

The Manson Family murders had a profound impact on American society and culture. They marked the end of the 1960s, a decade often associated with peace, love, and countercultural idealism, and ushered in a period of fear, disillusionment, and cynicism. The murders shattered the illusion of the "Summer of Love" and revealed the darker side of the counterculture movement.

The trial and its aftermath also had a lasting impact on the criminal justice system and the way cults and charismatic leaders are understood. The Manson case highlighted the dangers of unchecked charisma and the potential for psychological manipulation to lead to horrific acts of violence. It also raised questions about the role of the media in sensationalizing crime and the influence of popular culture on criminal behavior.

Manson himself became a symbol of evil and insanity, his image and persona exploited by the media and popular culture for decades. He was the subject of numerous books, documentaries, and films, and his face, with the swastika carved into his forehead, became one of the most recognizable images in the annals of crime. Manson's story continues to fascinate and horrify, a testament to the enduring power of his myth and the profound impact of the crimes he orchestrated.

Chapter 6: Albert Fish

Albert Fish, often referred to as the "Brooklyn Vampire," the "Moon Maniac," or the "Gray Man," is one of the most disturbing figures in the annals of American crime. Born Hamilton Howard Fish in 1870, Fish became infamous for his horrific acts of murder, cannibalism, and sadomasochistic torture, particularly of young children. His crimes were so grotesque and unsettling that they continue to evoke horror and disbelief even today. Fish's case is not only significant for the sheer brutality of his actions but also for what it reveals about the darkest corners of human psychology and the nature of evil.

Early Life and Psychological Foundations

Albert Fish was born on May 19, 1870, in Washington, D.C., into a family plagued by mental illness. His father, Randall Fish, was 75 years old at the time of Albert's birth, and his mother, Ellen Fish, was much younger. The Fish family had a history of mental instability; several members of his family were diagnosed with severe psychiatric conditions, including mania and religious psychosis. This background of genetic predisposition to mental illness likely played a significant role in shaping Fish's future behavior.

Fish's early life was marked by hardship and trauma. When he was just five years old, his father died of a heart attack, leaving the family in dire financial straits. Unable to care for her children, Ellen Fish placed Albert in St. John's Orphanage in Washington, D.C. It was in this orphanage that Fish's troubling behavior began to emerge. He was subjected to severe physical abuse at the hands of the orphanage staff, who regularly beat and whipped the children. Fish later recounted that he began to derive pleasure from the pain inflicted upon him, a key indicator of the sadomasochistic tendencies that would later define his crimes.

Fish's experiences in the orphanage were the foundation for his lifelong association of pain with pleasure. By the time he left the orphanage at age nine, Fish had developed a deep-seated obsession with physical suffering, both inflicting it and experiencing it. These early experiences of abuse and neglect undoubtedly contributed to the development of his deviant desires and his eventual descent into violence and madness.

The Development of a Monster

After leaving the orphanage, Fish moved to New York City, where he lived with his mother. As he grew older, his behavior became increasingly erratic and disturbing. In his early twenties, Fish began engaging in various sexual perversions, including self-mutilation, which involved inserting needles into his body, particularly into his groin and abdomen. He also developed an obsession with consuming raw meat, which was an early manifestation of his cannibalistic tendencies.

Fish's deviant sexual behavior was accompanied by a growing interest in sadomasochism and the occult. He became fascinated with religious themes of pain and suffering, often interpreting biblical passages in a twisted manner that justified his violent fantasies. This blend of religious fanaticism and sexual deviance created a dangerous psychological cocktail that would eventually drive him to commit some of the most heinous crimes in American history.

Throughout his adult life, Fish worked as a painter and handyman, often taking jobs that allowed him to move from place to place. This itinerant lifestyle provided him with ample opportunity to seek out and victimize vulnerable children. Fish was married twice and had six children, but his familial relationships did little to curb his monstrous impulses. In fact, he often subjected his own children to physical abuse, though he never directed his murderous tendencies towards them.

First Known Crimes and Escalation

Fish's criminal behavior began to escalate in the early 1900s. He started frequenting brothels where he could act out his sadomasochistic fantasies with willing partners, but this was not enough to satisfy his increasingly violent urges. Fish began targeting young children, whom he viewed as easy prey. His preferred victims were vulnerable children, often from poor or immigrant families, who would not be missed if they disappeared.

Fish's first known abduction occurred in 1910 when he lured a young boy named Thomas Kedden to a secluded location in Wilmington, Delaware. Over the course of two weeks, Fish tortured Kedden in horrific ways, including cutting off part of his penis. However, Fish decided not to kill Kedden, instead releasing him with a warning to never speak of what had happened. This incident marked the beginning of Fish's transition from sadistic fantasies to actual violence, setting the stage for the even more brutal crimes to come.

Throughout the 1910s and 1920s, Fish continued to indulge in his violent urges, often targeting children who were playing alone in parks or on the streets. He would lure them away with promises of treats or money, then subject them to unspeakable acts of torture and mutilation. Despite his escalating violence, Fish managed to avoid detection for many years, largely because of his unassuming appearance and the chaotic nature of his lifestyle, which allowed him to move from place to place without raising suspicion.

The Horrific Murder of Grace Budd

The crime that ultimately led to Fish's capture was the abduction and murder of 10-year-old Grace Budd in 1928. This case would become one of the most infamous in American history, not only for the brutality of the crime but also for the shocking details that emerged during the investigation and trial.

On May 25, 1928, Fish visited the Budd family in New York under the pretense of offering a job to Edward Budd, Grace's older brother. Fish, who introduced himself as "Frank Howard," claimed to be a successful farmer looking for help on his farm. During the visit, Fish's attention turned to Grace, and he convinced the Budds to allow him to take her to a party at his sister's house. Tragically, Grace never returned.

Fish took Grace to an abandoned house in Westchester County, where he subjected her to a gruesome and protracted death. According to Fish's later confession, he strangled Grace to death and then mutilated her body, eventually consuming parts of her flesh. Fish's cannibalistic tendencies were a deeply ingrained aspect of his pathology, driven by a combination of sadomasochism, religious delusion, and a desire to possess his victims in the most intimate way possible.

The Budd family was left devastated by Grace's disappearance, and the police launched an extensive investigation. However, Fish managed to evade capture for several years. It was not until 1934, when Fish sent an anonymous letter to Grace's mother, Delia Budd, detailing the horrific fate of her daughter, that the authorities were able to track him down. The letter, which described in graphic detail how Fish had murdered and eaten parts of Grace, remains one of the most chilling pieces of evidence in criminal history.

Arrest, Trial, and Confession

Fish was arrested on December 13, 1934, after police traced the letter back to him. During his interrogation, Fish initially denied any involvement in Grace Budd's murder, but he eventually confessed in excruciating detail. His confession revealed not only the horrific nature of Grace's murder but also the extent of his other crimes, including the murders of several other children.

Fish's trial began on March 11, 1935, in White Plains, New York. The trial quickly became a media sensation, with reporters and the public alike captivated by the gruesome details of Fish's crimes. The prosecution presented overwhelming evidence of Fish's guilt, including his detailed confession and the testimony of medical experts who examined the remains of Grace Budd.

One of the central issues in the trial was whether Fish was legally insane at the time of the murders. Fish's defense argued that he was suffering from severe mental illness, including psychosis and sadomasochistic disorders, which rendered him incapable of understanding the wrongfulness of his actions. However, the prosecution countered that Fish was fully aware of his crimes and had carefully planned and executed them, indicating that he was legally sane.

The jury ultimately rejected the insanity defense and found Fish guilty of first-degree murder. On March 22, 1935, Fish was sentenced to death by electrocution. Despite his defense team's efforts to appeal the verdict, Fish's execution was carried out on January 16, 1936, at Sing Sing Prison in Ossining, New York. Fish reportedly went to his death with little fear, even expressing a morbid curiosity about the sensation of being electrocuted.

Psychological Analysis and Legacy

Albert Fish's crimes have been the subject of extensive analysis by psychologists, criminologists, and forensic experts, all of whom have attempted to understand the mind of a man capable of such horrific acts. Fish exhibited a range of severe psychiatric disorders, including sadomasochism, cannibalism, and pedophilia, as well as possible schizophrenia or other psychotic disorders. His deep-seated need to inflict and experience pain, combined with his religious delusions and obsession with cannibalism, created a uniquely dangerous individual.

Fish's case also highlights the complex relationship between mental illness and criminal behavior. While there is no doubt that Fish was profoundly mentally disturbed, his ability to evade capture for so many years and the calculated nature of his crimes suggest a level of awareness and control that complicates the narrative of insanity. Fish's case has been used to explore the boundaries of legal insanity, the role of mental illness in criminal responsibility, and the challenges of identifying and treating individuals with similar psychological profiles.

Fish's legacy is one of horror and revulsion. His crimes are among the most disturbing in the history of American criminal justice, and his name has become synonymous with the darkest aspects of human nature. Fish's story serves as a chilling reminder of the capacity for evil that can exist within the human mind and the devastating consequences that can result when that evil is left unchecked.

Cultural Impact and Continued Fascination

The story of Albert Fish has left an indelible mark on American culture and the study of criminal psychology. His crimes were so grotesque and incomprehensible that they have continued to captivate and horrify the public long after his death. Fish's case has inspired numerous books, documentaries, and films, each attempting to dissect the mind of a man who seemed to embody pure evil.

One of the most significant cultural impacts of Fish's story is its role in the exploration of the "boogeyman" archetype in horror fiction and popular culture. Fish's acts of cannibalism, his targeting of innocent children, and his eerie, unassuming appearance make him a real-life embodiment of the kind of nightmarish figures that populate horror stories. His ability to blend into society while harboring such monstrous desires only adds to the terror his story evokes.

Fish's crimes have also prompted ongoing debates about the nature of evil and the extent to which mental illness can explain or excuse such behavior. Some view Fish as a case study in the extreme consequences of untreated mental illness, while others see him as a symbol of the inherent capacity for evil within the human psyche. His case has been referenced in discussions about criminal justice, particularly in the context of the death penalty and the treatment of mentally ill offenders.

Moreover, Fish's case has influenced the portrayal of serial killers in media. The macabre details of his crimes, his bizarre behavior, and his unsettling letters have served as a blueprint for fictional depictions of killers who defy understanding. Fish's life and actions challenge the boundaries of what society considers possible, forcing people to confront the darkest aspects of human nature.

Chapter 7: Ed Gein

Edward Theodore Gein, more commonly known as Ed Gein, was born on August 27, 1906, in La Crosse, Wisconsin. Gein's childhood was marked by a profound sense of isolation and an extremely dysfunctional family dynamic. His father, George Gein, was an alcoholic who was unable to hold down steady work, leading the family to endure financial hardship. His mother, Augusta Gein, was the dominant figure in his life, a devoutly religious woman who harbored a deep hatred for her husband and believed the world outside their home was corrupt and sinful. Augusta's influence on Ed was both profound and detrimental, shaping his view of the world and his relationships with women.

Augusta was a fervent Lutheran who instilled in her sons a fear of women and sexuality. She taught Ed and his older brother, Henry, that all women (except for herself) were instruments of the devil and that sexual desire was a sin. Augusta's rigid and oppressive beliefs created an environment where Ed had little social interaction outside his family, fostering a deep sense of dependence on his mother. This unhealthy attachment to Augusta became the cornerstone of Ed Gein's psychological development, ultimately contributing to his later actions.

The family eventually moved to a farm in Plainfield, Wisconsin, where Ed spent most of his formative years. The farm was isolated, and the boys were rarely allowed to leave, further intensifying Ed's social isolation. Despite the oppressive atmosphere at home, Ed was an obedient child who idolized his mother and absorbed her teachings without question. However, this obedience masked a growing internal turmoil that would later manifest in horrifying ways.

The Deaths of Ed Gein's Family Members

The first significant crack in Ed Gein's psyche appeared with the death of his father in 1940. George Gein's death was not particularly impactful on Ed, given that George had been a distant and uninvolved parent. However, it was the beginning of a series of losses that would destabilize Ed's already fragile mental state.

In 1944, Ed's brother Henry died under mysterious circumstances. The two brothers had been burning brush on the farm when the fire got out of control. When the authorities arrived, they found Henry's body lying face down in an area that had not been touched by the fire. Though there were bruises on Henry's head, the death was ruled as a result of asphyxiation from the fire. However, some speculate that Ed may have been involved in his brother's death, possibly due to Henry's increasing criticism of Augusta and his desire to leave the farm. This event is shrouded in ambiguity, but it may have been the first sign of Ed's capacity for violence.

The most significant loss in Ed's life came in 1945 with the death of his mother, Augusta. Her death was a devastating blow to Ed, leaving him utterly alone and without direction. Ed had lost the only person who had ever mattered to him, and the only anchor in his life was gone. This loss unmoored Ed completely, and it was after Augusta's death that his behavior began to spiral into the macabre.

The Descent into Madness

After his mother's death, Ed Gein became increasingly reclusive, living alone on the family farm. The farm itself fell into disrepair, mirroring Ed's deteriorating mental state. Inside the house, however, Ed kept certain rooms, including his mother's, immaculately preserved as a shrine to Augusta. The rest of the house was cluttered and filthy, reflecting Ed's chaotic inner world.

It was during this time that Ed's morbid obsessions began to take a dark and tangible form. Ed became fascinated with death, particularly with the female body. His deep-seated fear and hatred of women, instilled by his mother, combined with his inability to cope with her death, led him down a path of necrophilia and grave robbing. Ed began to visit local cemeteries, where he would exhume recently buried bodies, primarily those of middle-aged women who reminded him of his mother.

Ed would bring these bodies back to his farm, where he engaged in bizarre rituals. He used the skin and bones of the corpses to create various items, including masks, belts, and furniture. Ed's actions were driven by a twisted desire to recreate his mother, and he believed that by wearing the skin of these women, he could somehow bring Augusta back to life or embody her.

The Discovery of Ed Gein's Crimes

The full extent of Ed Gein's depravity was not uncovered until November 16, 1957, following the disappearance of Bernice Worden, a local hardware store owner in Plainfield. Suspicion quickly fell on Gein, who had been seen in the store on the morning of her disappearance. When the authorities arrived at Gein's farm, they made a series of gruesome discoveries that would shock the nation.

Inside the farmhouse, investigators found Worden's decapitated body hanging upside down, gutted like a deer. Her head was found in a burlap sack, and her heart was placed in a plastic bag near the stove. This was only the beginning of the horrors that the police would uncover. As they continued to search the property, they found a number of grotesque artifacts made from human remains, including a lampshade made from human skin, a belt made from nipples, a chair upholstered in human skin, and a collection of human skulls.

Perhaps the most chilling discovery was a "woman suit" made from the skin of several female corpses, which Gein admitted he wore.

The investigation revealed that Gein had exhumed numerous bodies from local cemeteries and used their remains to create his macabre collection. While Gein admitted to killing Bernice Worden and another local woman, Mary Hogan, he claimed that the majority of the remains in his possession were from bodies he had dug up. Despite this claim, the exact number of his victims remains unknown, as Gein's actions have left many questions unanswered.

The Psychological Profile of Ed Gein

Ed Gein's crimes and the bizarre nature of his behavior have made him a subject of intense study in the fields of psychology and criminology. Gein's actions were driven by a complex interplay of factors, including his abusive upbringing, his profound attachment to his mother, and his severe mental illness.

Psychologists who examined Gein after his arrest diagnosed him with schizophrenia and other severe mental disorders. Gein's attachment to his mother was seen as the central factor in his crimes; he was unable to accept her death and sought to resurrect or replace her through his gruesome activities. His desire to become his mother or to bring her back to life through the creation of a "woman suit" speaks to the depth of his psychological disturbance.

Gein's case also raised important questions about the influence of social isolation and upbringing on criminal behavior. The extreme isolation imposed by his mother, combined with her oppressive and puritanical views, created an environment in which Gein's mental illness could flourish unchecked. His lack of social interaction and his mother's teachings about the inherent evil of women distorted his view of the world and contributed to his development as a killer.

Trial and Incarceration

Ed Gein was arrested on November 16, 1957, and charged with the murders of Bernice Worden and Mary Hogan. Due to his severe mental illness, Gein was found unfit to stand trial and was committed to the Central State Hospital for the Criminally Insane (now the Dodge Correctional Institution) in Waupun, Wisconsin. In 1968, after ten years of treatment, Gein was deemed competent to stand trial. He was found guilty of the murder of Bernice Worden but was also found legally insane, which meant he would spend the rest of his life in a mental institution rather than in prison.

Gein remained in mental health facilities until his death from cancer on July 26, 1984, at the age of 77. He was buried in the Plainfield Cemetery, the same cemetery from which he had exhumed many of his victims. Over the years, his grave became a site of vandalism and theft, with people stealing pieces of the gravestone as macabre souvenirs.

Cultural Legacy and Influence

The horrific details of Ed Gein's crimes have left an enduring legacy in American culture, particularly in the horror genre. Gein's life and actions have inspired numerous films, books, and television shows, and he has become one of the most infamous figures in the annals of American crime.

One of the most notable cultural references to Gein is the character of Norman Bates in Alfred Hitchcock's 1960 film *Psycho*, which was based on the novel of the same name by Robert Bloch. The character of Bates, like Gein, was a reclusive man with an unhealthy attachment to his mother, and his crimes were similarly rooted in his inability to let go of her after her death. The idea of a killer who preserved his mother's body and took on her identity was directly inspired by Gein's story.

Gein also served as the inspiration for other iconic horror villains, including Leatherface in *The Texas Chain Saw Massacre* (1974) and Buffalo Bill in *The Silence of the Lambs* (1991). These characters, like Gein, engage in acts of necrophilia and use the skin of their victims to create grotesque artifacts or clothing. The portrayal of these characters in film and literature has cemented Gein's legacy as a symbol of ultimate horror.

Gein's influence extends beyond fiction; his case has been the subject of numerous documentaries, true crime books, and psychological studies. His crimes continue to fascinate and horrify the public, serving as a reminder of the darkness that can exist within the human psyche.

Chapter 8: Aileen Wuornos

Aileen Carol Wuornos was born on February 29, 1956, in Rochester, Michigan, into a deeply troubled family. Her early life was marked by significant hardship, abuse, and neglect, setting the stage for the tumultuous path she would follow later in life. Her mother, Diane Wuornos, was just 14 years old when she married Aileen's father, Leo Dale Pittman, a convicted child molester who was diagnosed with schizophrenia. Diane filed for divorce before Aileen was even born, and by the time Aileen was four years old, her mother had abandoned her and her brother Keith, leaving them to be raised by their maternal grandparents, Lauri and Britta Wuornos.

Aileen's upbringing with her grandparents was far from stable. Her grandmother, Britta, was an alcoholic, and her grandfather, Lauri, was physically abusive. This environment of violence and instability only exacerbated the psychological trauma that Aileen had already begun to experience. By the time she was 11 years old, Aileen was engaging in sexual activities in exchange for cigarettes, drugs, and food, often with older men in the neighborhood. These early experiences with sex and exploitation left deep emotional scars and contributed to her profound mistrust and hatred of men, themes that would later emerge in her criminal activities.

At age 14, Aileen became pregnant, reportedly after being raped by a friend of her grandfather's. She was sent to a home for unwed mothers, where she gave birth to a son who was put up for adoption. The shame and trauma of this experience only deepened her sense of alienation and despair. Shortly afterward, she dropped out of school and was expelled from her home by her grandfather. With nowhere else to turn, Aileen was forced to live on the streets, surviving through prostitution and petty crime.

Descent into Crime and Homelessness

Aileen's life on the streets was marked by a series of escalating criminal behaviors. She moved to Florida in her early 20s, where she continued to engage in sex work to support herself. Over the next several years, Aileen's criminal record grew as she was arrested multiple times for offenses such as DUI, disorderly conduct, and theft. Her life was characterized by a transient existence, moving from place to place, and relying on men for financial support, often through relationships that were volatile and abusive.

Despite her growing criminal record, Aileen did not see herself as a hardened criminal. Rather, she viewed herself as a victim of circumstance, someone who had been dealt an unfair hand in life and was merely trying to survive. This sense of victimization would later play a significant role in her self-perception and the justifications she offered for her crimes.

In 1986, Aileen met Tyria Moore, a hotel maid, at a Daytona Beach gay bar. The two women quickly became romantically involved and began living together. For Aileen, Tyria represented the first stable relationship in her life, and she was deeply in love with her. However, their relationship was fraught with financial difficulties, and Aileen continued to support them through prostitution. Despite the challenges, Aileen and Tyria's relationship was one of the few constants in Aileen's tumultuous life, and it became a central aspect of her identity.

The Murders

Between late 1989 and 1990, Aileen Wuornos embarked on a killing spree that would earn her the dubious distinction of being America's most notorious female serial killer. Over the course of 12 months, she killed seven men in Florida, all of whom she claimed had either assaulted her or attempted to do so while she was working as a prostitute. The first of these men was Richard Mallory, a convicted rapist who picked up Aileen along Interstate 75 in December 1989. Aileen later claimed that Mallory had brutally assaulted her, leading her to shoot him in self-defense.

Mallory's death was initially not linked to Aileen, as his body was discovered several miles away in a wooded area, and there was little evidence to connect the crime to her. However, over the next few months, Aileen continued to kill, each time using the same method: she would shoot her victims with a .22-caliber pistol, often multiple times, and then rob them of their money and possessions. The other victims included David Spears, Charles Carskaddon, Peter Siems (whose body was never found), Troy Burress, Charles Humphreys, and Walter Jeno Antonio.

Aileen's modus operandi was strikingly similar in each case, leading investigators to suspect that they were dealing with a serial killer. Despite the similarities, it took some time for law enforcement to piece together the connection between the murders. It wasn't until a car belonging to one of the victims, Peter Siems, was found abandoned and linked to two women, Aileen and Tyria, that the authorities began to close in on Aileen.

Arrest and Trial

In January 1991, Aileen Wuornos was arrested at a bar in Port Orange, Florida, on an outstanding warrant for a previous weapons charge. At the time of her arrest, Aileen had no idea that the authorities were investigating her for the murders, but the net was closing in. Tyria Moore, who had been living with Aileen throughout the killing spree, was picked up by police shortly afterward. Faced with the possibility of being charged as an accessory to murder, Tyria agreed to cooperate with the authorities and was instrumental in securing Aileen's confession.

Under pressure from Tyria and after several days of questioning, Aileen finally confessed to the murders. However, she insisted that she had acted in self-defense in each case, claiming that the men had either raped her or attempted to do so. Despite her claims, the prosecution argued that Aileen was a cold-blooded killer who had murdered the men for financial gain. The fact that she had robbed each of her victims and later pawned their belongings to support herself and Tyria was used as evidence of her motives.

Aileen's trial for the murder of Richard Mallory began in January 1992, and it quickly became a media sensation. The case was notable not only because Aileen was a female serial killer—a rarity in the annals of American crime—but also because of the sensational nature of the crimes and Aileen's troubled background. The prosecution painted a picture of Aileen as a manipulative, calculating predator who had lured her victims to their deaths under the guise of offering them sex. The defense, on the other hand, argued that Aileen was a deeply traumatized woman who had been driven to kill in self-defense.

Despite her claims of self-defense, Aileen was found guilty of first-degree murder in the Mallory case and was sentenced to death. She later pleaded no contest to the murders of the other six men, claiming that she wanted to "get right with God." She was subsequently sentenced to six additional death sentences, making her one of the few women in American history to be condemned to death for multiple murders.

Psychological Profile and Motivations

Aileen Wuornos's case has been the subject of extensive psychological analysis, as experts have sought to understand the motivations behind her crimes. Many psychologists have pointed to Aileen's deeply troubled upbringing as a key factor in her development as a killer. The abuse, neglect, and abandonment she experienced as a child left her with profound emotional scars, leading to a deep-seated mistrust of others, particularly men. Her early experiences with sexual exploitation also played a significant role in shaping her views on sex and relationships, contributing to her later belief that men were inherently dangerous and untrustworthy.

Some experts have suggested that Aileen may have suffered from borderline personality disorder, a mental illness characterized by intense emotional instability, impulsive behavior, and a distorted self-image. This disorder, combined with her traumatic past, may have contributed to her violent outbursts and her inability to form healthy relationships. Others have argued that Aileen's actions were driven by a desire for revenge against the men who had exploited and abused her throughout her life. In her mind, each of her victims represented the men who had hurt her in the past, and by killing them, she was exacting a form of retribution.

Aileen herself often vacillated between claiming that she killed in self-defense and admitting that she was driven by a deep-seated hatred of men. In interviews, she expressed a sense of bitterness and rage at the world, often blaming her actions on the abuse she had suffered and the harsh realities of life as a prostitute. This ambivalence made it difficult to fully understand her true motivations, as she seemed to be both a victim and a perpetrator of violence.

Media Sensation and Public Perception

Aileen Wuornos's case attracted widespread media attention, not only because of the sensational nature of the crimes but also because of the way Aileen was portrayed in the media. Dubbed the "Damsel of Death" and the "Highway Hooker," Aileen was often depicted as a femme fatale, a woman who used her sexuality to lure men to their deaths. This portrayal was both sensationalized and simplistic, reducing Aileen's complex and tragic life story to a lurid headline.

The media's fascination with Aileen also extended to her trial, which was covered extensively by the press. The image of Aileen, a tough, unrepentant woman with a troubled past, made for compelling news, and her case became a focal point for debates about the death penalty, mental illness, and the criminal justice system. Some saw her as a cold-blooded killer who deserved to be executed, while others viewed her as a victim of a system that had failed to protect her from a life of abuse and exploitation.

Aileen's story also captured the attention of filmmakers, writers, and artists, who sought to explore the deeper themes of her life and crimes. The most notable of these portrayals was the 2003 film *Monster*, in which actress Charlize Theron portrayed Aileen in a performance that earned her an Academy Award. The film offered a more nuanced and sympathetic portrayal of Aileen, focusing on her troubled background and the emotional turmoil that drove her to kill. However, even this portrayal has been criticized for oversimplifying Aileen's life and for glossing over the darker aspects of her personality.

Execution and Legacy

On October 9, 2002, after more than a decade on death row, Aileen Wuornos was executed by lethal injection at Florida State Prison. In her final statement, Aileen was cryptic, saying, "I'd just like to say I'm sailing with the rock, and I'll be back like Independence Day, with Jesus June 6th. Like the movie, big mother ship and all, I'll be back." Her words left many puzzled, reflecting the complex and often contradictory nature of her personality.

Aileen Wuornos's legacy is a complicated one. On one hand, she is remembered as one of the most infamous female serial killers in American history, a woman who killed seven men and showed little remorse for her actions. On the other hand, her life story has sparked important discussions about the impact of childhood trauma, mental illness, and the ways in which society fails those who are most vulnerable.

Aileen's case also highlights the unique challenges faced by women who commit violent crimes. As one of the few female serial killers, Aileen's actions defied traditional gender roles and expectations, making her an object of both fascination and fear. Her life and crimes continue to be studied by criminologists, psychologists, and sociologists, who seek to understand the factors that led her down such a dark path.

In the years since her death, Aileen Wuornos has become a symbol of the intersection between victimization and violence, a reminder of how deeply personal pain can manifest in destructive ways. Her story serves as both a cautionary tale and a call to address the underlying issues that contribute to crime, particularly among those who have been marginalized and abused.

Chapter 9: David Berkowitz (Son of Sam)

David Berkowitz, also known as the "Son of Sam," is one of the most infamous serial killers in American history. His reign of terror in New York City during the late 1970s left an indelible mark on the city and the collective psyche of the nation. Berkowitz's crimes, characterized by their randomness and brutality, fueled widespread panic and fear, making him one of the most notorious figures in the annals of American crime.

Early Life: A Troubled Beginning

David Richard Berkowitz was born Richard David Falco on June 1, 1953, in Brooklyn, New York. His biological mother, Elizabeth "Betty" Broder, had an affair with a married man, and when she became pregnant, she decided to give the baby up for adoption. Just a few days after his birth, Berkowitz was adopted by Nathan and Pearl Berkowitz, a Jewish couple who lived in the Bronx. His name was changed to David Richard Berkowitz, and he was raised in a relatively stable and loving environment.

Despite his adoptive parents' efforts to provide a good home, David Berkowitz's childhood was marked by feelings of rejection, anger, and confusion. He struggled with his identity and self-worth, feelings that were exacerbated when he learned of his adoption at a young age. This revelation deeply affected him, leading to a sense of abandonment and alienation. Berkowitz was known to be a troubled child who exhibited behavioral problems, including pyromania and cruelty to animals—early signs that are often associated with future violent behavior.

In 1967, when Berkowitz was 14 years old, his adoptive mother, Pearl, passed away from breast cancer. Her death was a devastating blow to Berkowitz, as he had been particularly close to her. The loss of his mother further intensified his feelings of loneliness and anger. After Pearl's death, Nathan Berkowitz remarried, but David's relationship with his stepmother was strained, and he grew increasingly distant from his adoptive father.

Adolescence and Military Service

Berkowitz's teenage years were marked by increasing social isolation and a growing fascination with violence and the occult. He struggled academically and had few friends, preferring to spend his time alone, indulging in dark fantasies and violent thoughts. By the time he graduated from high school in 1971, Berkowitz was a deeply troubled young man with a burgeoning obsession with death and destruction.

Seeking to escape his troubled life in New York, Berkowitz enlisted in the United States Army in 1971. He served as an infantryman and was stationed in South Korea for most of his service. While in the military, Berkowitz was reportedly a good soldier, but his fascination with violence and death continued to grow. It was during this time that he began experimenting with drugs and became more deeply involved in the occult, particularly Satanism.

After completing his military service in 1974, Berkowitz returned to New York City, where he worked a series of menial jobs. He struggled to adjust to civilian life, feeling increasingly isolated and disconnected from society. His relationships with others were superficial at best, and he had difficulty forming meaningful connections with people. As his loneliness and anger grew, so did his dark fantasies, which began to take on a more concrete and violent form.

The Descent into Madness: Berkowitz's Path to Murder

By the mid-1970s, David Berkowitz was living in a small apartment in Yonkers, New York, and his mental state was rapidly deteriorating. He became obsessed with the idea that he was being controlled by demonic forces, a belief that was fueled by his involvement in the occult and his growing interest in Satanism. Berkowitz claimed that he was receiving messages from a demon that had possessed his neighbor's dog, commanding him to kill.

Berkowitz's delusions and paranoia became more intense as he began to believe that he was on a mission to serve these demonic forces. He became convinced that the only way to appease the demons and silence the voices in his head was to commit murder. In 1976, he purchased a .44 caliber Bulldog revolver, the weapon that would become infamous in his killing spree.

The "Son of Sam" Murders: A City in Terror

David Berkowitz's killing spree began on July 29, 1976, when he shot and killed Donna Lauria, an 18-year-old medical technician, in the Bronx. Lauria was sitting in a car with her friend, Jody Valenti, when Berkowitz approached and fired three shots into the vehicle. Lauria was killed instantly, while Valenti was wounded but survived. The seemingly random nature of the attack left police baffled, and there were few clues to lead them to the killer.

Over the next year, Berkowitz would go on to commit a series of similar attacks, each one more brazen than the last. His victims were typically young women with long, dark hair, often accompanied by male companions. Berkowitz would approach his victims in parked cars or on the street, opening fire without warning. The randomness of the attacks and the lack of any clear motive made the case particularly difficult for law enforcement.

The media soon dubbed the unknown assailant the ".44 Caliber Killer" due to the distinctive weapon used in the murders. As the body count grew, so did the fear and panic among New Yorkers. Women with long, dark hair began cutting their hair short or dyeing it blonde in an attempt to avoid becoming the next victim. The entire city was gripped by terror, as the killer seemed to strike at random and without warning.

Berkowitz's murders continued into 1977, and with each attack, he became bolder. On January 30, 1977, he shot and killed Christine Freund, a 26-year-old secretary, as she sat in a car with her fiancé, John Diel. Freund was killed instantly, while Diel survived the attack. On March 8, 1977, Berkowitz struck again, shooting and killing 19-year-old college student Virginia Voskerichian as she walked home from school in Queens.

The "Son of Sam" Letters: A Killer Taunts the Police

As the investigation into the murders intensified, Berkowitz began to play a cat-and-mouse game with the police and the media. In April 1977, he sent a letter to New York Daily News columnist Jimmy Breslin, in which he introduced himself as the "Son of Sam." The letter was a chilling manifesto in which Berkowitz taunted the police, mocked their efforts to catch him, and claimed that he was compelled to kill by a demonic force.

The letter was published in the Daily News, and it only heightened the public's fear and fascination with the case. The nickname "Son of Sam" stuck, and Berkowitz reveled in the notoriety it brought him. He sent additional letters to the police and the media, each one more cryptic and disturbing than the last. In these letters, Berkowitz referred to himself as "Mr. Monster" and "The Duke of Death," and he described his killings as part of a larger, supernatural plan.

The letters were filled with bizarre references to demons, Satanic rituals, and his supposed connection to a larger cult of devil worshippers. While the police dismissed much of what Berkowitz wrote as the ramblings of a madman, they were concerned about the possibility that he might not be acting alone. The idea that the "Son of Sam" was part of a larger, organized group only added to the fear and confusion surrounding the case.

Capture and Confession: The End of the Reign of Terror

The break in the case came on July 31, 1977, when Berkowitz committed what would be his final murder. On that night, he shot and killed Stacy Moskowitz, a 20-year-old aspiring actress, and seriously wounded her boyfriend, Robert Violante, as they sat in a car in Brooklyn. Unbeknownst to Berkowitz, a woman had witnessed him near the scene of the crime and reported a suspicious man to the police. Her description of the man and his car—a yellow Ford Galaxie—matched the vehicle seen near several of the previous crime scenes.

The police were able to trace the car to David Berkowitz, who was living in Yonkers at the time. On August 10, 1977, detectives staked out Berkowitz's apartment and arrested him as he left his building. Inside his car, they found the .44 caliber Bulldog revolver that had been used in the murders, along with maps of the crime scenes and a letter addressed to the police. Berkowitz did not resist arrest and immediately confessed to being the "Son of Sam."

During his confession, Berkowitz claimed that he was driven to kill by the demonic voices in his head, particularly that of "Sam," a demon that he believed was speaking to him through his neighbor's dog. He described his crimes in detail, expressing little remorse for his actions and insisting that he was not in control of his behavior. Berkowitz's claims of demonic possession were initially met with skepticism, and many believed that he was feigning insanity to avoid the death penalty.

Trial and Incarceration

David Berkowitz was charged with six counts of murder and several counts of attempted murder. Given the overwhelming evidence against him, including his confession, the case never went to trial. On May 8, 1978, Berkowitz pleaded guilty to all charges, admitting to the murders and the attempted murders. During his sentencing, Berkowitz caused a scene in the courtroom, screaming that he wanted to kill again and claiming that his murderous impulses were still uncontrollable.

Despite his outbursts, the court found Berkowitz competent to stand trial, and he was sentenced to six consecutive life terms in prison, with no possibility of parole. He was incarcerated at the Attica Correctional Facility in upstate New York, one of the most notorious and secure prisons in the state.

Post-Conviction Life and Public Fascination

While in prison, Berkowitz's mental state appeared to stabilize, and he began to renounce his earlier claims of demonic possession. He later admitted that the story about the demon-possessed dog was a fabrication, a desperate attempt to create a sensational narrative that would explain his actions. Berkowitz claimed that he had been deeply unhappy and angry at the world, and that his murders were an expression of that inner turmoil.

In the 1980s, Berkowitz experienced a religious conversion, becoming a born-again Christian. He began referring to himself as the "Son of Hope" rather than the "Son of Sam," and he started writing letters and essays about his faith, urging others to turn away from violence and find redemption. Berkowitz also became involved in prison ministry work, counseling other inmates and sharing his story in an effort to prevent others from following the same path.

Despite his claims of reformation, Berkowitz remained a figure of public fascination. Over the years, he has been the subject of numerous books, documentaries, and films, all attempting to explore the psyche of one of America's most notorious serial killers. Berkowitz himself has expressed regret for his actions and has apologized to the families of his victims, though many remain skeptical of his sincerity.

The Legacy of the "Son of Sam"

David Berkowitz's crimes had a profound and lasting impact on New York City and the nation as a whole. The "Son of Sam" case changed the way law enforcement approached the investigation of serial crimes, leading to the development of new profiling techniques and the establishment of specialized task forces dedicated to tracking down serial killers.

The case also led to the creation of the "Son of Sam" laws, which prevent criminals from profiting from the publicity surrounding their crimes. These laws were enacted in response to concerns that Berkowitz might seek to profit from book or movie deals related to his story. The laws have since been expanded to apply to other criminals, ensuring that the proceeds from such deals are directed to the victims or their families.

Berkowitz's story also serves as a stark reminder of the potential for darkness within the human soul. His descent into madness and violence was fueled by a combination of personal trauma, social isolation, and a fascination with evil that ultimately led to the deaths of six innocent people. The "Son of Sam" case remains one of the most infamous chapters in the history of American crime, a testament to the terrifying power of the human mind when it is consumed by rage and delusion.

As of today, David Berkowitz remains incarcerated, serving his life sentence without the possibility of parole. His story continues to captivate and horrify, a chilling example of how an ordinary man can become one of the most feared and reviled killers in modern history.

Chapter 10: Dennis Rader (BTK Killer)

Dennis Rader, known by the moniker "BTK Killer"—an acronym for "Bind, Torture, Kill"—is one of the most notorious and terrifying serial killers in American history. Over the span of nearly two decades, Rader committed a series of brutal murders that left the Wichita, Kansas community in a state of perpetual fear and unease. His ability to lead a double life—being a family man, church leader, and an active member of the community by day, while indulging in his sadistic fantasies as a killer by night—makes his case particularly chilling. Rader's eventual capture in 2005 brought an end to one of the longest and most intense manhunts in the history of American criminal justice.

Early Life: A Troubled Foundation

Dennis Lynn Rader was born on March 9, 1945, in Pittsburg, Kansas, and raised in Wichita. He was the oldest of four sons born to William and Dorothea Rader. Outwardly, Rader's childhood appeared normal, but beneath the surface, there were early signs of the darkness that would later consume him. From a young age, Rader exhibited disturbing behaviors, such as torturing and killing small animals—one of the classic indicators of a potential serial killer. These acts of cruelty provided him with a sense of power and control that he found increasingly intoxicating.

Rader also developed a fascination with bondage, sadomasochism, and control, often fantasizing about tying up and torturing women. These fantasies grew more elaborate and violent over time, becoming the foundation of his later crimes. He would cut out pictures of women from magazines and draw ropes or chains around them, feeding his fantasies of domination and control.

Despite these dark tendencies, Rader was able to maintain an outward appearance of normalcy. He was an average student, active in the Boy Scouts, and attended church regularly with his family. However, the seeds of his future crimes were already deeply rooted in his psyche, and they would continue to grow throughout his adolescence and into adulthood.

Adulthood: A Double Life Begins

After graduating from high school in 1963, Rader enrolled at Kansas Wesleyan University but dropped out after one year. In 1966, he joined the United States Air Force, where he served for four years. During his time in the military, Rader's outward demeanor remained that of a disciplined and responsible serviceman, but his dark fantasies continued to fester.

Upon his discharge from the Air Force in 1970, Rader returned to Wichita, where he worked in a variety of jobs, including as an assembler at the Coleman Company and as an installer for ADT Security Services. His job at ADT, where he worked from 1974 to 1988, gave him access to the homes of potential victims and provided him with the knowledge and tools to disable security systems—a skill that would prove useful in his later crimes.

In 1971, Rader married Paula Dietz, and the couple went on to have two children. By all outward appearances, Rader was a devoted husband and father. He was an active member of Christ Lutheran Church, where he served as president of the church council, and he was also a Cub Scout leader. To those who knew him, Rader was a pillar of the community—responsible, dependable, and seemingly ordinary. But beneath this veneer of normalcy lay a dark and dangerous alter ego.

The BTK Murders: A Reign of Terror

Dennis Rader's transformation from a man with dark fantasies to a cold-blooded killer began in the early 1970s. In January 1974, he committed his first known murders, an event that would mark the beginning of his reign of terror as the BTK Killer.

On January 15, 1974, Rader targeted the Otero family in their Wichita home. Rader had been stalking the family for some time, and on that fateful morning, he broke into their house, armed with a gun and ropes. Inside the home were Joseph Otero, his wife Julie, and their two youngest children, 11-year-old Joseph Jr. and 9-year-old Josephine. Rader bound, tortured, and killed all four family members in a manner that reflected his sadistic fantasies. He later described the experience as intensely satisfying, referring to it as a "hit" that fulfilled his deep-seated desires.

The brutality of the Otero murders shocked the Wichita community, but no one could have imagined that this was only the beginning of a long and terrifying killing spree. Over the next few years, Rader continued to kill, each time following a similar pattern: he would stalk his victims, learn their routines, and then strike when they were most vulnerable. His victims were usually women or young girls, and he would bind them, torture them, and then kill them, often by strangulation.

Rader's second known victim was Kathryn Bright, whom he murdered on April 4, 1974. Rader broke into her home and waited for her to return. When she arrived home with her brother, Kevin, Rader attacked them both. Although Kevin managed to survive despite being shot twice, Kathryn was not as fortunate; she was bound and stabbed multiple times before succumbing to her injuries.

In March 1977, Rader struck again, this time targeting Shirley Vian. He broke into her home, where she was alone with her three children. After forcing the children into the bathroom and barricading the door, Rader bound and strangled Vian to death. Later that same year, on December 8, Rader killed his next victim, Nancy Fox, after breaking into her home and binding and strangling her.

The "BTK" Moniker: A Killer's Need for Attention

Unlike many serial killers who attempt to evade capture, Rader craved attention and recognition for his crimes. This desire led him to send taunting letters to the media and the police, detailing his murders and signing them with the initials "BTK," which stood for "Bind, Torture, Kill." Rader's letters were filled with graphic descriptions of his crimes, as well as cryptic clues that hinted at his identity and motives. These letters served to further terrorize the Wichita community and frustrated law enforcement officials, who were unable to identify the killer despite his brazen communications.

Rader's first known communication with the media occurred in October 1974, when he sent a letter to The Wichita Eagle newspaper, taking credit for the Otero murders. The letter contained specific details about the crime scene that had not been released to the public, confirming that the writer was indeed the killer. In the letter, Rader also expressed his frustration at not receiving more media attention, writing, "How many do I have to kill before I get a name in the paper or some national attention?"

Over the next few years, Rader sent several more letters, each one more taunting than the last. He would often include items taken from his victims, such as jewelry or clothing, as "trophies" of his kills. Rader's letters also revealed his obsession with power and control, as well as his belief that he was smarter than the police and the media.

Despite the detailed information Rader provided in his letters, law enforcement was unable to track him down. He was careful not to leave fingerprints or DNA at the crime scenes, and his communications were anonymous and untraceable. This ability to evade capture only fueled Rader's arrogance and sense of invincibility.

A Decade of Silence: The BTK Killer Goes Dormant

After the murder of Nancy Fox in 1977, Rader went silent for several years. His sudden disappearance from the public eye led some to believe that the BTK Killer had either died, been imprisoned for another crime, or moved away from the area. However, Rader had simply chosen to lay low, perhaps to avoid drawing too much attention to himself as the investigation into the BTK murders intensified.

During this period of dormancy, Rader continued to live a seemingly normal life. He remained active in his church and community, all while harboring the dark secrets of his past. His ability to compartmentalize his life—separating his role as a husband, father, and community leader from his identity as a sadistic killer—allowed him to go undetected for so long.

Resurfacing: BTK Returns to the Public Eye

In 1985, after nearly eight years of silence, Rader resurfaced and claimed another victim. On April 27, 1985, he murdered Marine Hedge, a neighbor who lived just a few houses down from his own home in Park City, Kansas. Rader broke into Hedge's house, strangled her to death, and then took her body to his church, where he photographed her in various poses before dumping her body in a ditch.

Following Hedge's murder, Rader killed again in 1986, targeting Vicki Wegerle in her home. After gaining entry to her house under the pretense of being a repairman, Rader bound and strangled

Wegerle to death, taking photographs of her body as a keepsake. He then sent a copy of Wegerle's driver's license to the media as proof of his crime, once again taunting the police and showcasing his desire for recognition.

Rader's final known murder occurred in January 1991, when he killed Dolores Davis, another neighbor, by breaking into her home, binding, and strangling her. As with his previous victims, Rader took photographs of Davis's body and kept items from the crime scene as souvenirs.

The BTK Killer's Downfall: A Deadly Game of Cat and Mouse

Despite Rader's attempts to outsmart law enforcement, advancements in forensic technology and his own hubris eventually led to his capture. In 2004, after more than a decade of silence, Rader began sending letters to the media and police again, reigniting public fear and interest in the BTK case. However, this renewed communication would prove to be his undoing.

In one of his letters, Rader asked the police if they could trace a floppy disk back to its source if he were to send one with information about his crimes. The police, eager to finally catch the elusive killer, responded via a newspaper ad, assuring him that the disk could not be traced. Trusting their word, Rader sent a floppy disk containing a message to a local TV station in February 2005.

Unbeknownst to Rader, the disk contained metadata that led investigators to a computer at Christ Lutheran Church, where Rader served as president of the church council. The metadata also revealed that the last person to modify the disk was someone named "Dennis." Armed with this information, investigators began to focus their attention on Dennis Rader, a well-known and respected member of the community.

To confirm their suspicions, the police obtained a warrant to test a DNA sample from Rader's daughter, which they compared to DNA evidence collected from the BTK crime scenes. The results were a match, and on February 25, 2005, Dennis Rader was arrested outside his home in Park City.

Confession and Trial: The End of the BTK Killer

Following his arrest, Rader quickly confessed to the murders, providing chillingly detailed accounts of each crime. He described his methods of stalking and killing his victims, often referring to them as "projects" and speaking in a cold, detached manner. Rader also admitted to being the author of the BTK letters and expressed a perverse pride in his ability to evade capture for so long.

Rader's trial began in June 2005, and he pleaded guilty to 10 counts of first-degree murder. During his sentencing hearing, Rader's lack of remorse and his chilling descriptions of the murders shocked both the court and the public. He was sentenced to 10 consecutive life terms in prison, with no possibility of parole.

Rader's incarceration at the El Dorado Correctional Facility in Kansas marked the end of his reign of terror, but the psychological scars he left on the Wichita community and the families of his victims remain to this day.

Legacy: The Impact of the BTK Case

The case of Dennis Rader, the BTK Killer, is one of the most studied and analyzed in the history of American criminology. Rader's ability to lead a double life for so many years—escaping detection while committing such heinous crimes—has been the subject of numerous books, documentaries, and academic studies. His case has provided valuable insights into the mind of a serial killer, particularly the ways in which individuals can compartmentalize their lives and hide their dark impulses behind a mask of normalcy.

The BTK case also had a profound impact on law enforcement, leading to the development of new investigative techniques and the advancement of forensic science. The use of metadata to track down Rader was a groundbreaking moment in criminal investigation, demonstrating the importance of digital evidence in solving crimes.

In addition to its contributions to criminal justice, the BTK case has also had a lasting effect on the Wichita community. The fear and anxiety that gripped the city during Rader's reign of terror have left deep psychological scars, and the memory of his crimes continues to haunt the area.

Chapter 11: Charles Starkweather

Charles Raymond Starkweather, an American spree killer who terrorized the United States during the late 1950s, is one of the most infamous figures in American criminal history. His killing spree, which took place over a two-month period in 1957 and 1958, left 11 people dead and shocked the nation. Starkweather's crimes, fueled by a volatile mix of teenage rebellion, alienation, and a troubled love affair, would go on to inspire numerous books, films, and songs. This detailed account of Charles Starkweather's life and crimes delves into the psychology, motivations, and consequences of his actions, providing a comprehensive look at one of America's most notorious murderers.

Early Life: The Making of a Killer

Charles Starkweather was born on November 24, 1938, in Lincoln, Nebraska, to Guy and Helen Starkweather. He was the third of seven children in a working-class family. Starkweather's early years were marked by poverty and a sense of inadequacy. His father struggled with unemployment due to rheumatoid arthritis, while his mother worked as a waitress to support the family.

From an early age, Starkweather experienced difficulties in school, both academically and socially. He was born with genu varum, a condition commonly known as "bow legs," which made him a target for bullying. His speech impediment and poor eyesight further isolated him from his peers. Starkweather's anger and frustration at his inability to fit in led him to develop a deep-seated resentment towards those who tormented him.

Starkweather's behavior began to deteriorate during his teenage years. He became increasingly rebellious and turned to petty crime as a way to assert control over his life. He dropped out of high school at the age of 16 and took a job as a garbage collector. Starkweather idolized the image of the outlaw and found solace in the stories of notorious criminals like Billy the Kid and Jesse James. These influences, combined with his pent-up rage and feelings of alienation, set the stage for the violent spree that would soon follow.

The Love Affair: Caril Ann Fugate

A pivotal figure in Starkweather's life was Caril Ann Fugate, a 13-year-old girl he met in 1956. Despite the significant age difference—Starkweather was 18 at the time—the two quickly became romantically involved. Fugate, like Starkweather, came from a troubled background, and their relationship was marked by a shared sense of disillusionment and rebellion against authority.

Starkweather was intensely possessive of Fugate, and their relationship became increasingly volatile. He dropped out of school and began to spiral further into delinquency, committing a series of petty crimes to impress his young girlfriend. Fugate's family disapproved of the relationship, but Starkweather refused to let her go, becoming more obsessive and controlling as time went on.

As the relationship intensified, Starkweather began to fantasize about a life of crime and adventure with Fugate by his side. He envisioned himself as a modern-day outlaw, living outside the bounds of society and taking what he wanted by force. These fantasies would soon manifest in a horrifying reality.

The First Murder: Prelude to a Spree

Starkweather's descent into murder began on November 30, 1957, with the killing of Robert Colvert, a gas station attendant in Lincoln, Nebraska. Starkweather, who had been planning a robbery, attempted to purchase a stuffed animal for Fugate with stolen money. When Colvert refused to sell the toy, Starkweather returned later that night with a shotgun. After forcing Colvert to drive to a remote area, Starkweather shot him in the head, making Colvert his first victim.

The murder of Robert Colvert marked a turning point in Starkweather's life. The act of taking another person's life seemed to embolden him, fueling his delusions of power and invincibility. Starkweather now saw himself as a figure to be feared, someone who could impose his will on the world through violence.

The Murder Spree: A Trail of Death Across Nebraska and Wyoming

Following the murder of Colvert, Starkweather's behavior became increasingly erratic. On January 21, 1958, he argued with Fugate's mother, Velda Bartlett, and stepfather, Marion Bartlett, over their disapproval of his relationship with their daughter. In a fit of rage, Starkweather shot and killed both of them, as well as Fugate's two-year-old half-sister, Betty Jean Bartlett. He then hid their bodies in outbuildings on the property.

With the Bartlett family dead, Starkweather and Fugate went on the run. Over the next eight days, the couple embarked on a killing spree that spanned two states, leaving a trail of bodies in their wake. The victims ranged in age from teenagers to elderly adults, and their murders were often brutal and senseless.

- **The Murder of August Meyer and the Ward Family**

Their first stop was the farm of August Meyer, a 70-year-old family friend. Starkweather shot Meyer in the head, then brutally beat his dog to death. After fleeing the scene, Starkweather and Fugate became stuck in the mud near the town of Bennet, Nebraska. When teenage sweethearts Robert Jensen and Carol King stopped to offer assistance, Starkweather abducted them at gunpoint, driving them to an abandoned storm cellar. There, he shot Jensen multiple times and attempted to sexually assault King before shooting her in the face. The bodies of Jensen and King were discovered the next day, sparking a massive manhunt.

- **The Murder of C. Lauer and Clara Ward**

Starkweather and Fugate then headed to Lincoln, where they entered the home of wealthy industrialist C. Lauer Ward. Starkweather shot and killed both Ward and his wife, Clara, before stabbing their maid, Lillian Fencl, to death. The couple ransacked the house, stealing money and valuables before fleeing in Ward's black Packard.

- **The Capture: The End of the Road**

Starkweather and Fugate's final victim was traveling salesman Merle Collison, who they encountered on a highway near Douglas, Wyoming. Starkweather shot Collison in his car and attempted to steal the vehicle, but the car's brake was engaged, and Starkweather was unable to release it. As Starkweather struggled with the car, a passerby stopped to offer help. Suspicious of Starkweather's behavior, the passerby engaged in a scuffle with him, which attracted the attention of a nearby Wyoming state trooper.

The trooper, along with local law enforcement, gave chase to Starkweather and Fugate as they fled in the stolen Packard. After a high-speed pursuit, Starkweather was eventually cornered and surrendered. Fugate, who had been with him throughout the spree, claimed she was a hostage and not a willing participant.

Starkweather, however, insisted that she had been an active accomplice.

The Trial: A Nation Gripped by Sensationalism

The trial of Charles Starkweather quickly became a media sensation, with newspapers across the country providing extensive coverage of the case. Starkweather was charged with multiple counts of first-degree murder, and the question of Fugate's involvement became a central issue. Prosecutors painted Starkweather as a cold-blooded killer, while his defense team attempted to argue that he was insane and unable to control his actions.

During the trial, Starkweather maintained that Fugate was a willing participant in the murders, a claim that she vehemently denied. The prosecution, however, argued that Fugate had ample opportunity to escape or alert authorities if she had been a true hostage. Despite Fugate's claims, she was also charged with murder.

On May 23, 1958, Starkweather was found guilty of first-degree murder and sentenced to death. Fugate was convicted of being an accessory to murder and sentenced to life in prison, although she would be paroled after serving 17 years. Starkweather's death sentence was carried out on June 25, 1959, when he was executed in the electric chair at the Nebraska State Penitentiary. His final words before his execution were, "They are blaming me for everything."

Psychological Profile: The Mind of a Teenage Killer

The case of Charles Starkweather has been the subject of extensive psychological analysis, with experts attempting to understand what drove a seemingly ordinary teenager to commit such heinous acts. Starkweather's background, marked by feelings of inadequacy, social isolation, and a fascination with violence, provides some insight into his motivations.

Starkweather's troubled relationship with his family, particularly his strained relationship with his father, may have contributed to his feelings of anger and resentment. His idolization of outlaws and criminals, combined with his own sense of powerlessness, likely fueled his desire to assert control through violence. Starkweather's relationship with Fugate, which was characterized by possessiveness and obsession, further exacerbated his instability.

Some experts have suggested that Starkweather exhibited traits of antisocial personality disorder, characterized by a lack of empathy, impulsivity, and a disregard for the rights of others. His behavior during the murders—marked by cold-blooded brutality and a lack of remorse—supports this diagnosis. Starkweather's actions were not driven by a clear motive, such as financial gain or revenge, but rather by a desire for power and recognition.

Cultural Impact: Starkweather in Popular Media

The Starkweather case has left an indelible mark on American culture, inspiring numerous films, books, and songs. The stark contrast between Starkweather's youth and the brutality of his crimes captured the public's imagination and made him a symbol of teenage rebellion gone horribly wrong.

One of the most famous works inspired by Starkweather is the 1973 film "Badlands," directed by Terrence Malick and starring Martin Sheen and Sissy Spacek. "Badlands" is a fictionalized account of the Starkweather-Fugate killing spree, and it explores themes of alienation, violence, and the allure of the outlaw lifestyle. The film's depiction of Starkweather's character, though renamed Kit Carruthers, captures the sense of aimless rebellion and the twisted romanticism that surrounded his crimes.

Another notable work inspired by Starkweather is the 1994 film "Natural Born Killers," directed by Oliver Stone and written by Quentin Tarantino. Although the film is a satirical and hyper-violent take on the media's fascination with crime and criminals, it draws clear parallels to Starkweather's spree, particularly in its portrayal of a young couple on a murderous rampage across the country. The film's protagonists, Mickey and Mallory Knox, echo the dynamic between Starkweather and Fugate, with a similar blend of charisma, nihilism, and brutality.

Starkweather's crimes also found their way into music, with Bruce Springsteen's song "Nebraska" from his 1982 album of the same name being a direct reference to the killer. The haunting ballad, told from Starkweather's perspective, reflects on the senselessness of his actions and the inevitability of his downfall. Springsteen's lyrics capture the bleakness of Starkweather's world and the cold, emotionless nature of his crimes.

In addition to films and music, Starkweather's story has been the subject of numerous books and documentaries, each seeking to understand the motivations behind his killing spree and its impact on American society. These works often explore the broader social and cultural context of the 1950s, a time when post-war prosperity was juxtaposed with the emergence of teenage rebellion and a growing sense of disillusionment among the youth.

Legacy: Lessons from Starkweather's Crimes

The legacy of Charles Starkweather is one of horror, fascination, and caution. His crimes serve as a stark reminder of the potential for violence that can exist within seemingly ordinary individuals. Starkweather's story is a case study in the dangers of unchecked anger, alienation, and the romanticization of criminal behavior.

In the years following Starkweather's execution, his case has been used as an example in discussions about juvenile delinquency, mental health, and the influence of media on young minds. His crimes have prompted debates about the role of society in preventing such tragedies and the responsibility of parents, educators, and communities in identifying and addressing the early signs of troubled behavior.

Moreover, Starkweather's story has become a cautionary tale about the perils of obsession and toxic relationships. The destructive bond between Starkweather and Fugate highlights the potential for young, impressionable individuals to be drawn into dangerous situations by more dominant or manipulative partners. It also raises questions about the degree of culpability in such cases, particularly when one party claims to be acting under duress or coercion.

Finally, the Starkweather case remains a chilling example of the unpredictability of human behavior. Despite the numerous attempts to analyze and understand his motives, Starkweather's killing spree ultimately defies easy categorization. His actions were a terrifying blend of calculated violence and impulsive rage, leaving a legacy that continues to haunt and intrigue those who study the darker aspects of human nature.

Chapter 12: John List

John Emil List stands out as one of America's most notorious family annihilators. His name evokes a chilling blend of calculated coldness, meticulous planning, and a deep, disturbing disconnect from the basic tenets of human empathy. Born on September 17, 1925, List's actions on November 9, 1971, left an indelible mark on American criminal history. His crime, the systematic murder of his entire family in their home in Westfield, New Jersey, shocked the nation and became a macabre case study in the psychology of murder, guilt, and religious fanaticism.

Early Life and Background: The Formation of a Rigid Personality

John List was born to German-American parents in Bay City, Michigan. His father, John Frederick List, and his mother, Alma List, were devout Lutherans, and they raised their only child in a strictly religious household. List's upbringing was marked by discipline, conservative values, and an unwavering commitment to religion. These early influences would profoundly shape his personality, creating a man who was rigid, emotionally distant, and deeply religious.

List was a bright student, and after graduating high school in 1943, he enlisted in the United States Army during World War II. He served as a laboratory technician and was discharged in 1946. Utilizing the G.I. Bill, List attended the University of Michigan, where he earned a bachelor's degree in business administration and later a master's degree in accounting. His education provided him with a stable career, but it also reinforced his methodical and calculating nature.

In 1951, List was recalled to active military duty during the Korean War, where he served as an officer in the finance corps. It was during this period that he met his future wife, Helen Morris Taylor, a widow with a young daughter, Brenda. The couple married in 1951, and List adopted Brenda. Together, they had three more children: Patricia, John Jr., and Frederick. The List family appeared to be the epitome of the American Dream—successful, devout, and respectable. However, beneath this façade lay a growing storm of financial troubles, domestic tensions, and List's increasingly fanatical religious beliefs.

The Road to Murder: Financial Ruin and Religious Obsession

By the late 1960s, John List's life began to unravel. After a series of job losses and financial setbacks, the family was living well beyond their means in a 19-room Victorian mansion known as Breeze Knoll. List's pride and his strict Lutheran upbringing prevented him from seeking help or admitting his failures. Instead, he meticulously concealed the family's financial ruin from his wife and children, all while sinking deeper into debt.

List's religious beliefs became more extreme during this period. He began to view his inability to provide for his family as a moral failing, a sin that could only be rectified by ensuring their salvation. He believed that by killing his family, he could save them from the shame of poverty and the temptations of the modern world. In his twisted logic, List convinced himself that murder was a merciful act, sparing his loved ones from damnation and allowing them to enter Heaven with their souls intact.

List's wife, Helen, had her own struggles. She was an alcoholic, and her health was deteriorating due to untreated syphilis contracted from her first husband. Her illness exacerbated the tension in the household, and List became increasingly resentful and detached. He saw his wife as an obstacle to his own religious purity and as a burden that further strained his already fragile psyche.

The Murders: A Chilling Execution

On the morning of November 9, 1971, John List carried out a meticulously planned massacre of his family. He first shot his wife, Helen, in the back of the head as she drank her morning coffee in the kitchen. He then moved upstairs to his mother, Alma, who lived with the family in an upstairs apartment. List shot her in the head as well, ensuring that she would not hear the gunshots and come downstairs. He placed her body in the attic.

Next, List waited for his children to return home from school. Patricia, 16, and Frederick, 13, were the first to arrive. List shot them both in the head, placing their bodies on sleeping bags in the ballroom of their mansion. His oldest son, John Jr., 15, was last to arrive. Unlike the others, John Jr. struggled with his father. After missing several shots, List finally killed his son with a volley of bullets to the head and chest. He placed John Jr.'s body alongside his siblings and mother in the ballroom.

After the murders, List calmly cleaned up, sat down to eat lunch, and then systematically began to erase his existence. He wrote detailed letters to his pastor and employer, explaining that the financial ruin and moral decay of his family had driven him to murder. He canceled the family's newspaper and milk deliveries, informed the children's school that they would be on a long vacation, and turned down the thermostat to preserve the bodies. Then, he vanished.

The Escape: Eighteen Years on the Run

John List's disappearance became one of the most notorious manhunts in U.S. history. For nearly two decades, he eluded capture, living under an assumed identity and building a new life for himself.

After leaving his family home, List drove to Kennedy Airport, parked his car, and took a train to Michigan. From there, he traveled to Colorado, where he assumed the name Robert Peter "Bob" Clark, a name he had taken from a former college classmate who had died in 1943.

In Denver, List began a new life. He found work as an accountant, joined a Lutheran church, and eventually remarried a woman named Delores Miller in 1985. The couple moved to Midlothian, Virginia, where List continued to live quietly, evading the law and maintaining his new identity for 18 years.

The List mansion, Breeze Knoll, burned down in a mysterious fire in 1972, destroying evidence and further complicating the search for the killer. List's letters, however, provided investigators with critical insights into his mindset and the rationale behind his actions. Despite their best efforts, the FBI and local authorities were unable to locate List, who had effectively vanished without a trace.

Capture and Trial: The Fall of a Family Annihilator

John List might have remained free if not for the advent of television crime programs. In May 1989, the popular TV show "America's Most Wanted" aired a segment on the List murders. The program featured a forensic sculptor named Frank Bender, who created an age-progressed clay bust of List, imagining what he might look like nearly two decades after the murders. The sculpture was astonishingly accurate, down to the large, square glasses that had become a part of List's new persona.

A former neighbor of List's from Denver recognized him immediately and contacted the authorities. On June 1, 1989, List was arrested at his home in Virginia. He initially denied his true identity, but fingerprints taken from his military records confirmed that he was indeed John Emil List.

List's trial began in April 1990. The prosecution argued that List had meticulously planned the murders for months, citing his calculated actions in the days leading up to the crime. The defense attempted to portray List as a man who had been driven to madness by financial stress and religious obsession. However, the jury was not swayed. After deliberating for nine hours, they found List guilty of five counts of first-degree murder.

During his sentencing, List expressed remorse for his actions but maintained that he believed he was saving his family from eternal damnation. The judge sentenced him to five consecutive life terms without the possibility of parole, ensuring that List would spend the rest of his life behind bars.

Legacy: The Psychological and Cultural Impact of John List

The case of John List has had a lasting impact on both the field of criminal psychology and popular culture. List's crimes are often cited in discussions of family annihilation, a rare but particularly disturbing form of multiple homicide in which a parent kills their entire family. Experts have analyzed List's personality and actions, attempting to understand the motivations behind such an extreme act of violence.

List is often described as a classic example of a narcissistic personality disorder. His inability to cope with failure, combined with his rigid moral and religious beliefs, created a perfect storm of delusion and desperation. In his mind, he was not committing a crime, but rather a righteous act of salvation. This distorted thinking allowed him to carry out the murders with a chilling lack of emotion.

The List case also highlighted the challenges of investigating and prosecuting family annihilators. These crimes often occur in private, with little warning or opportunity for intervention. The perpetrators are usually seen as upstanding members of society, making it difficult for others to recognize the warning signs. In List's case, his meticulous planning and subsequent disappearance made it nearly impossible for authorities to track him down, underscoring the need for more sophisticated investigative techniques.

In popular culture, John List has been the subject of numerous books, documentaries, and films. His story continues to fascinate and horrify audiences, serving as a grim reminder of the potential for evil that can exist behind closed doors. The meticulous nature of his crimes, combined with his ability to evade capture for so long, has cemented his place in the annals of American criminal history.

Chapter 13: Jerry Brudos

Jerry Brudos, also known as "The Lust Killer" or "The Shoe Fetish Slayer," is a name synonymous with some of the most grotesque and deviant acts of violence in the history of American serial killers. His crimes, committed between 1968 and 1969, reflect a mind deeply entrenched in sexual sadism, misogyny, and an obsession with female footwear. Brudos's acts of murder, mutilation, and fetishism have left an indelible mark on criminal psychology, making him one of the most notorious and studied figures in the annals of criminal history.

Born Jerome Henry Brudos on January 31, 1939, in Webster, South Dakota, Brudos's life and crimes offer a chilling glimpse into the development of a serial killer driven by extreme fetishes and deep-seated rage against women. His story is one of psychological torment, escalating violence, and ultimately, brutal murder.

Early Life: The Roots of a Dark Obsession

Jerry Brudos's early life was marked by a complex mixture of neglect, abuse, and the development of disturbing sexual fetishes. The youngest of two sons, Brudos was an unwanted child. His mother, Eileen Brudos, had longed for a daughter and expressed open disappointment at Jerry's birth. This lack of maternal affection would have profound effects on his psyche, sowing seeds of resentment and anger that would later manifest in violent ways.

The Brudos family moved frequently during Jerry's childhood, contributing to his feelings of instability and isolation. His father, Henry Brudos, was largely absent, both physically and emotionally, leaving Jerry to the cold and often cruel whims of his mother. Eileen's harsh treatment of Jerry included verbal abuse and a dismissive attitude toward his needs, further alienating him from normal familial bonds.

From an early age, Brudos exhibited signs of a troubled mind. At the age of five, he discovered a pair of high-heeled shoes in a junkyard, sparking what would become a lifelong obsession with women's footwear. When his mother discovered him wearing the shoes, she reacted with anger and disgust, a response that likely reinforced Brudos's association of shame with his budding fetish. Despite his mother's attempts to suppress his interests, Brudos's fascination with shoes only grew, evolving into a full-blown sexual fetish as he reached adolescence.

As Brudos entered puberty, his fetishes expanded to include women's underwear and clothing. He began stealing shoes and lingerie from neighbors and classmates, often keeping the items hidden as trophies. These behaviors were early indicators of the criminal compulsions that would later drive him to commit murder. Brudos's fantasies became increasingly violent, focusing on the domination, humiliation, and control of women. His inability to form healthy relationships with women, combined with his growing sexual deviancy, created a dangerous cocktail of frustration and anger.

Escalation to Violence: The Making of a Killer

By the time Brudos reached adulthood, his fetishes and fantasies had grown darker and more extreme. He served in the U.S. Army for a brief period but was discharged for his bizarre behavior and inability to adapt to military life. After his discharge, Brudos attempted to settle into a normal life, marrying a young woman named Darcy and fathering two children. However, the veneer of normalcy could not mask the seething darkness within him.

Brudos's relationship with his wife was deeply dysfunctional. He demanded that Darcy remain subservient and often forced her to walk around the house naked, wearing only high heels while he photographed her. These acts of control and humiliation were a clear extension of his earlier fetishes and a sign that his need for domination was growing stronger.

In 1967, Brudos's fantasies crossed a dangerous line from thought to action. He began prowling the streets in search of women who fit his idealized image of femininity—young, attractive, and slender, with a particular focus on their feet and shoes. His first known attack occurred in January 1968, when he lured a young woman into his car under the pretense of needing directions. He choked her into unconsciousness and raped her, but she survived and managed to escape. This attack was the first of many that would culminate in a series of brutal murders.

The Murders: A Pattern of Depravity

Brudos's murder spree began in earnest in January 1968, when he abducted and killed 19-year-old Linda Slawson. Slawson was a door-to-door encyclopedia saleswoman who made the fatal mistake of knocking on Brudos's door. He invited her in, knocked her unconscious, and then strangled her to death. After killing her, Brudos indulged in his fetishes by dressing her in various outfits and shoes he had collected, photographing her corpse in a macabre fashion shoot. He then cut off her left foot, which he kept as a trophy, using it to model his collection of stolen high-heeled shoes. He disposed of the rest of her body by dumping it into the Willamette River, weighted down to ensure it wouldn't resurface.

Over the next year, Brudos would go on to murder three more women in similar fashion, each time escalating the level of violence and depravity. His next victim, 23-year-old Jan Susan Whitney, was killed in November 1968 after her car broke down on Interstate 5. Brudos offered her a ride, but instead, he strangled her with a leather strap. He took her body to his garage, where he suspended it from the ceiling using a pulley system he had rigged for such purposes. Over the next few days, Brudos continued to dress and photograph Whitney's corpse, eventually cutting off her breasts to make plastic molds, which he kept as mementos.

Brudos's third victim was Karen Sprinker, an 18-year-old college student abducted from a department store parking lot in March 1969. Sprinker's fate mirrored that of Brudos's earlier victims. He took her to his home, where he forced her to model for him in various outfits before killing her. Like Whitney, her body was suspended from the ceiling while Brudos engaged in his gruesome rituals. He amputated her breasts and disposed of her body in the Willamette River, weighed down with an engine block to prevent it from floating to the surface.

The final victim, 22-year-old Linda Salee, was abducted in April 1969. Brudos's modus operandi remained consistent—he lured her into his car, took her to his home, and killed her. Her body was also discarded in the river after being subjected to similar post-mortem mutilations.

The Investigation and Capture: A Trail of Horror

Brudos's crimes went undetected for several months, but the disappearances of multiple young women in the same area raised alarm among law enforcement. The police began to notice a pattern in the abductions—each victim had been last seen in or near department stores, and each had been wearing fashionable clothing, particularly shoes. This led investigators to suspect that the killer had a shoe fetish, a crucial detail that would eventually lead to Brudos's capture.

In May 1969, the police received a breakthrough when a fisherman discovered the bodies of two of Brudos's victims in the Long Tom River, a tributary of the Willamette. The bodies were heavily weighted down and bore signs of extreme mutilation. This discovery intensified the investigation, and police began to focus on known sex offenders and individuals with a history of violence against women.

Brudos's name surfaced during the investigation when one of his earlier attempted victims, who had managed to escape, provided a description of her attacker and his car. This led police to Brudos, who was placed under surveillance. During this time, police gathered enough evidence to obtain a search warrant for Brudos's home.

The search of Brudos's garage revealed a treasure trove of incriminating evidence. Police found photographs of the victims, as well as various personal items belonging to them. The most damning evidence was the collection of body parts Brudos had kept as trophies, including the amputated breasts of two victims. Brudos was arrested and, after being confronted with the overwhelming evidence against him, he confessed to the murders.

Trial and Imprisonment: The End of a Killer's Reign

Jerry Brudos was charged with three counts of first-degree murder, and in June 1969, he pleaded guilty to all charges in an attempt to avoid the death penalty. He was sentenced to three consecutive life terms in prison, with no possibility of parole.

During his trial, Brudos showed little remorse for his actions. He described his crimes in a detached, almost clinical manner, focusing more on the details of his fetishes than on the lives he had destroyed. His lack of empathy and his obsession with his sexual fantasies shocked both the court and the public. Psychiatrists who examined Brudos diagnosed him with antisocial personality disorder, as well as extreme sexual sadism, noting that his behavior was driven by a deep-seated hatred of women, combined with a compulsion to dominate and control them.

Brudos's life in prison was largely uneventful. He was housed at the Oregon State Penitentiary, where he remained until his death in 2006 from liver cancer. Even in prison, Brudos's obsessions persisted. He reportedly requested women's shoe catalogs from several mail-order companies, which he used to fuel his fantasies.

Psychological Analysis: Understanding the Mind of Jerry Brudos

Jerry Brudos's case is often studied by psychologists and criminologists seeking to understand the intersection of sexual fetishes and violent behavior. Brudos's crimes were not driven by a need for power or financial gain but by his overwhelming and deviant sexual desires. His obsession with women's shoes and clothing was the foundation of his criminal behavior, and it gradually escalated into violence as he sought to fulfill increasingly extreme fantasies.

- **The Role of Fetishism in Brudos's Crimes**

Fetishism, in Brudos's case, was not merely a sexual preference but an all-consuming compulsion that dictated his actions. His fixation on women's shoes and underwear began at a young age and evolved into a full-blown paraphilia. This fetishism was intertwined with feelings of anger and resentment towards women, likely stemming from his tumultuous relationship with his mother. His need to dominate and control women through these objects of desire reflected a deep-seated psychological disturbance.

Brudos's acts of murder and mutilation were an extension of his fetishistic behavior. By killing women and then dressing them up in the objects of his desire, he was able to exert total control over them, turning them into lifeless mannequins that he could manipulate at will. The removal of body parts, such as feet and breasts, and the creation of trophies from these parts, further emphasized his desire to possess and objectify women.

- **Antisocial Personality Disorder and Sexual Sadism**

Psychiatrists who studied Brudos diagnosed him with antisocial personality disorder, characterized by a lack of empathy, disregard for the rights of others, and an inability to conform to social norms. Individuals with this disorder often exhibit manipulative behavior, a superficial charm, and a propensity for lying, all traits that Brudos displayed during his interactions with others, including his family.

In addition to antisocial personality disorder, Brudos was also diagnosed with sexual sadism, a condition where an individual derives pleasure from inflicting pain, humiliation, or suffering on others. This sadism was evident in the way Brudos treated his victims—he not only killed them but also engaged in acts of post-mortem mutilation, which he found sexually gratifying. His need to relive the killings through photographs and trophies further underscored his sadistic tendencies.

- **The Influence of Early Childhood Experiences**

Brudos's early childhood experiences played a significant role in shaping his deviant behavior. His mother's rejection and harsh treatment created a foundation of anger and resentment towards women, which was later expressed through his crimes. The lack of a positive maternal figure in his life may have contributed to his inability to form healthy relationships with women, leading to his objectification and dehumanization of them.

Furthermore, the early discovery of his shoe fetish and the subsequent shame and punishment he experienced likely reinforced the association between his sexual desires and feelings of guilt and anger. As he grew older, these emotions became increasingly intertwined with his fantasies, driving him to act out violently as a way to assert control and dominance over the objects of his fixation.

Legacy and Impact: Lessons from Brudos's Crimes

The crimes of Jerry Brudos continue to be a subject of study in criminal psychology, providing valuable insights into the development and behavior of sexually motivated serial killers. His case highlights the dangers of untreated paraphilias and the potential for such conditions to escalate into violent behavior when combined with underlying psychological disorders.

Brudos's crimes also underscore the importance of early intervention and treatment for individuals exhibiting deviant sexual behaviors. Had Brudos received psychological help during his childhood or adolescence, it is possible that his fetishes could have been managed in a way that did not lead to violence. His case serves as a reminder of the need for greater awareness and understanding of sexual disorders and their potential impact on behavior.

Chapter 14: Joel Rifkin

Joel Rifkin is one of the most notorious serial killers in American history, responsible for the brutal murders of at least 17 women between 1989 and 1993. His killing spree, marked by extreme violence and the systematic targeting of vulnerable women, has left a lasting scar on the collective consciousness. Rifkin's life, his crimes, and the psychological underpinnings of his actions offer a disturbing glimpse into the mind of a serial killer driven by deep-seated psychological issues and an uncontrollable compulsion to kill.

Early Life and Troubled Beginnings

Joel David Rifkin was born on January 20, 1959, in New York City. His early life was marked by feelings of isolation, rejection, and inadequacy. Adopted as an infant by Bernard and Jeanne Rifkin, Joel struggled to fit in from a young age. His adoptive parents provided a stable home, but Rifkin's early years were plagued by severe social difficulties and academic struggles. He was often bullied by his peers due to his awkward demeanor and slow learning abilities, which only exacerbated his feelings of inadequacy and low self-esteem.

Rifkin's struggles in school were compounded by dyslexia, which went undiagnosed for much of his childhood. His inability to keep up with his classmates led to further ostracization and ridicule. As a result, Rifkin became increasingly withdrawn, retreating into a world of fantasy to escape the harsh realities of his life. He developed an obsession with violent fantasies, which he later admitted played a significant role in shaping his homicidal tendencies.

During his teenage years, Rifkin's behavior became increasingly erratic. He dropped out of high school and briefly attended college, but his academic performance continued to suffer. His social isolation deepened, and he began to engage in petty crimes and theft. It was during this time that Rifkin's fascination with violent fantasies began to take on a darker, more dangerous dimension. He started fantasizing about dominating and killing women, a fantasy that would later evolve into a horrifying reality.

The Descent into Murder

Rifkin's descent into murder began in 1989, when he claimed his first victim, a woman named Susie. He picked her up in Manhattan and brought her back to his home in East Meadow, Long Island, where he brutally beat and strangled her. After killing Susie, Rifkin dismembered her body and disposed of the remains in various locations, including the East River. The murder provided Rifkin with a sense of power and control that he had never experienced before, and it marked the beginning of a four-year killing spree that would claim the lives of at least 17 women.

Over the next several years, Rifkin continued to prey on vulnerable women, most of whom were sex workers. He would pick them up, bring them back to his home or a secluded location, and then kill them in a frenzy of violence. After the murders, Rifkin would often dismember the bodies and dispose of the remains in different locations around New York. His methods of disposal varied, ranging from dumping body parts in rivers to burying them in remote areas.

Rifkin's ability to evade capture for so long was due in part to his careful selection of victims. He targeted women who were on the fringes of society, often homeless or struggling with addiction, making it less likely that their disappearances would be immediately noticed or investigated. Additionally, the transient nature of his victims' lifestyles made it difficult for authorities to establish a pattern or link the murders together.

Despite the brutality of his crimes, Rifkin maintained a seemingly normal life on the surface. He lived with his mother in a suburban neighborhood and held various jobs, including working as a landscaper and at a print shop. His ability to compartmentalize his life allowed him to continue his killing spree without arousing suspicion. However, behind the facade of normalcy, Rifkin was consumed by his violent urges, which he later described as an uncontrollable addiction.

The Psychological Profile of a Killer

Understanding Joel Rifkin's psychological makeup is key to understanding the motivations behind his horrific crimes. Rifkin exhibited many of the traits commonly associated with serial killers, including a deep-seated sense of inadequacy, social isolation, and a lack of empathy. These traits were compounded by his obsessive fantasies about violence and domination, which fueled his compulsion to kill.

One of the most striking aspects of Rifkin's psychological profile is his intense feelings of inadequacy and self-loathing. Throughout his life, Rifkin struggled with a pervasive sense of failure and worthlessness, stemming from his difficulties in school and his inability to form meaningful relationships. These feelings of inadequacy were exacerbated by the bullying and rejection he experienced as a child, leading him to retreat into a world of violent fantasies where he could assert control and power.

Rifkin's fantasies about violence and domination were likely a way for him to compensate for his feelings of powerlessness in real life. By killing women, Rifkin was able to exert total control over them, transforming them from living beings into objects that he could manipulate and dispose of at will. This need for control was a driving force behind his crimes, and it provided him with a sense of satisfaction that he could not achieve in any other aspect of his life.

In addition to his feelings of inadequacy, Rifkin also exhibited a profound lack of empathy, a common trait among serial killers. He viewed his victims not as human beings, but as objects to be used and discarded. This dehumanization of his victims allowed Rifkin to commit acts of extreme violence without any apparent remorse or guilt. Even after his arrest, Rifkin showed little remorse for his actions, instead focusing on the details of his crimes and the methods he used to evade capture.

Rifkin's lack of empathy was likely a result of his deep-seated psychological issues, including his inability to form meaningful connections with others. His social isolation and rejection by his peers may have led him to view the world in a detached and dehumanized manner, where people were merely objects to be manipulated for his own gratification.

The Arrest and Trial

Joel Rifkin's killing spree came to an end on June 28, 1993, when he was arrested after a routine traffic stop turned into a high-speed chase. Rifkin had been driving without a license plate, and when police attempted to pull him over, he fled, leading officers on a chase through the streets of Long Island. The chase ended when Rifkin crashed his car into a utility pole, and when officers approached the vehicle, they discovered the decomposing body of his final victim, Tiffany Bresciani, in the trunk.

Rifkin was immediately arrested and taken into custody, where he quickly confessed to the murders of 17 women. His detailed confessions provided authorities with a horrifying insight into the mind of a serial killer who had been operating undetected for years.

Rifkin's calm and matter-of-fact demeanor during his confession was chilling, as he recounted the details of each murder with a disturbing lack of emotion.

During his trial, Rifkin's defense team attempted to argue that he was not guilty by reason of insanity, citing his long history of psychological issues and violent fantasies. However, the prosecution successfully argued that Rifkin was fully aware of his actions and their consequences, and that he had gone to great lengths to cover up his crimes. The jury ultimately found Rifkin guilty of nine counts of second-degree murder, and he was sentenced to 203 years to life in prison.

Rifkin's trial and subsequent conviction brought closure to the families of his victims, many of whom had been living with the uncertainty of their loved ones' disappearances for years. However, the trial also raised questions about the role of society in creating the conditions that allowed Rifkin to operate for so long without detection. The fact that so many of Rifkin's victims were marginalized women highlights the vulnerability of certain populations and the need for greater societal support and protection for those at risk.

Legacy and Impact

Joel Rifkin's crimes have left a lasting impact on both the public consciousness and the field of criminal psychology. His case is often cited as an example of how a seemingly ordinary individual can harbor deep-seated psychological issues that manifest in violent and destructive behavior. Rifkin's ability to lead a double life, maintaining a facade of normalcy while committing horrific acts of violence, serves as a reminder of the complexities of human psychology and the potential for darkness that exists within us all.

In the years since his conviction, Rifkin has become a subject of study for criminologists and psychologists seeking to understand the motivations and behaviors of serial killers. His case provides valuable insights into the psychological and environmental factors that can contribute to the development of violent tendencies, and it underscores the importance of early intervention and treatment for individuals exhibiting signs of psychological distress.

Rifkin's crimes have also had a lasting impact on the victims' families and the communities in which he operated. The fear and uncertainty that gripped these communities during Rifkin's killing spree have left a lasting mark, and the memories of his victims continue to serve as a sobering reminder of the fragility of life and the dangers that can lurk beneath the surface of seemingly ordinary individuals.

Chapter 15: H. H. Holmes

Herman Webster Mudgett, who would later become infamous as H. H. Holmes, was born on May 16, 1861, in Gilmanton, New Hampshire. Raised in a relatively affluent family, Holmes exhibited signs of unusual behavior from a young age. His early life was marked by a fascination with death and dissection, foreshadowing the horrors he would later unleash. Holmes was reportedly bullied by his peers, and there are stories, though not confirmed, that he was once forced to stand face-to-face with a skeleton in a doctor's office, sparking a lifelong obsession with anatomy and the macabre.

Holmes excelled academically and eventually enrolled in the University of Michigan Medical School, where he began honing his skills in dissection and surgery. It was during this time that he also developed a penchant for criminal activity, particularly in the realm of insurance fraud. Holmes was known to steal cadavers from the medical school, disfigure them, and then claim they had died accidentally to collect insurance money. These early crimes were just the beginning of a career that would blend medical knowledge with a twisted penchant for murder.

The Birth of a New Identity

After several years of engaging in small-scale fraud and deceit, Holmes adopted the alias "Dr. Henry Howard Holmes" and moved to Chicago in 1886. This new identity allowed him to reinvent himself as a legitimate physician and businessman, but it also provided a convenient cover for his increasingly sinister activities. By this time, Holmes had married three different women without ever divorcing the previous wives, further highlighting his manipulative and deceptive nature.

In Chicago, Holmes initially worked at a pharmacy before buying it outright. This establishment, however, was just a stepping stone to his most infamous venture: the construction of a massive, labyrinthine building that would later be known as the "Murder Castle."

The Construction of the Murder Castle

The "Murder Castle," located at the corner of South Wallace Avenue and West 63rd Street in the Englewood neighborhood of Chicago, stands as one of the most chilling examples of premeditated murder in history. Construction on the building began in 1887, and Holmes designed it to serve multiple purposes, one of which was to facilitate his homicidal desires. The building was a bizarre, multi-story structure with over 100 rooms, many of which had no windows, doors that opened into brick walls, and staircases that led nowhere. The structure also featured secret passageways, trapdoors, hidden chambers, and soundproof rooms.

Holmes employed a series of different contractors to work on the building, frequently dismissing them and hiring new ones to ensure that no one person would understand the complete layout. This allowed Holmes to keep the true purpose of the building hidden from everyone. While the ground floor of the building housed shops, the upper floors contained apartments and offices that Holmes rented out, luring in potential victims under the guise of providing affordable housing during the 1893 World's Columbian Exposition, also known as the Chicago World's Fair.

The Methods of Murder

Holmes' "Murder Castle" was a veritable house of horrors, where he employed a variety of methods to kill his victims. Some rooms were outfitted as gas chambers, with pipes leading into the walls that Holmes could control from his own office, allowing him to asphyxiate his victims at will. Other rooms were soundproofed, allowing Holmes to torture his victims without their screams being heard by the outside world. There were also chutes that led directly from the upper floors to the basement, where Holmes had set up a dissection table, a crematorium, and vats of acid. After murdering his victims, Holmes would often dissect their bodies and sell the skeletons to medical schools, further profiting from his gruesome activities.

Holmes targeted a wide range of victims, including hotel guests, employees, and even romantic partners. He was known to charm and manipulate women, often promising marriage, only to kill them once they were under his control. Many of his victims were young women who had come to Chicago seeking employment during the World's Fair, only to meet a tragic and terrifying end at the hands of Holmes.

Capture and Trial

Despite the scale of his crimes, Holmes' downfall began not with murder but with yet another instance of insurance fraud. He had concocted a plan with an associate, Benjamin Pitezel, to fake Pitezel's death and collect the insurance money. However, Holmes ultimately murdered Pitezel and went on to kill three of Pitezel's children as well. These murders, combined with Holmes' increasingly reckless behavior, led to his arrest in 1894.

Holmes' trial, which took place in 1895, was a media sensation. Dubbed "America's First Serial Killer," Holmes' cold, calculating demeanor shocked the public. During the trial, Holmes confessed to 27 murders, though the actual number of his victims is believed to be much higher, possibly even in the hundreds. His detailed confessions were both chilling and bizarre, filled with contradictory statements that made it difficult to determine the full extent of his crimes. Nevertheless, he was convicted and sentenced to death.

Execution and Legacy

On May 7, 1896, H. H. Holmes was hanged at Moyamensing Prison in Philadelphia. Even in death, Holmes remained a figure of macabre curiosity. It was reported that his neck did not snap immediately upon the drop, leading to a slow and agonizing death by strangulation, a fate that some saw as poetic justice for the man who had inflicted so much pain on others.

Holmes' legacy as one of America's most infamous serial killers endures to this day. His "Murder Castle" was eventually torn down, but the story of his crimes continues to fascinate and horrify people around the world. The tale of H. H. Holmes is often cited as a case study in the psychology of a psychopath, illustrating how charm, intelligence, and a complete lack of empathy can combine to create a killer of terrifying proportions.

Cultural Impact and Modern Interpretations

The story of H. H. Holmes has been the subject of numerous books, documentaries, and films, most notably Erik Larson's best-selling book *The Devil in the White City*. Larson's book juxtaposes the grandeur of the 1893 World's Fair with the dark underbelly of Holmes' murderous activities, offering a gripping narrative that has captivated readers since its publication. There have been talks of adapting the book into a film or television series, with various high-profile directors and actors attached to the project over the years.

Holmes' life and crimes have also inspired a range of fictional portrayals, from characters in horror novels to villains in television shows. His "Murder Castle" has become a symbol of the extreme lengths to which a killer can go to satisfy their dark desires, and his story serves as a grim reminder of the potential for evil that can lurk behind a seemingly charming exterior.

Chapter 16: Andrei Chikatilo (the Butcher of Rostov)

Andrei Romanovich Chikatilo, born on October 16, 1936, in the village of Yabluchne, Ukrainian SSR (then part of the Soviet Union), is one of the most notorious and horrifying serial killers in history. His early life was marked by extreme hardship, deprivation, and emotional turmoil, which likely played a significant role in shaping the monster he would become. Chikatilo's childhood was during a time of great suffering for the Soviet Union, particularly during the Holodomor, a man-made famine that devastated Ukraine from 1932 to 1933, resulting in the deaths of millions.

Chikatilo was born into a poor, rural family. His father, Roman, was conscripted into the Red Army during World War II and was captured by the Germans, spending the war years as a prisoner. This brought shame upon the family, as Soviet society viewed prisoners of war as traitors. Chikatilo's mother, Anna, was a harsh and strict woman, who often told her son terrifying stories to keep him obedient. One such story involved Chikatilo's older brother, Stepan, who was allegedly kidnapped and eaten by starving neighbors during the famine. Although this story may have been fabricated, it left a profound impact on Chikatilo's psyche, contributing to his lifelong fear of abandonment and death.

Growing up, Chikatilo was frequently bullied and ostracized by his peers due to his shyness, introverted nature, and poor eyesight. He also suffered from enuresis, or bedwetting, which led to further humiliation. As a child, Chikatilo developed a fascination with power and control, likely as a defense mechanism against the helplessness he felt in his harsh environment. These early experiences of trauma, isolation, and ridicule laid the groundwork for his later, horrific acts.

Sexual Dysfunction and Psychological Issues

Chikatilo's sexual development was deeply troubled and marred by dysfunction. From a young age, he struggled with impotence, which severely impacted his self-esteem and ability to form healthy relationships. In his teenage years, he attempted to engage in sexual activities with his peers, but his inability to perform sexually led to intense feelings of inadequacy and humiliation. These experiences further fueled his deep-seated rage and resentment toward women, which would later manifest in his violent attacks.

Throughout his life, Chikatilo sought control and dominance to compensate for his feelings of powerlessness, particularly in sexual contexts. He found that he could only achieve sexual gratification through acts of violence, often involving the mutilation and murder of his victims. This perverse connection between violence and sexual arousal became the driving force behind his killing spree.

The Emergence of a Killer

Despite his troubled personal life, Chikatilo was able to lead a relatively normal existence on the surface. He attended Rostov University, where he studied Russian literature, and later became a teacher. However, his career was plagued by accusations of inappropriate behavior towards his students, particularly young girls. Chikatilo was reported for molesting children on several occasions, but due to the inefficiencies and corruption within the Soviet system, he was never formally charged. Instead, he was quietly dismissed from his teaching positions and moved to new schools, where the pattern of abuse continued.

It wasn't until the late 1970s that Chikatilo's deviant urges escalated into murder. His first known victim was a nine-year-old girl named Yelena Zakotnova, whom he lured into a secluded area in 1978. Chikatilo attempted to rape her, but when he failed to achieve an erection, he became enraged and stabbed her to death. This act marked the beginning of a series of brutal murders that would span over a decade, claiming the lives of at least 52 victims, though the actual number is believed to be higher.

The Modus Operandi

Andrei Chikatilo's methods of killing were marked by extreme brutality and savagery. His victims, who ranged in age from young children to women in their forties, were often lured into isolated areas with promises of food, money, or companionship. Once alone with his victims, Chikatilo would attack them, typically starting with a violent assault. He would then proceed to mutilate their bodies, often stabbing them dozens of times in a frenzied manner. Chikatilo's preferred method of killing was stabbing or slashing, which he found sexually arousing.

In many cases, Chikatilo would mutilate the genitals of his victims, sometimes removing internal organs, eyes, or breasts. This gruesome dismemberment was not only a means of venting his rage and frustration but also a source of perverse pleasure. Chikatilo claimed that the sight of his victims' blood, along with the act of cutting into their flesh, provided him with a sense of power and sexual gratification that he could not achieve through consensual sexual acts.

Chikatilo's murders were often committed in remote, wooded areas near train stations or bus stops, making it difficult for authorities to find witnesses or evidence. He was careful to cover his tracks, disposing of his victims' belongings and scattering body parts to prevent identification. Despite the horrifying nature of his crimes, Chikatilo was able to evade capture for many years, in part due to the limitations of Soviet law enforcement at the time.

The Manhunt and Arrest

The authorities were slow to connect the series of murders to a single perpetrator, largely due to the chaotic and inefficient nature of Soviet policing during the 1980s. The country was still recovering from the stagnation of the Brezhnev era, and the police were ill-equipped to handle such a complex case. Additionally, the Soviet government was reluctant to admit that a serial killer was on the loose, as it contradicted their propaganda of a safe and crime-free society.

Despite these challenges, a dedicated task force was eventually assembled to track down the killer. Led by Major Mikhail Fetisov and forensic psychologist Alexander Bukhanovsky, the investigation took years to gain momentum. Bukhanovsky's psychological profile of the killer, which accurately described Chikatilo's personality and behavioral patterns, played a crucial role in narrowing down the suspect pool.

Chikatilo was first arrested in 1984, but due to a lack of evidence, he was released. During this time, another man was wrongfully convicted and executed for some of the murders, further delaying Chikatilo's capture. It wasn't until November 20, 1990, that Chikatilo was finally arrested after being observed by an undercover officer near a train station in Rostov, acting suspiciously and attempting to approach young children.

When Chikatilo was taken into custody, investigators found blood and dirt under his fingernails, and further forensic evidence linked him to several of the murders. During his interrogation, Chikatilo initially denied any involvement, but after days of intense questioning, he finally confessed. His detailed confessions were chilling, as he described his crimes with a detached, almost clinical precision. He admitted to killing 56 people, though the official count stands at 52, and he provided investigators with horrifying details about the methods he used and the reasons behind his actions.

Trial and Execution

Andrei Chikatilo's trial, which began in April 1992, was a spectacle that drew widespread media attention. The courtroom was packed with journalists, survivors, and relatives of the victims, all eager to see the man responsible for such unimaginable atrocities. Chikatilo, often referred to as the "Butcher of Rostov" or the "Red Ripper," remained emotionless throughout much of the proceedings, occasionally making bizarre outbursts or gestures that suggested a disturbed mind.

Chikatilo's defense team attempted to argue that he was insane and therefore not responsible for his actions. However, the court-appointed psychiatrists found him mentally competent to stand trial, despite his obvious psychological issues. The trial was a harrowing experience for the families of the victims, as they were forced to listen to the gruesome details of how their loved ones had been tortured and killed.

In October 1992, Chikatilo was found guilty of 52 murders and sentenced to death. The judge described his crimes as "inhuman" and "evil beyond comprehension." Chikatilo was placed on death row, where he spent the next few years in solitary confinement. His appeal was denied, and on February 14, 1994, Andrei Chikatilo was executed by a single gunshot to the back of the head at a prison in Novocherkassk, Russia.

The Legacy of Terror

The story of Andrei Chikatilo is one of the darkest chapters in the history of crime, not only in the Soviet Union but in the world. His reign of terror lasted over 12 years, during which he preyed on the most vulnerable members of society, leaving behind a trail of broken families and devastated communities. Chikatilo's crimes were a direct challenge to the Soviet regime's claims of social harmony and safety, exposing the deep flaws in a system that allowed such a predator to operate with impunity for so long.

Chikatilo's case has been the subject of numerous books, documentaries, and films, including the 1995 movie *Citizen X*, which dramatizes the investigation and eventual capture of the killer. His story serves as a grim reminder of the potential for human depravity and the capacity for evil that can exist within an individual. It also highlights the importance of effective law enforcement and psychological profiling in the pursuit of justice.

Psychological Analysis and Aftermath

Andrei Chikatilo's case has been extensively studied by criminologists and psychologists, who have sought to understand the factors that drove him to commit such heinous acts. His combination of sexual dysfunction, childhood trauma, and deep-seated feelings of inadequacy likely contributed to the development of his murderous impulses. Chikatilo himself admitted that he derived sexual pleasure from the act of killing, which he viewed as a way to assert control and power over his victims.

Chikatilo's crimes also prompted significant changes in the Soviet and later Russian criminal justice system. His case exposed the inadequacies of Soviet policing, particularly in handling serial crimes, and led to improvements in forensic techniques and criminal profiling. The introduction of more sophisticated methods of investigation, including DNA analysis, has since helped prevent similar cases from going undetected for so long.

Chapter 17: Donald Henry Gaskins

Donald Henry Gaskins, also known as "Pee Wee" Gaskins, is remembered as one of the most ruthless and violent serial killers in American history. Born on March 13, 1933, in Florence County, South Carolina, Gaskins was the product of an abusive and chaotic environment that seemed to nurture his violent tendencies from an early age. His early life was marked by instability, neglect, and exposure to violence, all of which played a significant role in shaping the man he would become.

Gaskins was the last of several illegitimate children born to his mother, Eulea Parrott, who was a poor and uneducated woman. His father, whom Gaskins never met, had no role in his life. Growing up, Gaskins was often left to fend for himself, receiving little attention or care from his mother. The lack of a stable family structure and parental guidance led to his involvement in criminal activities at a very young age.

Nicknamed "Pee Wee" due to his small stature—he was undersized for his age—Gaskins was constantly bullied and ridiculed by his peers. This bullying fostered a deep sense of resentment and anger within him, which he would later channel into acts of extreme violence. By the time he was a teenager, Gaskins had already established himself as a troublemaker and a delinquent, engaging in theft, assault, and other criminal activities.

Early Crimes and Imprisonment

Gaskins' criminal behavior escalated rapidly during his adolescence. At the age of 13, he and a group of friends formed a gang known as the "Trouble Trio." The gang specialized in breaking into homes, stealing valuables, and committing acts of vandalism. However, their activities soon took a darker turn, as they began raping young girls in the area. Gaskins, who harbored a deep-seated hatred for women, was particularly vicious in these attacks.

In 1946, Gaskins was caught breaking into a home and was sent to reform school. His time in the reform school only served to harden him further. He was repeatedly abused, both physically and sexually, by older boys and even the staff. This abuse reinforced his belief that violence was the only way to survive and assert dominance. Gaskins eventually escaped from the reform school but was soon caught and sent to a state industrial school for boys, where he continued to be a problematic inmate.

At the age of 18, Gaskins was released from the industrial school but quickly returned to a life of crime. He began working in a traveling carnival, where he committed burglaries and assaults. His first known murder occurred in 1953 when he killed a young girl after she insulted him. Gaskins later claimed that this murder gave him a sense of power and control, sparking his desire to kill again.

The Formation of a Serial Killer

Gaskins' life of crime continued unabated throughout the 1950s and 1960s. He was arrested multiple times for various offenses, including assault, attempted murder, and theft. Each time he was incarcerated, Gaskins found himself in violent confrontations with other inmates, often resulting in him being placed in solitary confinement. Despite his frequent imprisonment, Gaskins managed to escape from custody on several occasions, further adding to his reputation as a dangerous and unpredictable criminal.

It was during his time in prison that Gaskins honed his ability to manipulate and intimidate others. He learned to exploit the weaknesses of those around him, often using violence or the threat of violence to get what he wanted. Gaskins' small stature belied his ferocity, earning him a reputation as a man not to be trifled with. He was known for his ability to turn the tables on larger, more physically imposing inmates, often resorting to brutal tactics to maintain his position of power.

Gaskins' most significant period of criminal activity began in the late 1960s, following his release from prison. He moved back to South Carolina, where he embarked on a killing spree that would last for nearly a decade. Gaskins later divided his murders into two categories: "coastal kills" and "serious murders." The coastal kills were victims of opportunity—hitchhikers, drifters, and strangers whom Gaskins would pick up, torture, and murder. He claimed that these murders were purely for his pleasure, as he derived great satisfaction from the act of killing.

The serious murders, on the other hand, involved people Gaskins knew personally or had some connection to. These killings were often motivated by a desire for revenge, financial gain, or the need to eliminate a potential threat. Gaskins was meticulous in planning these murders, often spending weeks or even months stalking his victims before finally striking. His method of killing was typically brutal and sadistic, involving prolonged torture and mutilation.

The Methods of Murder

Donald Henry Gaskins was notorious for the sheer brutality of his murders. His preferred method of killing was a slow, methodical process designed to inflict as much pain and terror as possible. He often kidnapped his victims, taking them to remote, isolated locations where he could carry out his gruesome acts without fear of being interrupted. Gaskins would tie up his victims, subjecting them to hours or even days of torture before finally killing them.

One of his favorite methods of torture involved inserting needles and nails under his victims' fingernails, a practice that caused excruciating pain. He also enjoyed mutilating his victims with knives, cutting them in specific patterns that he found aesthetically pleasing. Gaskins would often dismember his victims, sometimes while they were still alive, and scatter the body parts in different locations to hinder identification.

Gaskins' depravity knew no bounds. He took pleasure in the terror and helplessness of his victims, relishing the control he exerted over them. In some cases, he would sexually assault his victims before killing them, further asserting his dominance. Gaskins' crimes were not driven by a singular motive but rather by a compulsion to exert power and control over others, fueled by a deep-seated hatred and anger that had been festering since childhood.

The Killing Spree and Capture

Gaskins' killing spree continued throughout the 1970s, with his body count steadily rising. He was particularly active along the coastal highways of South Carolina, where he preyed on hitchhikers and transients. These "coastal kills" were random and opportunistic, allowing Gaskins to kill without arousing suspicion. However, it was his "serious murders" that ultimately led to his downfall.

In 1975, Gaskins was hired by a local criminal named Silas Yates to kill Yates' ex-girlfriend, Martha Ann Dicks, also known as "Clyde." Yates offered Gaskins $1,500 to carry out the murder, which Gaskins accepted. However, Gaskins' involvement in the murder eventually came to light, leading to his arrest. During the investigation, law enforcement officials discovered evidence linking Gaskins to multiple other murders, both coastal kills and serious murders.

Faced with the overwhelming evidence against him, Gaskins initially denied any involvement in the murders. However, under intense questioning, he eventually confessed to killing over a dozen people, though the true number of his victims is believed to be much higher. Gaskins' confessions were chilling in their detail, as he described each murder with a cold, emotionless demeanor that shocked even the most seasoned investigators.

Gaskins' arrest marked the end of his reign of terror, but it also opened the door to further revelations about his crimes. As investigators dug deeper into his past, they uncovered more and more evidence of his involvement in unsolved murders, leading to additional charges being brought against him.

Trial and Sentencing

The trial of Donald Henry Gaskins was one of the most sensational in South Carolina's history. The media dubbed him "The Meanest Man in America," a moniker that captured the public's horror at the extent of his crimes. Gaskins showed little remorse during the trial, often smirking or laughing as witnesses recounted the details of his atrocities. His lack of empathy and cold-blooded nature only served to solidify his reputation as a monster.

Gaskins' defense team attempted to argue that he was mentally ill and therefore not responsible for his actions. However, the prosecution presented overwhelming evidence of premeditation and planning in Gaskins' murders, arguing that he was fully aware of what he was doing and enjoyed it. The jury agreed, and in 1976, Gaskins was found guilty of multiple counts of murder and sentenced to death.

Gaskins was sent to death row at the South Carolina Penitentiary, where he would spend the next several years awaiting execution.

However, his story did not end there. While on death row, Gaskins managed to commit one final murder, an act that would go down in history as one of the most brazen crimes ever committed by a condemned man.

The Death Row Murder

While on death row, Gaskins was approached by a fellow inmate, Tony Cimo, the son of one of Gaskins' victims, who offered him $2,000 to kill another death row inmate, Rudolph Tyner. Tyner had been convicted of murdering Cimo's parents during a botched robbery, and Cimo wanted revenge. Gaskins agreed to carry out the hit, seeing it as an opportunity to prove that he still had power even while facing his own death.

Gaskins initially attempted to poison Tyner by lacing his food with arsenic. When that plan failed, he devised a more elaborate scheme. Demonstrating his resourcefulness and cunning, Gaskins crafted a makeshift bomb using plastic explosives and a radio speaker. He convinced Rudolph Tyner that the radio device was a means for communication between their cells. In reality, the device was a bomb disguised as a two-way communication system. Gaskins then instructed Tyner to hold the speaker up to his ear and press the button, promising that it would facilitate clearer communication between them.

On September 2, 1982, Gaskins set off the bomb remotely, killing Tyner instantly. The explosion was so powerful that it blew Tyner's head apart. This murder, committed while Gaskins was already on death row, stunned the authorities and further solidified his reputation as one of the most cold-blooded killers in American history.

After Tyner's murder, Gaskins made a full confession, openly admitting his role in the crime. He was proud of his ability to kill even while under constant surveillance and on death row, and he reportedly laughed about the incident with fellow inmates. His actions led to an additional death sentence, though this made little practical difference, as Gaskins was already sentenced to die.

Execution and Final Confessions

Donald Henry Gaskins was finally executed on September 6, 1991, in the electric chair at the Central Correctional Institution in Columbia, South Carolina. In his final days, Gaskins continued to show no remorse for his actions. He remained defiant until the end, insisting that he had done what he had to do to survive and that he enjoyed the power and control he had over his victims.

Before his execution, Gaskins spent time writing his autobiography, *Final Truth*, with the help of author Wilton Earle. In the book, Gaskins confessed to killing over 100 people, far more than the number officially attributed to him. While some of these claims are likely exaggerated, there is no doubt that Gaskins was responsible for a significant number of murders.

Gaskins described his killings in graphic detail, showing a complete lack of empathy for his victims. He portrayed himself as a man who was driven by a need to assert dominance and who took pleasure in the suffering of others. His autobiography provided a rare and disturbing glimpse into the mind of a serial killer, revealing the depths of his depravity.

Legacy of Violence

Donald Henry Gaskins' life and crimes left an indelible mark on American criminal history. He is remembered as one of the most violent and sadistic serial killers the country has ever seen. His crimes were not only brutal in their execution but also random in nature, which made them all the more terrifying. Gaskins did not have a specific victim profile; he killed men, women, and children, choosing his victims based on convenience and his own twisted desires.

Gaskins' legacy is a reminder of the darkest aspects of human nature and the potential for evil that can exist within an individual. His story also underscores the importance of effective law enforcement and the challenges involved in capturing and prosecuting serial killers, particularly those who are as cunning and elusive as Gaskins was.

Psychological Profile

Gaskins' psychological profile is that of a deeply disturbed individual who exhibited psychopathic tendencies from an early age. His lack of empathy, coupled with his need for control and power, made him a dangerous and unpredictable predator. Psychologists who have studied Gaskins believe that his childhood experiences, including the abuse he suffered and the environment of violence in which he was raised, played a significant role in shaping his criminal behavior.

Gaskins' small stature and the bullying he endured likely contributed to his feelings of inadequacy and rage, which he later expressed through violence. His ability to manipulate others, even from behind bars, and his willingness to kill without hesitation or remorse, mark him as one of the most dangerous types of serial killers—one who kills not out of necessity, but for the sheer pleasure of it.

Chapter 18: Angelo Buono and Kenneth Bianchi

Angelo Buono and Kenneth Bianchi, infamous for their gruesome murders in Los Angeles during the late 1970s, were two of the most notorious serial killers in American history. Known as the "Hillside Stranglers," their killing spree left a trail of terror throughout the city and shocked the nation with its brutality. The duo's methodical approach to selecting, torturing, and murdering their victims demonstrated a chilling disregard for human life and a calculated cruelty that placed them among the most feared criminals of their time.

Background: Childhood and Early Life

- **Angelo Buono**

Angelo Buono was born on October 5, 1934, in Rochester, New York. He grew up in a troubled environment, marked by a dysfunctional family dynamic. Buono's mother was a strict and overbearing figure, which instilled in him a deep-seated resentment towards women. This misogyny would later manifest in his treatment of women and fuel his sadistic tendencies.

Buono's early life was characterized by a lack of direction and a propensity for delinquent behavior. He dropped out of high school and began a life of petty crime, engaging in theft, burglary, and other criminal activities. Buono had a string of relationships with women, all of which ended badly due to his abusive behavior. By the time he was in his twenties, Buono had developed a reputation as a violent and controlling individual, particularly towards women.

Buono eventually moved to Los Angeles, where he continued his life of crime. He opened an auto upholstery business, which he used as a front for various illegal activities, including pimping and running a prostitution ring. Buono's business provided him with access to vulnerable women, whom he would later exploit and victimize.

- **Kenneth Bianchi**

Kenneth Bianchi was born on May 22, 1951, in Rochester, New York, and was adopted by Nicholas and Frances Bianchi shortly after his birth. Despite being raised in a relatively stable and loving home, Bianchi exhibited troubling behavior from a young age. He was a chronic liar and frequently engaged in manipulative behavior to get his way. Bianchi also showed signs of a split personality, a condition that would later play a significant role in his defense during his trial.

Bianchi struggled academically and socially throughout his childhood. He was described as lazy and unmotivated by his teachers, and he had difficulty forming meaningful relationships with his peers. His adoptive mother, Frances, was overly protective and indulgent, which may have contributed to Bianchi's sense of entitlement and his inability to accept responsibility for his actions.

After graduating from high school, Bianchi attempted to pursue various career paths, including becoming a police officer and a psychologist, but he failed to achieve any lasting success. His lack of direction and growing frustration with his life led him to engage in increasingly risky and criminal behavior. In 1976, Bianchi moved to Los Angeles to live with his cousin, Angelo Buono, a decision that would set the stage for their deadly partnership.

The Formation of a Deadly Partnership

When Kenneth Bianchi moved to Los Angeles, he and Angelo Buono quickly formed a close bond. Despite their age difference—Buono was 17 years older than Bianchi—the two cousins shared a similar disdain for women and a fascination with power and control. Buono, who had already established himself as a violent and manipulative individual, became a mentor of sorts to Bianchi, introducing him to his world of crime and exploitation.

The two cousins began working together in Buono's auto upholstery business, but they soon discovered that their true interests lay in more sinister activities. They initially started by kidnapping women and forcing them into prostitution, using threats and violence to keep them in line. However, this criminal enterprise eventually escalated into something far more dangerous.

Buono and Bianchi began to fantasize about committing murder, seeing it as the ultimate expression of power and control. Their shared sadism and misogyny created a deadly synergy, with each man encouraging the other's worst impulses. In late 1977, their fantasies became a horrifying reality when they embarked on a killing spree that would leave Los Angeles in a state of terror.

The Hillside Strangler Murders

The Hillside Strangler murders, so named because many of the victims were found on the hillsides of Los Angeles, began in October 1977 and continued until February 1978. Over this period, Buono and Bianchi abducted, tortured, raped, and murdered at least 10 young women, although the true number of their victims may never be known.

The victims were typically young women between the ages of 12 and 28, most of whom were either prostitutes or runaways. Buono and Bianchi used a variety of ruses to lure their victims into their car, often posing as police officers and claiming they needed to take the women in for questioning. Once the victims were in their custody, the cousins would take them to Buono's home, where they would subject them to unimaginable torture.

The methods of torture used by Buono and Bianchi were particularly brutal. The women were often bound, gagged, and subjected to prolonged physical and sexual abuse. Buono and Bianchi would strangle their victims with a rope or cord, tightening it slowly to prolong their suffering. In some cases, the killers would revive their victims after they had lost consciousness, only to continue the torture. The killers derived sadistic pleasure from the power they held over their victims, and they took great care to ensure that the women suffered as much as possible before they died.

After killing their victims, Buono and Bianchi would dump the bodies in remote areas around Los Angeles, often leaving them in poses designed to shock and humiliate. The discovery of the bodies sparked widespread fear and panic in the city, with women becoming increasingly afraid to go out alone. The police were under immense pressure to catch the killers, but Buono and Bianchi's careful planning and lack of connection to their victims made the investigation difficult.

The Investigation and Capture

The Hillside Strangler murders attracted significant media attention, and the Los Angeles Police Department (LAPD) launched one of the largest manhunts in its history to catch the killers. Despite the intense scrutiny, Buono and Bianchi managed to avoid capture for several months, thanks in large part to their careful planning and ability to cover their tracks.

However, their killing spree came to an end in early 1978, when Kenneth Bianchi made a critical mistake. Bianchi, who had grown increasingly reckless, decided to move to Bellingham, Washington, in an attempt to start a new life. Despite the distance, he could not resist the urge to kill again, and on January 11, 1979, he murdered two young women, Karen Mandic and Diane Wilder, in a manner similar to the Hillside Strangler killings.

The murders in Bellingham were Bianchi's undoing. Unlike the Los Angeles murders, Bianchi left behind several pieces of evidence, including his fingerprints, that linked him to the crime scene. The local police quickly arrested him, and under intense interrogation, Bianchi eventually confessed to the murders. He also implicated Angelo Buono as his partner in the Hillside Strangler killings.

The Trials of Angelo Buono and Kenneth Bianchi

After his arrest, Kenneth Bianchi attempted to avoid the death penalty by claiming that he suffered from multiple personality disorder (now known as dissociative identity disorder). He claimed that one of his alternate personalities, "Steve Walker," was responsible for the murders and that he had no control over his actions. However, psychiatric experts quickly saw through Bianchi's ruse, and his defense was dismissed as an attempt to manipulate the legal system.

In exchange for avoiding the death penalty, Bianchi agreed to testify against his cousin, Angelo Buono. His testimony was crucial in securing Buono's conviction, as it provided detailed accounts of their crimes and the roles each man played. Bianchi's cooperation with the prosecution allowed him to receive a life sentence without the possibility of parole, rather than facing execution.

Angelo Buono's trial began in November 1981 and lasted nearly two years, making it one of the longest and most complex criminal trials in U.S. history. The prosecution presented overwhelming evidence of Buono's involvement in the murders, including Bianchi's testimony, forensic evidence, and the testimony of surviving victims who had been forced into prostitution by Buono and Bianchi.

Throughout the trial, Buono maintained his innocence, claiming that Bianchi was lying to save himself. However, the jury was unconvinced by Buono's defense, and on November 18, 1983, he was found guilty of nine counts of murder. Buono was sentenced to life in prison without the possibility of parole.

Psychological Profiles of Buono and Bianchi

The psychological profiles of Angelo Buono and Kenneth Bianchi reveal a disturbing combination of personality disorders, sadism, and deep-seated misogyny. Both men exhibited traits commonly associated with psychopathy, including a lack of empathy, a propensity for violence, and a need for control and power over others.

- **Angelo Buono**

Angelo Buono was the dominant partner in the Hillside Strangler killings, a man driven by a deep hatred of women and a desire to assert his dominance through violence. Buono's abusive behavior towards women was a reflection of his misogynistic beliefs, which were likely shaped by his troubled childhood and the dysfunctional relationships he had with his mother and other female figures in his life.

Buono was a classic example of a psychopath—charming and manipulative on the surface, but cold and calculating underneath.

He was able to maintain a façade of respectability, running a business and interacting with the community, while secretly engaging in horrific acts of violence. Buono's ability to compartmentalize his violent tendencies allowed him to evade suspicion for so long, even as the bodies of his victims continued to be discovered across Los Angeles.

Buono's psychological makeup was marked by a sadistic need to inflict pain and suffering on others, particularly women. He derived pleasure not only from the act of killing but also from the fear and helplessness of his victims. His controlling nature extended to every aspect of his life, and he used manipulation and intimidation to maintain power over those around him. Buono's lack of remorse and his willingness to continue his criminal activities even after the police investigation intensified demonstrate his complete disregard for human life.

- **Kenneth Bianchi**

Kenneth Bianchi, while influenced by his older cousin, was equally disturbed in his own right. Bianchi exhibited traits of both psychopathy and narcissism, characterized by his manipulative behavior, superficial charm, and an inflated sense of self-importance. Despite his outward appearance as a polite and mild-mannered individual, Bianchi harbored a deep-seated rage and a desire for control, which he expressed through his participation in the Hillside Strangler murders.

Bianchi's psychological profile also suggests that he struggled with a fragmented identity. His claims of multiple personality disorder, while ultimately dismissed as a fabrication, hinted at his attempts to dissociate from the heinous acts he committed. Whether or not Bianchi genuinely believed in his alternate personalities, his ability to compartmentalize his crimes and present himself as a normal, law-abiding citizen speaks to the depth of his psychological disturbance.

Bianchi's decision to cooperate with authorities and testify against Buono can be seen as both a survival tactic and a reflection of his self-serving nature. While he may have feared the death penalty, Bianchi's willingness to betray his cousin also suggests a lack of loyalty and a desperate attempt to distance himself from the full extent of his crimes.

The Legacy of the Hillside Stranglers

The crimes of Angelo Buono and Kenneth Bianchi left an indelible mark on the history of American serial killers. The Hillside Strangler murders not only terrorized Los Angeles but also highlighted the dark undercurrents of violence and misogyny that can drive individuals to commit such heinous acts. The sheer brutality of their crimes, combined with the randomness of their victim selection, created an atmosphere of fear and uncertainty that gripped the city for months.

The case also had a significant impact on law enforcement and forensic investigation techniques. The extensive manhunt and the eventual capture of Buono and Bianchi underscored the importance of inter-agency cooperation, the need for advances in forensic science, and the challenges posed by serial offenders who operate without a clear pattern or motive.

In popular culture, the Hillside Stranglers have been the subject of numerous books, documentaries, and films, which have sought to explore the psychology behind their crimes and the impact of their actions on the victims and the community. The case remains a chilling example of how ordinary-looking individuals can harbor monstrous tendencies, and it continues to serve as a cautionary tale about the potential for evil that exists within human nature.

The Aftermath and Continuing Infamy

After their convictions, both Angelo Buono and Kenneth Bianchi spent the remainder of their lives in prison. Buono, who was sentenced to life without parole, died of a heart attack in his cell on September 21, 2002, at the age of 67. Bianchi, on the other hand, remains incarcerated, serving his life sentence in Washington state. Over the years, Bianchi has continued to seek attention, making various attempts to manipulate the legal system and the media, but his efforts have largely been ignored.

The legacy of the Hillside Stranglers lives on, not only in the memories of the victims' families but also in the broader cultural consciousness. The case has been studied extensively by criminologists, psychologists, and law enforcement professionals as a means of understanding the dynamics of serial killing partnerships and the factors that contribute to such extreme behavior.

The Hillside Strangler murders also serve as a stark reminder of the vulnerability of certain populations, particularly women, to predatory violence. The case prompted changes in how law enforcement agencies approach the investigation of serial crimes and how they communicate with the public during such crises. It also highlighted the importance of public awareness and vigilance in preventing such atrocities from occurring.

Chapter 19: Carl Panzram

Carl Panzram, one of the most infamous and cold-blooded serial killers in American history, is often remembered for his sheer brutality and unapologetic embrace of evil. Born into a life of hardship and abuse, Panzram's criminal career spanned several decades and included a wide range of violent crimes, from petty theft to murder and rape. His autobiography, written while he was on death row, offers a chilling insight into the mind of a man who reveled in causing pain and suffering. Panzram's story is one of unrelenting violence, fueled by a deep-seated hatred for humanity and a desire to inflict as much harm as possible before meeting his own end.

Early Life and Childhood: The Seeds of Hatred

Carl Panzram was born on June 28, 1891, in East Grand Forks, Minnesota, to German immigrants Johann and Matilda Panzram. He was the youngest of five children in a poor farming family. His childhood was marked by extreme hardship, abuse, and neglect. Panzram's father abandoned the family when Carl was young, leaving Matilda to raise the children on her own. The Panzram family struggled to survive, and Carl quickly became bitter and resentful towards the world.

From a young age, Panzram exhibited signs of severe behavioral problems. He was rebellious, defiant, and prone to violent outbursts. His first encounter with the law occurred when he was just eight years old, after he stole some apples and a cake from a neighbor's house. This petty theft would mark the beginning of a long and brutal criminal career.

At the age of 11, Panzram was sent to the Minnesota State Training School, a reform school for troubled boys. It was here that Panzram's hatred for authority and society truly began to take root. The school was notorious for its harsh treatment of inmates, and Panzram was frequently beaten and sexually abused by the staff. These experiences left a lasting impact on him, fueling his rage and solidifying his belief that the world was a cruel and unjust place. In his later writings, Panzram would often cite his time at the reform school as a turning point in his life, where any remnants of innocence or goodness were destroyed.

After two years at the reform school, Panzram was released, but the damage had already been done. He returned home with a hardened heart and an unquenchable thirst for revenge against the world that had wronged him. His criminal activities escalated rapidly, and by the age of 14, he had become a full-fledged delinquent, committing burglaries, thefts, and acts of arson with increasing frequency.

Early Criminal Career: From Juvenile Delinquent to Hardened Criminal

In 1906, at the age of 15, Carl Panzram enlisted in the United States Army, hoping to find a sense of purpose and discipline. However, his rebellious nature quickly led to trouble, and he was court-martialed for larceny just a year later. Panzram was sentenced to three years in the United States Disciplinary Barracks at Fort Leavenworth, Kansas, where he would continue to endure brutal treatment at the hands of prison guards. The harsh conditions and relentless abuse further deepened Panzram's hatred for authority and fueled his desire for revenge.

After his release from Leavenworth in 1910, Panzram began a life of itinerant crime, traveling across the United States and committing a wide range of offenses. He adopted a series of aliases to evade capture and became skilled at escaping from custody whenever he was caught. His crimes during this period included burglary, theft, and arson, but Panzram's true calling would soon become apparent: he had developed an insatiable appetite for violence and murder.

Panzram's hatred for humanity knew no bounds, and he took every opportunity to act on his violent impulses. He later claimed that he had committed his first murder in 1911, killing a man who had attempted to rob him in a train yard. However, this claim has never been confirmed, and it is likely that Panzram's first confirmed murders occurred several years later.

The Murderous Rampage Begins: A Trail of Blood Across Continents

In 1920, Panzram embarked on a journey that would take him across the United States and to several foreign countries, leaving a trail of blood and destruction in his wake. He traveled extensively, often stowing away on ships or hopping freight trains to avoid detection. During this time, Panzram committed a series of heinous crimes, including numerous murders, rapes, and acts of piracy.

One of Panzram's most infamous crimes occurred in 1920, when he stole a yacht in New York City and sailed it to Africa. During his journey, Panzram lured sailors on board with promises of employment, only to rob, rape, and murder them before dumping their bodies overboard. He later claimed to have killed at least ten men in this manner. Once he arrived in Africa, Panzram continued his killing spree, murdering several locals and engaging in acts of violence and exploitation.

After leaving Africa, Panzram traveled to Portugal and then to South America, where he committed additional murders and other violent crimes. His time abroad only served to further harden him, as he encountered new opportunities to indulge his sadistic tendencies. Panzram's international crime spree demonstrated his complete disregard for human life and his belief that he was above the law, no matter where he went.

In 1922, Panzram returned to the United States, where he continued his murderous rampage. He committed a series of brutal murders in cities across the country, including New York, Philadelphia, and Chicago. His preferred method of killing involved shooting his victims at close range or bludgeoning them to death with a heavy object. In some cases, Panzram would rob his victims after killing them, using the money to fund his travels and continue his life of crime.

The Capture and Imprisonment: A Cycle of Escape and Violence

Despite his cunning and ability to evade capture, Carl Panzram was eventually arrested several times throughout his criminal career. However, his time in custody was often short-lived, as he frequently managed to escape from jails and prisons. Each time he was recaptured, Panzram's hatred for authority and society deepened, and he became even more determined to exact revenge on those who had wronged him.

One of Panzram's most notable escapes occurred in 1920, when he broke out of a jail in Oregon after being arrested for burglary. After his escape, Panzram embarked on a cross-country crime spree that included the murders of several men and boys. He was eventually recaptured in 1922 in Yonkers, New York, but escaped once again and continued his life of crime.

In 1928, Panzram was arrested in Washington, D.C., for burglary. During his time in custody, Panzram confessed to killing at least 21 people and committing more than 1,000 acts of sodomy. His confessions shocked law enforcement officials, who were unaccustomed to dealing with such a brazen and unrepentant criminal. Panzram showed no remorse for his actions, instead expressing pride in the pain and suffering he had caused.

While awaiting trial for his crimes, Panzram began writing his autobiography, in which he detailed his life of violence and hatred. The manuscript, which he titled *Killer: A Journal of Murder*, provides a chilling insight into Panzram's twisted mind and his unwavering commitment to evil. In the book, Panzram expressed his belief that the world was full of "filthy, rotten, evil people" who deserved nothing but pain and death. He also claimed that he took pleasure in killing, describing it as a "thrill" that gave him a sense of power and satisfaction.

Psychological Profile: The Mind of a Monster

Carl Panzram's psychological profile is that of a deeply disturbed individual who exhibited traits commonly associated with psychopathy and sociopathy. His complete lack of empathy, combined with his sadistic tendencies and desire for power and control, made him one of the most dangerous and unpredictable criminals of his time. Panzram's early experiences of abuse and neglect likely played a significant role in shaping his violent behavior, but his actions also suggest an inherent capacity for evil that went beyond his environment.

Panzram's hatred for humanity was all-consuming, and he viewed himself as a predator among prey. He believed that the world was a cruel and unjust place, and he saw his actions as a form of retribution against a society that had wronged him. Panzram's writings are filled with vitriol and contempt for humanity, and he took great pleasure in recounting his crimes in graphic detail. His autobiography reveals a man who was not only unrepentant but also proud of the pain and suffering he had caused.

Panzram's psychological makeup was marked by a profound sense of alienation and a belief that he was fundamentally different from—and superior to—other people. He saw himself as an agent of chaos, free from the moral constraints that governed the rest of society. This sense of superiority, combined with his sadistic tendencies, made Panzram a particularly dangerous and unpredictable criminal.

The Final Years: Confession and Execution

Carl Panzram's final years were marked by a sense of resignation and acceptance of his fate. After his arrest in Washington, D.C., he was sentenced to 25 years in Leavenworth Federal Penitentiary for burglary. While in prison, Panzram continued to engage in violent behavior, attacking guards and fellow inmates whenever the opportunity arose. His conduct in prison was so violent that he was eventually placed in solitary confinement.

Despite his confinement, Panzram continued to write prolifically, detailing his crimes and his hatred for humanity in his autobiography. He also corresponded with a young prison guard named Henry Lesser, who showed Panzram an unexpected kindness by giving him writing materials. Panzram's letters to Lesser reveal a man who was fully aware of the evil he had committed but who felt no remorse for his actions. Instead, he viewed his crimes as a form of justice against a world that had treated him unfairly.

In 1929, Panzram killed a prison laundry foreman named Robert Warnke by bashing his head in with an iron bar. This murder led to Panzram being charged with first-degree murder and sentenced to death. Panzram welcomed the death sentence, seeing it as a release from the misery of his existence. He refused to appeal his sentence and actively sought to hasten his execution.

On September 5, 1930, Carl Panzram was hanged at Leavenworth Federal Penitentiary. As he stood on the gallows, he showed no fear or remorse. When asked if he had any last words, Panzram reportedly replied, "Hurry it up, you Hoosier bastard! I could kill a dozen men while you're screwing around!" These final words encapsulate the essence of Carl Panzram—a man who, until the very end, remained defiant, unrepentant, and consumed by hatred.

Legacy: The Infamy of Carl Panzram

Carl Panzram's legacy is one of infamy and horror. His life story has been the subject of numerous books, documentaries, and academic studies, all of which seek to understand the mind of a man who reveled in violence and destruction. Panzram's autobiography, *Killer: A Journal of Murder*, remains one of the most disturbing and revealing accounts of a serial killer's inner thoughts, offering a rare glimpse into the psyche of a man who embraced evil with open arms.

Panzram's crimes continue to serve as a stark reminder of the potential for darkness within the human soul. His complete lack of empathy, his sadistic pleasure in causing pain, and his unrelenting hatred for humanity make him one of the most terrifying figures in the history of American crime. Despite his death, Panzram's story continues to resonate, serving as a cautionary tale about the consequences of a life fueled by anger, resentment, and a desire for revenge.

In the years since his execution, Carl Panzram has become a symbol of pure, unrepentant evil. His name is often mentioned alongside other notorious serial killers, such as Ted Bundy, Jeffrey Dahmer, and John Wayne Gacy, as an example of the worst that humanity has to offer. However, Panzram's story also serves as a reminder of the importance of addressing the root causes of violence and crime, particularly in the lives of those who have experienced severe abuse and neglect.

Panzram's life and crimes raise important questions about the nature of evil and the factors that contribute to the development of violent behavior. Was Panzram born a killer, or was he shaped by the abuse and mistreatment he endured as a child? Could his violent tendencies have been prevented if he had received proper care and support at a young age? These are questions that continue to be debated by criminologists, psychologists, and historians.

Chapter 20: Richard Chase (the Vampire of Sacramento)

Richard Trenton Chase, infamously known as the "Vampire of Sacramento," is one of the most disturbing figures in the annals of American criminal history. His moniker, "Vampire," was not a mere metaphor; Chase believed that consuming the blood of his victims was essential to his survival, driven by delusions that were born from his severe mental illness. His crimes were shocking not just for their brutality but for the profound and eerie detachment with which he carried them out. Chase's descent into madness, fueled by untreated schizophrenia, substance abuse, and a bizarre obsession with blood, led to a spree of horrific murders in Sacramento, California, in the late 1970s. The sheer savagery of his acts and the twisted logic behind them make Richard Chase a case study in the lethal potential of unchecked mental illness.

Early Life: A Troubled Beginning

Richard Trenton Chase was born on May 23, 1950, in Santa Clara County, California. His early life was marked by a series of troubling behaviors that hinted at the psychological issues that would later manifest in terrifying ways. Chase grew up in what appeared to be a typical middle-class family, but beneath the surface, his home life was far from stable. His father was reportedly strict and abusive, and the environment at home was tense, with frequent arguments between his parents. This dysfunctional upbringing likely contributed to the early signs of mental instability that Chase exhibited.

From a young age, Chase displayed behaviors consistent with the "Macdonald triad," a set of three indicators often associated with future violent tendencies: bedwetting, cruelty to animals, and fire-setting. These behaviors are seen as red flags for deep-seated psychological issues, and in Chase's case, they foreshadowed the extreme violence that would later define his life.

As he entered adolescence, Chase's problems became more pronounced. He struggled academically and socially, finding it difficult to form meaningful relationships. He began experimenting with drugs and alcohol, which exacerbated his already fragile mental state. By the time he was in high school, Chase's behavior had become increasingly erratic. He developed a preoccupation with his health, convinced that he was suffering from a variety of ailments. This obsession with his body and health would later evolve into full-blown hypochondria, a condition that played a significant role in his descent into madness.

The Onset of Mental Illness: A Life Unraveling

After graduating from high school, Chase's mental health continued to deteriorate. He enrolled in American River College in Sacramento but struggled to cope with the demands of higher education. He began using drugs more heavily, including marijuana and LSD, which only served to amplify his delusions and paranoia. His behavior became increasingly bizarre, and he started to exhibit symptoms of schizophrenia, a severe mental disorder characterized by distorted thinking, hallucinations, and delusions.

One of Chase's most persistent delusions was the belief that his body was deteriorating. He became convinced that his blood was turning to powder and that his organs were slowly failing. To combat this perceived decay, Chase began drinking the blood of animals, believing that it would prevent his body from wasting away. He would capture and kill small animals, such as rabbits and birds, and drink their blood, sometimes mixing it with Coca-Cola in a grotesque attempt to "replenish" his own blood supply. This obsession with blood, combined with his growing detachment from reality, set the stage for the horrific acts he would later commit.

In 1973, at the age of 23, Chase was involuntarily committed to a mental institution after being found injecting rabbit's blood into his veins. During his stay, he was diagnosed with paranoid schizophrenia, but despite his alarming behavior and clear signs of severe mental illness, he was released after a short period. The doctors believed that with medication, Chase could manage his symptoms, but he soon stopped taking his prescribed antipsychotic drugs, leading to a rapid and dangerous decline in his mental state.

After his release, Chase moved into an apartment on his own, where his isolation and paranoia grew more intense. He became increasingly obsessed with the idea that he needed blood to survive and began fixating on the idea of human blood as the ultimate solution to his perceived physical ailments. This delusion would soon lead him down a path of unimaginable horror.

The Murders: A Spree of Unimaginable Horror

Richard Chase's murderous spree began on December 29, 1977, when he committed his first known murder. His victim was Ambrose Griffin, a 51-year-old engineer and father of two. Griffin was helping his wife bring groceries into their home when Chase randomly shot him in a drive-by shooting. This seemingly senseless act of violence was just the beginning of what would become a series of increasingly brutal and gruesome murders.

On January 23, 1978, Chase broke into the home of Teresa Wallin, a 22-year-old woman who was three months pregnant. He shot her three times before mutilating her body in a manner that shocked even the most seasoned investigators. Chase drank her blood and removed several of her internal organs, taking some with him as he left the scene. The brutality of this murder, coupled with the clear indications of necrophilia and cannibalism, earned Chase the nickname "The Vampire of Sacramento."

Just four days later, on January 27, 1978, Chase committed his most heinous crime. He entered the home of 38-year-old Evelyn Miroth, where he encountered not only Evelyn but also her 6-year-old son Jason, her 22-month-old nephew David Ferreira, and a family friend, 51-year-old Dan Meredith. Chase shot Meredith first, then proceeded to kill Evelyn, Jason, and David in a blood-soaked rampage. After killing Evelyn, he engaged in horrific acts of necrophilia and cannibalism, mutilating her body and drinking her blood. He also removed the infant David's body from the scene, later consuming parts of his body before discarding the remains.

The sheer savagery of these murders stunned the Sacramento community and law enforcement alike. Chase's actions were not just acts of violence but of deep-seated madness, driven by his belief that drinking blood was necessary for his survival. The randomness of his attacks, coupled with the brutality of the crimes, created an atmosphere of fear and panic in the city.

The Investigation and Capture: Unraveling the Vampire's Madness

The investigation into the murders was complicated by the sheer randomness of Chase's attacks. He had no connection to his victims, choosing them at random, which made it difficult for law enforcement to identify a pattern or motive. However, the extreme brutality of the crimes provided investigators with crucial forensic evidence, including Chase's fingerprints and shoe prints at the scenes.

After the discovery of the bodies at Evelyn Miroth's home, the Sacramento Police Department launched a massive manhunt for the killer. The nature of the crimes led investigators to believe that the perpetrator was mentally disturbed, and they focused their efforts on identifying individuals with a history of mental illness or bizarre behavior.

Chase's capture came about due to a combination of good police work and a tip from a former classmate who recognized his description in the media. The classmate had seen Chase in the neighborhood on the day of the Miroth murders and reported his suspicious behavior to the authorities. This tip, combined with the forensic evidence, led the police to Chase's apartment, where they discovered a scene of utter horror.

Inside Chase's apartment, investigators found bloodstains on the walls, floor, and ceiling, as well as numerous blood-soaked rags and containers. They also found remains of his victims, including organs and body parts stored in the refrigerator. The apartment was a chilling reflection of Chase's delusions, filled with disturbing evidence of his obsession with blood and his belief that he needed it to survive.

Chase was arrested on January 27, 1978, the same day as his final murders. He offered no resistance and confessed to the crimes almost immediately, providing investigators with detailed accounts of his actions. His confessions were chilling in their lack of remorse; Chase viewed his murders not as crimes but as necessary acts to save himself from what he believed was his inevitable demise.

The Trial: A Battle of Insanity and Justice

Richard Chase's trial began in 1979, and it quickly became clear that his mental state would be the central issue. The defense argued that Chase was not guilty by reason of insanity, pointing to his long history of schizophrenia, his bizarre delusions, and the fact that he genuinely believed that drinking blood was necessary for his survival. They contended that Chase's actions were the result of his severe mental illness and that he should be committed to a psychiatric institution rather than executed.

The prosecution, however, argued that Chase knew what he was doing was wrong and that his premeditated actions demonstrated an awareness of the criminal nature of his behavior. They pointed out that Chase had taken steps to avoid detection, such as using gloves and carefully choosing his victims, which indicated a level of planning and understanding that was inconsistent with a complete lack of awareness.

The trial featured extensive testimony from psychiatrists and psychologists, who provided conflicting opinions on Chase's mental state. Some experts testified that Chase was clearly psychotic and unable to control his actions, while others argued that he was aware of the wrongfulness of his actions and therefore should be held accountable.

Ultimately, the jury found Richard Chase guilty of six counts of first-degree murder, rejecting the insanity defense. He was sentenced to death and sent to San Quentin State Prison to await execution. Chase's reaction to the verdict was one of indifference; he had already resigned himself to the belief that he would not live long and even expressed a desire to be executed as soon as possible.

Imprisonment and Death: The Final Chapter

While on death row at San Quentin, Richard Chase continued to exhibit bizarre and troubling behavior. He was isolated from other prisoners due to the extreme nature of his crimes and the fear that he might be attacked by other inmates. Chase's mental state remained deeply disturbed; he was plagued by delusions and continued to express his belief that he needed blood to survive. He refused most of his meals, often claiming that his food was poisoned, and his health deteriorated as a result.

Prison psychiatrists closely monitored Chase, recognizing the severity of his mental illness. Despite the guilty verdict at his trial, there was little doubt among those who interacted with him that Chase was profoundly disturbed. His letters from prison, filled with ramblings about conspiracies and his delusional beliefs, further illustrated the depth of his psychosis.

Chase's time on death row was brief. On December 26, 1980, less than two years after his conviction, Richard Chase was found dead in his cell. He had committed suicide by overdosing on a stash of antidepressants that he had saved over time. His death marked the end of a life defined by unimaginable horror, both for his victims and for Chase himself, who was tormented by a mind that had long since lost touch with reality.

Legacy: The Vampire of Sacramento in Criminal History

Richard Chase's legacy is one of infamy and terror. His crimes shocked the nation and left a lasting impact on the city of Sacramento. The sheer brutality of his actions, coupled with the disturbing nature of his delusions, make him one of the most infamous serial killers in American history. Chase's case has been the subject of numerous books, documentaries, and academic studies, all of which seek to understand the mind of a man who believed that drinking blood was the only way to keep himself alive.

The case of Richard Chase also highlights the tragic consequences of untreated mental illness. Despite numerous signs that he was severely disturbed, Chase fell through the cracks of the mental health system, receiving inadequate care and being released from institutions when he clearly needed ongoing treatment. His story serves as a cautionary tale about the dangers of neglecting mental health issues and the importance of proper intervention and care.

In the years since his death, Richard Chase has become a symbol of the dark and terrifying potential of the human mind when it is consumed by delusion and madness. His name is often mentioned alongside other notorious serial killers, but Chase stands out for the uniquely horrifying nature of his crimes and the profound mental illness that drove him to commit them. His story continues to be a source of fascination and horror, a reminder of the fragility of the human psyche and the devastating impact of untreated mental illness.

Chapter 21: Alexander Pichushkin (the Chessboard Killer)

Alexander Pichushkin, also known as the "Chessboard Killer," is one of Russia's most notorious serial killers, infamous for his gruesome murders and his chilling goal of filling every square on a chessboard with a victim. His moniker comes from his claim that he intended to kill 64 people—the number of squares on a chessboard—although his actual victim count is believed to be at least 49. Pichushkin's crimes were not only brutal but also meticulously planned, revealing a methodical mind driven by a deep-seated need for domination and control. His story is one of twisted ambition, shocking violence, and a relentless pursuit of a grim and macabre goal.

Early Life: A Foundation of Violence and Isolation

Alexander Yuryevich Pichushkin was born on April 9, 1974, in Moscow, Russia. His early life was marked by hardship, loneliness, and an environment that may have contributed to his later violent tendencies. Raised primarily by his mother, Pichushkin's father abandoned the family when he was still a child, leaving him without a male role model during his formative years. This lack of paternal influence and the absence of a stable family structure had a significant impact on Pichushkin's development.

As a child, Pichushkin suffered a severe head injury after falling off a swing. The injury reportedly caused damage to his frontal lobe, a part of the brain responsible for impulse control and decision-making. This traumatic event is often cited as a potential catalyst for his later behavior, as frontal lobe injuries are sometimes associated with increased aggression, poor judgment, and difficulty controlling violent impulses.

In school, Pichushkin was bullied and ostracized by his peers, further contributing to his feelings of isolation and anger. He was described as a shy and introverted child, often struggling academically and socially. However, despite these difficulties, Pichushkin demonstrated a high level of intelligence, particularly in the realm of strategy games like chess. He quickly developed a talent for the game, using it as an outlet for his frustrations and as a way to assert control in a world where he often felt powerless.

Pichushkin's relationship with his mother was complex and strained. She was reportedly strict and overbearing, and their interactions were often characterized by tension and conflict. This difficult home life, combined with his social struggles at school, created an environment in which Pichushkin's anger and resentment festered, laying the groundwork for the violent behavior that would emerge later in his life.

The Evolution of a Killer: From Animal Cruelty to Human Prey

Like many serial killers, Pichushkin's early criminal behavior began with acts of cruelty toward animals. As a teenager, he would capture stray dogs and cats, torturing and killing them as a way to vent his anger and frustration. These acts of animal cruelty served as a precursor to the far more horrific crimes he would later commit against humans. They also provided him with a sense of power and control, which he found intoxicating and addictive.

During his teenage years, Pichushkin's interest in chess grew into an obsession. He spent countless hours playing the game, often at the Bitsevsky Park in Moscow, where he would challenge strangers to matches. Chess became more than just a game for Pichushkin; it was a way for him to exercise his strategic thinking and to prove his intellectual superiority over others. However, as his obsession with chess deepened, so too did his fascination with the idea of murder.

Pichushkin's first known attempt at murder occurred in 1992, when he was just 18 years old. He lured a classmate, Mikhail Odiychuk, to the same Bitsevsky Park where he played chess, under the pretense of drinking vodka together. Pichushkin had planned to kill Odiychuk, but at the last moment, Odiychuk managed to escape, sensing something was wrong. This failed attempt did not deter Pichushkin; instead, it seemed to solidify his desire to kill, setting him on a path of increasingly violent behavior.

For the next several years, Pichushkin's violent tendencies simmered beneath the surface. He continued to play chess and lived a seemingly normal life, but the desire to kill remained ever-present in his mind. It wasn't until the early 2000s that Pichushkin began to act on his homicidal impulses in earnest, embarking on a killing spree that would make him one of Russia's most feared serial killers.

The Killing Spree: A Methodical and Merciless Approach

Alexander Pichushkin's killing spree began in 2001, and for the next five years, he would go on to commit a series of brutal murders, primarily in Bitsevsky Park, the same location where he had honed his chess skills. Pichushkin's victims were often elderly men, homeless individuals, or alcoholics—people who were vulnerable and unlikely to be missed if they disappeared.

Pichushkin's method was chillingly simple but effective. He would approach his victims in the park, often under the guise of offering them a drink or inviting them to share a bottle of vodka. Once he had gained their trust, he would lead them to a secluded area of the park, where he would bludgeon them to death with a hammer or other blunt instrument. After killing his victims, Pichushkin would sometimes force objects, such as vodka bottles or sticks, into their skulls through the wounds he had inflicted. This gruesome act was a signature of his murders, a macabre calling card that added an extra layer of horror to his already brutal crimes.

The choice of a hammer as his weapon was no coincidence. Pichushkin viewed the act of killing as a game, and the hammer, with its association with the construction and destruction of objects, symbolized his belief that he was playing a deadly game of strategy. In his mind, each murder was a move on the chessboard, a calculated step toward his ultimate goal of filling all 64 squares.

Pichushkin's murders were methodical, and he was careful to leave few clues behind. He often disposed of the bodies in the park's dense undergrowth, making them difficult to find. Despite the growing number of disappearances in the area, law enforcement was slow to connect the dots, largely due to the fact that Pichushkin targeted individuals who were already marginalized or living on the fringes of society.

For several years, Pichushkin was able to carry out his killings without detection. He grew more confident with each murder, reveling in the power he felt over his victims and the ability to evade capture. His killing spree continued unabated, and by 2006, he had claimed the lives of at least 49 people, with some estimates suggesting the number could be higher.

The Chessboard Killer's Downfall: A Fatal Mistake

Pichushkin's reign of terror came to an end in June 2006, when he made a critical mistake that led to his capture. His final known victim was Marina Moskalyova, a 36-year-old woman who worked with Pichushkin at a local supermarket. Unlike many of his previous victims, Moskalyova was not a vulnerable or marginalized individual, but someone who had a family and was well-known in her community.

On the day of her murder, Pichushkin convinced Moskalyova to accompany him to Bitsevsky Park for a walk. Before leaving, Moskalyova left a note for her son, detailing her plans to meet with Pichushkin. She also mentioned that she would be taking the same metro route as him, providing a crucial piece of evidence that would later lead to Pichushkin's arrest.

After luring Moskalyova to a secluded area of the park, Pichushkin killed her in his usual manner, bludgeoning her with a hammer and leaving her body in the undergrowth. However, this time, the authorities were able to quickly piece together what had happened. Moskalyova's note, along with CCTV footage from the metro station showing her in Pichushkin's company, provided investigators with the evidence they needed to identify him as the prime suspect.

On June 16, 2006, Alexander Pichushkin was arrested at his home. During the search of his apartment, police found a chessboard with 61 of its 64 squares filled in, each square representing a victim. Pichushkin later confessed to the murders, detailing his crimes with a chilling lack of remorse. He claimed that he had intended to kill 64 people, enough to fill every square on the chessboard, and expressed regret only that he had not been able to achieve his goal.

The Trial: A Chilling Confession and the Search for Justice

The trial of Alexander Pichushkin began in September 2007 and quickly became a media sensation in Russia. Pichushkin's calm and composed demeanor in court, combined with the horrifying details of his crimes, captivated the public's attention. He showed no remorse for his actions, instead expressing pride in his killings and viewing them as a form of art or game that he had mastered.

During the trial, Pichushkin openly confessed to 61 murders, although he was officially charged with 49. He provided detailed accounts of his methods and motivations, describing how he selected his victims, lured them to the park, and methodically carried out their murders. His testimony was chilling in its lack of emotion; Pichushkin spoke about his crimes as if he were discussing a routine activity, devoid of any sense of morality or empathy.

Pichushkin's defense argued that he was mentally ill, suffering from a form of paranoid schizophrenia that had driven him to commit the murders. However, a psychiatric evaluation determined that while Pichushkin did exhibit signs of personality disorders, he was legally sane and fully aware of his actions. This meant that he could be held accountable for his crimes and face the full extent of the law.

On October 29, 2007, Alexander Pichushkin was found guilty of 48 counts of murder and three counts of attempted murder. The court sentenced him to life imprisonment, with the first 15 years to be spent in solitary confinement. Despite his conviction, Pichushkin remained unapologetic, stating that he would have continued killing if he had not been caught. He claimed that the act of murder gave him a sense of completeness and power, and that he had no intention of stopping until he had reached his goal of 64 victims.

The Legacy of the Chessboard Killer: A Dark Chapter in Criminal History

Alexander Pichushkin's crimes left a lasting impact on Russian society and the world at large. His methodical approach to murder, coupled with his chilling lack of remorse, has made him one of the most infamous serial killers of the 21st century. The sheer brutality of his actions, combined with his strategic thinking and cold calculation, set him apart from other killers and earned him the moniker of the "Chessboard Killer."

Pichushkin's case has been the subject of extensive media coverage, books, documentaries, and academic studies, all of which seek to understand the mind of a man who was driven by a twisted desire to dominate and control. His story is often compared to that of other infamous Russian serial killers, such as Andrei Chikatilo, but Pichushkin's unique approach to murder and his obsession with filling the chessboard make his case particularly disturbing.

The Chessboard Killer's legacy is one of horror and fascination, a stark reminder of the depths of human depravity and the potential for evil that lies within us all. His story serves as a cautionary tale about the dangers of unchecked violence and the importance of addressing mental health issues before they manifest in such horrific ways.

Chapter 22: Richard Kuklinski (the Iceman)

Richard Kuklinski, infamously known as "The Iceman," is one of the most notorious contract killers in American history. A cold-blooded murderer who worked as a hitman for various mafia families, Kuklinski earned his chilling nickname from his method of freezing the bodies of his victims to obscure their time of death. His criminal career, which spanned several decades, was marked by brutality, cunning, and an unnerving lack of remorse. Kuklinski's story is one of a man who lived a double life—on the surface, a devoted family man, but in reality, a ruthless killer responsible for the deaths of over 100 people. His tale offers a disturbing glimpse into the life of a man who was able to compartmentalize his violent profession from his seemingly normal personal life, making him one of the most terrifying figures in the history of organized crime.

Early Life: The Making of a Monster

Richard Leonard Kuklinski was born on April 11, 1935, in Jersey City, New Jersey, into a family marred by poverty, abuse, and violence. The second of four children, Kuklinski's early life was a brutal introduction to the harsh realities of the world. His father, Stanley Kuklinski, was an alcoholic who frequently beat Richard and his siblings. His mother, Anna McNally, was a devoutly religious woman of Polish descent who also resorted to physical violence as a means of discipline. The Kuklinski household was a place of constant fear and tension, and young Richard learned early on that violence was a tool for survival.

The abuse Kuklinski endured at the hands of his parents left deep psychological scars. His father's beatings were particularly severe; on one occasion, Stanley beat Richard's older brother, Florian, so severely that the boy died from his injuries. The family covered up the death by claiming it was an accident, and no charges were ever brought against Stanley. This incident profoundly affected Richard, teaching him that violence could be committed with impunity if it was kept hidden—a lesson that would later become central to his career as a contract killer.

As a child, Kuklinski was shy, introverted, and prone to violent outbursts. He struggled in school, both academically and socially, and was often bullied by his peers. These early experiences of victimization fueled a deep-seated rage that would eventually manifest in his violent tendencies. By his early teens, Kuklinski had already committed his first murder, beating a neighborhood bully to death with a wooden pole. This initial act of violence was a turning point in his life; Kuklinski later claimed that he felt no remorse for the killing and that it gave him a sense of power and control that he had never experienced before.

In his late teens and early twenties, Kuklinski began to establish himself as a petty criminal, engaging in theft, burglary, and other illegal activities. He quickly gained a reputation for his violent temper and his willingness to resort to extreme measures to get what he wanted. It wasn't long before Kuklinski caught the attention of local mobsters, who recognized his potential as a hired gun.

The Transition to Contract Killing: A Killer for Hire

Kuklinski's entry into the world of contract killing was a gradual process. He started by performing small tasks for local mafia families, such as debt collection and intimidation. His imposing physical presence—Kuklinski stood 6 feet 5 inches tall and weighed over 270 pounds—made him an effective enforcer, and his willingness to commit acts of violence without hesitation quickly earned him the trust of his criminal employers.

As Kuklinski's reputation grew, so did the scope of his assignments. He began taking on more serious jobs, including murder. Kuklinski's first confirmed contract killing occurred in the early 1970s when he was hired by the DeCavalcante crime family to kill a rival mobster. Kuklinski carried out the hit with precision, leaving no evidence that could be traced back to him. His success on this job solidified his status as a reliable hitman, and he began receiving more lucrative contracts from various organized crime families, including the Gambino, Genovese, and Lucchese families.

Kuklinski's methods were as varied as they were brutal. He used guns, knives, explosives, and even his bare hands to kill his victims. One of his favorite methods was to use cyanide, which he would administer in drinks, food, or by spraying it in his victim's face. Cyanide was particularly appealing to Kuklinski because it killed quickly and left little evidence. He also developed a macabre technique of freezing his victims' bodies to obscure the time of death, a practice that earned him the nickname "The Iceman." By freezing the corpses and then thawing them out later, Kuklinski was able to mislead law enforcement investigators, making it difficult for them to determine when the murders had taken place.

Over the years, Kuklinski became increasingly detached from the violence he inflicted. He described his killings as purely business transactions, devoid of emotion or personal involvement. According to Kuklinski, he never took pleasure in the act of murder itself; instead, he saw it as a necessary part of his job, a means to an end that provided him with financial stability and a sense of power. Despite this, some of his actions suggest a deep-seated sadism. Kuklinski admitted to torturing some of his victims before killing them, using methods such as beating, stabbing, or burning to inflict maximum pain. He also claimed to have killed stray animals as a child, an early sign of the violent tendencies that would later define his adult life.

The Double Life: Family Man by Day, Killer by Night

One of the most chilling aspects of Richard Kuklinski's life was his ability to maintain a double life. While he was a ruthless killer for hire, he also portrayed himself as a devoted husband and father. Kuklinski married Barbara Pedrici in 1961, and the couple had three children together. To the outside world, they appeared to be a typical suburban family. Kuklinski was described by neighbors and friends as a doting father who was deeply involved in his children's lives, attending school events, and taking them on family vacations.

Barbara Kuklinski was aware that her husband had a violent streak, but she had no idea about the true nature of his activities. Kuklinski was careful to keep his criminal life separate from his family life, often telling Barbara that he worked in "business" or that he was involved in the distribution of adult films, which was partially true. This façade allowed him to maintain a veneer of respectability while continuing to commit his crimes in secret.

However, the reality of living with Kuklinski was far from idyllic. Behind closed doors, he was abusive and controlling, subjecting Barbara to frequent physical and emotional abuse. Kuklinski's violent outbursts were unpredictable, and Barbara lived in constant fear of provoking his wrath. Despite this, she stayed with him for many years, raising their children and trying to maintain a semblance of normalcy in their lives.

Kuklinski's ability to compartmentalize his life was a key factor in his success as a hitman. He was able to switch between his roles as a family man and a killer with ease, never allowing one to interfere with the other. This duality made him an enigma to those who knew him; many of his friends and neighbors were shocked when they learned the truth about his criminal activities, unable to reconcile the loving father they knew with the cold-blooded killer who had terrorized the underworld for decades.

The Fall of the Iceman: Undercover Operation and Arrest

Richard Kuklinski's downfall began in the mid-1980s when law enforcement agencies started to take a closer look at his activities. Despite his efforts to cover his tracks, Kuklinski had become a suspect in several unsolved murders, and the authorities were beginning to connect the dots. In 1985, a joint task force composed of agents from the New Jersey State Police, the Bureau of Alcohol, Tobacco, and Firearms (ATF), and the Federal Bureau of Investigation (FBI) was formed to investigate Kuklinski and gather evidence against him.

The key to Kuklinski's capture was an undercover operation involving an informant named Dominic Polifrone, a federal agent who posed as a hitman looking to do business with Kuklinski. Over the course of several meetings, Polifrone gained Kuklinski's trust and persuaded him to discuss his methods and past killings. Kuklinski, who had become increasingly careless and overconfident, openly bragged about his crimes, detailing how he had killed his victims and describing the different methods he had used.

During one of these meetings, Polifrone asked Kuklinski to carry out a hit on a fictitious target, offering him a payment of $50,000. Kuklinski agreed and began making preparations for the murder. However, before he could carry out the hit, Kuklinski was arrested on December 17, 1986, as part of a coordinated sting operation. The authorities had finally gathered enough evidence to charge him with multiple counts of murder.

The arrest marked the end of Kuklinski's reign as one of the most feared contract killers in the United States. The double life he had so carefully maintained for decades came crashing down, and the full extent of his crimes was revealed to the public.

The Trial and Sentencing: A Monster Unmasked

Richard Kuklinski's trial began in 1988 and quickly became a media sensation. The public was captivated by the story of the seemingly ordinary family man who had secretly been one of the most prolific killers in American history. The trial revealed the shocking details of Kuklinski's criminal career, including his methods of killing, his connections to organized crime, and the sheer number of victims he had claimed.

Throughout the trial, Kuklinski showed little emotion, maintaining a calm and composed demeanor as the evidence against him was presented. He admitted to some of the murders but denied others, often downplaying his role in the killings or shifting the blame onto others. Despite his attempts to minimize his culpability, the evidence against Kuklinski was overwhelming. Witness testimony, physical evidence, and his own recorded confessions left little doubt about his guilt.

In March 1988, Richard Kuklinski was convicted of five counts of murder and sentenced to life in prison without the possibility of parole. The sentencing judge described Kuklinski as a "dangerous, cold-blooded killer" who had shown no remorse for his actions. Kuklinski was sent to Trenton State Prison in New Jersey, where he would spend the rest of his life.

Life in Prison and Final Years

Richard Kuklinski spent the last 18 years of his life in prison, where he continued to maintain a reputation as a dangerous and unpredictable individual. Even behind bars, Kuklinski's presence was intimidating; he was known to get into altercations with other inmates and was kept in solitary confinement for much of his time in prison to prevent him from harming others.

While in prison, Kuklinski gave several interviews to journalists, psychologists, and criminologists, providing insights into his life and the motivations behind his crimes. These interviews formed the basis for several documentaries and books, most notably the HBO documentary "The Iceman Tapes: Conversations with a Killer," which featured Kuklinski speaking candidly about his murders. In these interviews, Kuklinski often claimed that he regretted the impact his actions had on his family but showed little remorse for the victims he had killed. He continued to emphasize the idea that his killings were simply a part of his "business," a necessary evil in the world of organized crime.

Kuklinski also provided information about other murders that he claimed to have committed, though some of these claims were met with skepticism. He claimed to have killed Jimmy Hoffa, the former president of the Teamsters Union, and boasted of involvement in high-profile mob hits. However, many of these claims were never substantiated, leading some to believe that Kuklinski was exaggerating his role in certain crimes to enhance his reputation.

On March 5, 2006, Richard Kuklinski died at the age of 70 in the prison's secure wing. He had been diagnosed with Kawasaki disease, a rare condition that causes inflammation of the blood vessels, and had been in poor health for several years. Kuklinski's death marked the end of a life that had been defined by violence and brutality, a life that left a trail of devastation in its wake.

The Legacy of the Iceman: A Study in Cold-Blooded Ruthlessness

Richard Kuklinski's story is one of the most chilling and complex in the annals of American crime. His ability to live a double life, his cunning and brutality, and his lack of remorse set him apart from other killers. Kuklinski's case has been the subject of extensive study by criminologists, psychologists, and law enforcement professionals, all of whom have sought to understand the mind of a man who could kill so easily and without apparent emotion.

Kuklinski's life and crimes have also captured the public's imagination, inspiring numerous books, films, and documentaries. His story serves as a stark reminder of the capacity for evil that exists within some individuals and the devastating impact that a single person can have on the lives of countless others. The Iceman's legacy is one of horror and fascination, a cautionary tale about the dangers of unchecked violence and the dark side of human nature.

Despite his death, Richard Kuklinski's name continues to evoke fear and intrigue, a symbol of the cold-blooded ruthlessness that can lurk behind even the most ordinary of façades. His story remains a haunting chapter in the history of crime, a reminder of the depths of depravity to which some individuals can descend.

Chapter 23: Leonard Lake and Charles Ng

Leonard Lake and Charles Ng are two of the most notorious serial killers in American history. Their crimes, committed in the mid-1980s, were marked by unparalleled brutality, sadism, and a disturbing level of premeditation. Together, they carried out a series of abductions, tortures, sexual assaults, and murders, targeting men, women, and children. Their heinous acts took place in a remote cabin in Wilseyville, California, a location that would later be described as a "house of horrors." The partnership between Lake and Ng was one of mutual sadism, fueled by shared fantasies of power and control over their victims. Their story is a harrowing reminder of the depths of human depravity and the devastating impact that can result when two like-minded individuals join forces in the pursuit of evil.

Leonard Lake: A Troubled Mind

Leonard Thomas Lake was born on October 29, 1945, in San Francisco, California. His early life was marked by instability and dysfunction. After his parents' divorce, Lake and his siblings were raised by their grandmother, a woman who allegedly encouraged his interest in pornography from a young age. This early exposure to sexual content, combined with a troubled family environment, played a significant role in shaping Lake's disturbed psyche.

As a child, Lake was known to be intelligent but withdrawn, with a penchant for cruelty. He reportedly began taking nude photographs of his sisters, a behavior that hinted at the darker impulses he would later act upon. Lake's fascination with domination and control over others grew stronger as he aged, and by the time he reached adulthood, these desires had evolved into violent fantasies.

Lake joined the U.S. Marine Corps in 1965 and served in Vietnam. The experience left him with deep psychological scars, including post-traumatic stress disorder (PTSD). During his time in the military, Lake developed survivalist tendencies and became obsessed with the idea of a societal collapse. He stockpiled weapons, food, and supplies, preparing for a future where he believed he would need to rely on his own resources to survive.

After leaving the Marines, Lake's life continued to spiral downward. He married twice, but both marriages ended in divorce. His relationships were marked by his controlling behavior and violent temper. Lake also became involved in various criminal activities, including theft and fraud, which eventually led to his first encounters with law enforcement. Despite these early brushes with the law, Lake managed to avoid significant legal consequences, allowing him to continue his descent into a world of dark fantasies and criminal behavior.

Charles Ng: A Troubled Youth

Charles Chi-Tat Ng was born on December 24, 1960, in Hong Kong. Ng came from a wealthy and prominent family, but his upbringing was far from stable. His father was reportedly strict and abusive, and Ng struggled to meet his family's high expectations. From a young age, Ng exhibited antisocial behavior, including stealing and engaging in violent outbursts. His troubled behavior led to his expulsion from multiple schools, and his parents eventually sent him to a boarding school in England in an attempt to reform him.

Ng's time in England did little to curb his destructive tendencies. He continued to get into trouble and eventually returned to Hong Kong, where his behavior only worsened. In 1978, Ng moved to the United States to attend college in California, but he quickly dropped out and drifted into a life of petty crime. In 1980, Ng enlisted in the U.S. Marine Corps using forged documents. His time in the Marines was brief but eventful; Ng was soon caught stealing weapons from a military armory and was court-martialed. He escaped custody and fled to Northern California, where he eventually crossed paths with Leonard Lake.

The Meeting of Two Minds: Lake and Ng's Deadly Partnership

Leonard Lake and Charles Ng met in 1981 through a shared interest in survivalism and a mutual disdain for societal norms. The two men quickly formed a close bond, with Lake taking on a mentor-like role for the younger Ng. Lake, who was nearly 15 years older than Ng, was drawn to Ng's willingness to engage in criminal activities and his apparent lack of moral boundaries. Ng, for his part, was captivated by Lake's vision of a post-apocalyptic world where they could live out their twisted fantasies without consequence.

Lake had long harbored fantasies of creating a "sex slave" bunker, a place where he could imprison and dominate women at will. He found in Ng a willing accomplice who shared his sadistic desires. Together, they began to plan and execute a series of crimes that would shock the world.

The Wilseyville Compound: A House of Horrors

In the early 1980s, Leonard Lake purchased a remote property in Wilseyville, California, where he and Ng began constructing a fortified bunker. The property, surrounded by dense woods and isolated from neighbors, was the perfect location for the two men to carry out their horrific plans without fear of detection. The bunker was equipped with soundproof walls, hidden rooms, and various tools and devices designed for torture and imprisonment. Lake and

Ng referred to this place as their "Operation Miranda," named after a character in a science fiction novel who was abducted and enslaved.

The Wilseyville compound soon became the site of unimaginable atrocities. Lake and Ng would lure their victims to the property under various pretexts, including offers of work or promises of friendship. Once there, the victims were overpowered, bound, and taken to the bunker, where they were subjected to horrific acts of torture and sexual assault. Many of the victims were videotaped as they were tortured, with Lake and Ng taking sadistic pleasure in documenting their crimes.

The victims were not limited to adults; Lake and Ng also targeted entire families, including children. After satisfying their twisted desires, the killers would murder their victims, often disposing of the bodies by burning them or burying them on the property. The exact number of victims is unknown, but it is believed that Lake and Ng may have killed as many as 25 people during their spree.

The Downfall: Capture and Legal Proceedings

The downfall of Leonard Lake and Charles Ng began on June 2, 1985, when Ng was caught shoplifting at a hardware store in South San Francisco. When the police arrived, they discovered that Ng was driving a car registered to a man who had been reported missing. A search of the vehicle revealed a gun with a silencer, leading to Ng's arrest. Leonard Lake, who was with Ng at the time, was also taken into custody. However, Lake managed to swallow a cyanide pill that he had hidden in his clothing, a suicide method he had long planned in the event of capture. He fell into a coma and died a few days later, taking many of his secrets to the grave.

Ng, meanwhile, fled the scene but was eventually captured in Canada after a lengthy manhunt. The investigation into Lake and

Ng's activities led police to the Wilseyville property, where they made a series of gruesome discoveries. The bunker was filled with evidence of the duo's crimes, including videotapes of their victims, personal belongings, and human remains. The tapes, in particular, provided chilling proof of the torture and murders that had taken place at the compound.

Charles Ng fought extradition to the United States for several years, but he was eventually returned to California to stand trial. The legal proceedings were drawn out, with numerous delays and complications, but in 1999, Ng was finally convicted of 11 counts of murder. He was sentenced to death and remains on death row at San Quentin State Prison.

The Aftermath: The Legacy of Lake and Ng's Crimes

The crimes of Leonard Lake and Charles Ng left a lasting scar on the communities affected by their actions. The sheer brutality of their murders, combined with the calculated and sadistic manner in which they were carried out, made the case one of the most shocking in American criminal history. The Wilseyville compound, once a place of unspeakable horror, was eventually dismantled, but the memories of what occurred there continue to haunt those who were involved in the investigation and the families of the victims.

The case also raised important questions about the nature of evil and the factors that can lead individuals to commit such heinous acts. Both Lake and Ng had troubled childhoods and exhibited signs of deep psychological disturbances, yet their partnership created a synergy of sadism that far exceeded what either might have done alone. Their story serves as a grim reminder of the dangers posed by individuals who are driven by dark fantasies and the potential for unimaginable harm when such individuals find others who share their twisted desires.

Chapter 24: Herb Baumeister

Herb Baumeister's life is one of the most chilling examples of how a seemingly ordinary individual can harbor a dark and deadly secret. Born in the 1940s and raised in a middle-class family, Baumeister outwardly appeared to lead a successful life. He was a husband, father, and the owner of a thriving business in Indianapolis, Indiana. However, beneath this veneer of normalcy lay a deeply disturbed individual who would become one of America's most notorious serial killers.

Baumeister is believed to have murdered at least 11 young men in the 1980s and 1990s, luring them to his sprawling estate on the outskirts of Indianapolis, where he subjected them to horrific fates. His crimes went undetected for years, in part because of his outward respectability and his ability to maintain a double life. Baumeister's story is a haunting reminder that evil can lurk behind even the most ordinary of façades, and that the pursuit of truth and justice can sometimes be hampered by the very masks that people wear.

Early Life: The Seeds of Darkness

Herbert Richard Baumeister was born on April 7, 1947, in Indianapolis, Indiana, the eldest of four children. His father, Dr. Herbert E. Baumeister, was an anesthesiologist, and his mother, Elizabeth Baumeister, was a homemaker. The Baumeister family lived a comfortable, middle-class life, and by all accounts, Herb's early childhood was relatively uneventful. However, as he grew older, signs of troubling behavior began to emerge.

During his adolescence, Baumeister exhibited increasingly bizarre and antisocial behavior. He developed a fascination with death and decay, often engaging in disturbing activities that alarmed his family and peers. For instance, he was known to play with dead animals, and on one occasion, he reportedly urinated on a teacher's desk. These acts were dismissed as mere "eccentricities" at the time, but they hinted at the deeper psychological issues that would later drive him to commit horrific crimes.

Baumeister's father, concerned about his son's erratic behavior, sought psychiatric help for him. During his teenage years, Herb was diagnosed with schizophrenia, a condition characterized by disordered thinking, delusions, and hallucinations. Despite this diagnosis, Baumeister did not receive the intensive treatment he needed, and his mental health issues were largely ignored or downplayed by those around him. He managed to graduate from high school and briefly attended Indiana University, but his academic performance was poor, and he eventually dropped out.

The Mask of Normalcy: Marriage, Family, and Business

In 1971, Herb Baumeister married Juliana "Julie" Saiter, a teacher he had met while attending Indiana University. The couple seemed an unlikely match, given Herb's eccentricities, but they shared a desire for a stable, conventional life. They would go on to have three children together and eventually move to the affluent suburb of Westfield, just outside of Indianapolis.

Baumeister struggled to find steady employment during the early years of his marriage. He held a series of jobs, including stints at the Indianapolis Star and the Indiana Bureau of Motor Vehicles (BMV). At the BMV, Baumeister's strange behavior and odd sense of humor made him an outcast among his colleagues, and he was eventually fired. His inability to hold down a job put a strain on his marriage, but Julie remained supportive, hoping that her husband would eventually find his footing.

In 1988, Herb Baumeister opened a thrift store called Sav-A-Lot, specializing in secondhand goods. The business was initially successful, providing the Baumeisters with a comfortable income and allowing them to purchase a 15-acre estate called Fox Hollow Farm. The property, located in the quiet, wooded suburb of Westfield, became the family's primary residence and was where Baumeister would later commit his most heinous crimes.

Despite his business success, Baumeister's behavior became increasingly erratic. He began drinking heavily and became more withdrawn from his family. Julie noticed her husband's strange habits, such as spending long hours away from home and avoiding physical intimacy, but she did not suspect the dark secret he was hiding. Herb's ability to maintain a façade of normalcy while harboring such a dark side is a testament to his cunning and the effectiveness of his "mask."

The Murders: A Hidden House of Horrors

Between 1980 and 1996, a series of young men began disappearing from the Indianapolis area, particularly from the city's gay bars. The disappearances were initially treated as isolated incidents, and the police had few leads to go on. It would be years before authorities realized that a serial killer was targeting the city's gay community, and even longer before they connected the crimes to Herb Baumeister.

Baumeister's method of operation was chillingly calculated. He would frequent gay bars in Indianapolis, posing as a friendly and approachable man. He would engage young men in conversation, often offering them a ride or an invitation to continue the evening at his home. Once he had gained their trust, Baumeister would lure them back to Fox Hollow Farm, where he would carry out his horrific plans.

At his secluded estate, Baumeister subjected his victims to terrifying and brutal acts. He is believed to have strangled many of his victims to death, often during sexual encounters. The secluded nature of the property allowed Baumeister to commit these crimes without fear of being overheard or interrupted. Once he had killed his victims, he would dispose of their bodies by burning them or burying the remains on the property.

Baumeister's wife and children were often away at their lake house during the weekends, providing him with the perfect opportunity to carry out his murders without arousing suspicion. For years, he was able to maintain this double life, presenting himself as a respectable businessman and family man by day while indulging his dark and deadly desires by night.

The Investigation: A Break in the Case

The investigation into the disappearances of the young men in Indianapolis gained momentum in the mid-1990s when a tip from a man named Tony Harris (a pseudonym) led police to suspect that Herb Baumeister might be involved. Harris had met Baumeister at a gay bar and had been invited back to Fox Hollow Farm. There, Harris witnessed behavior that made him fear for his life, and he managed to escape. He reported the incident to the police, describing the interior of Baumeister's home and the strange behavior he had observed.

At the same time, investigators were working to solve the mystery of a series of unidentified human remains found along the banks of the White River in Hamilton County, Indiana. The remains had been discovered by children playing in the area, but the police had been unable to identify the victims or determine how they had ended up in the river. The investigation into these remains had gone cold until Harris's tip provided a new direction.

With Harris's information in hand, investigators began to build a case against Herb Baumeister. They requested a search warrant for Fox Hollow Farm, but because there was not yet enough concrete evidence linking Baumeister to the murders, the request was denied. Frustrated but undeterred, detectives continued to monitor Baumeister, hoping for a break that would allow them to search his property.

In June 1996, Julie Baumeister, who had grown increasingly suspicious of her husband's behavior, filed for divorce. During the divorce proceedings, she allowed police to search Fox Hollow Farm while Herb was away. What they found was horrifying.

The Discovery: Uncovering the Truth

When police searched Fox Hollow Farm, they uncovered a grisly scene. The property was littered with human remains, some of which had been buried, while others had been burned and scattered. Investigators recovered over 5,500 bone fragments, representing the remains of at least 11 different individuals. The discovery confirmed their worst fears: Herb Baumeister was a serial killer who had been murdering young men and disposing of their bodies on his property for years.

The sheer scale of the carnage shocked even the most seasoned investigators. The remains were so fragmented and degraded that identifying the victims proved to be a monumental task. However, forensic experts were eventually able to link some of the remains to men who had been reported missing in the Indianapolis area, providing the families of those victims with a measure of closure.

By the time the police uncovered the evidence at Fox Hollow Farm, Herb Baumeister had fled to Canada. He was aware that the investigation was closing in on him, and rather than face the consequences of his actions, he chose to end his life. On July 3, 1996, Baumeister was found dead in his car at Pinery Provincial Park in Ontario, Canada, from a self-inflicted gunshot wound. In his suicide note, Baumeister made no mention of the murders, instead blaming his actions on his failing marriage and business troubles.

The Aftermath: A Legacy of Horror

The discovery of Herb Baumeister's crimes sent shockwaves through the community, leaving a trail of devastation in its wake. The families of the victims were left to grapple with the knowledge that their loved ones had met such brutal and senseless ends. The case also highlighted the vulnerability of marginalized communities, as many of Baumeister's victims were young, gay men who had been largely ignored by society and the media at the time of their disappearances.

Fox Hollow Farm, once a symbol of the Baumeisters' success, became a symbol of horror and death. The property was eventually sold, but its dark history continues to cast a long shadow over the estate. The new owners reported strange occurrences on the property, leading some to believe that the spirits of Baumeister's victims still haunt the grounds.

The case of Herb Baumeister not only left a lasting scar on the community but also sparked ongoing discussions about the nature of evil, mental illness, and the hidden dangers that can lurk behind the façades of normalcy. Fox Hollow Farm, once the Baumeister family's idyllic estate, became infamous as the site where unspeakable horrors took place. The new owners of the property reported paranormal activity, including apparitions and unexplained sounds, leading to speculation that the restless spirits of Baumeister's victims might still be present. These stories have attracted ghost hunters and curious visitors, further cementing the farm's dark reputation.

The legal and psychological ramifications of Baumeister's crimes were profound. His ability to maintain a double life—a devoted family man by day and a sadistic killer by night—led to a reexamination of how such individuals can evade detection for so long. Experts have since analyzed Baumeister's actions in an attempt to understand what drives a person to commit such atrocities. His case has become a topic of study in criminal psychology, particularly in understanding how certain personality disorders, like schizophrenia, combined with environmental factors, can manifest in violent behavior.

The Victims: Remembering Those Lost

The exact number of Baumeister's victims remains uncertain, though it is believed to be at least 11 and possibly many more. The young men who fell prey to Baumeister's deadly charm were mostly from the LGBTQ+ community, a fact that initially contributed to the lack of urgency in investigating their disappearances. This aspect of the case has been a sobering reminder of the need for law enforcement to treat all missing persons cases with equal seriousness, regardless of the victim's background or lifestyle.

The identities of some of Baumeister's victims were never fully established, leaving their families without the closure they desperately sought. For those families who did receive confirmation of their loved ones' fate, the pain of their loss was compounded by the horrific nature of their deaths. Memorials and vigils have been held in honor of the victims, ensuring that their lives are remembered and that their suffering is not forgotten.

The Investigation: Lessons Learned

The investigation into Herb Baumeister's crimes exposed significant gaps in how serial killers are detected and how vulnerable communities are protected. Law enforcement agencies have since improved their coordination and communication across jurisdictions, recognizing that serial killers often operate over large areas and target marginalized groups. The case also highlighted the importance of community involvement and vigilance; it was the bravery of Tony Harris in coming forward with his story that ultimately led to the unraveling of Baumeister's deadly activities.

The case also prompted a reevaluation of how mental health issues are addressed within the criminal justice system. Baumeister's schizophrenia and other psychological problems were never adequately treated, which likely contributed to his descent into violence. This has led to increased advocacy for better mental health care and intervention strategies that could potentially prevent individuals with severe psychological disorders from committing violent acts.

Chapter 25: Albert DeSalvo (the Boston Strangler)

Albert DeSalvo, known as the Boston Strangler, is one of the most infamous serial killers in American history, a name that evokes fear and curiosity alike. Operating during the early 1960s, DeSalvo's crimes terrorized the city of Boston, leading to widespread panic and intense media coverage. Over a span of nearly two years, 13 women were brutally murdered, and the city was left in a state of fear, with people locking their doors and windows in a desperate attempt to protect themselves from the unseen predator.

DeSalvo's case is not only infamous for the horrific nature of the crimes but also for the complex legal and psychological questions it raised. Despite his confession to the murders, there remains controversy over whether he was truly the Boston Strangler, or if he took the blame for crimes he didn't commit. The story of Albert DeSalvo is one that delves deep into the psyche of a troubled man, the failures of the criminal justice system, and the lingering questions that still haunt the case.

Early Life: The Making of a Killer

Albert Henry DeSalvo was born on September 3, 1931, in Chelsea, Massachusetts, a small city just outside of Boston. His childhood was marred by violence, abuse, and instability, factors that would later be seen as contributing to his troubled psyche. DeSalvo was one of six children born to Frank and Charlotte DeSalvo, and his early life was anything but ordinary.

Frank DeSalvo, Albert's father, was a violent alcoholic who frequently abused his wife and children. He would beat Charlotte in front of the children, and there are reports that he even forced

Albert to watch as he engaged in sexual acts with prostitutes. This exposure to such extreme violence and sexual deviance at a young age had a profound impact on Albert, shaping his views on sex, power, and control.

The DeSalvo family was extremely poor, living in a dilapidated tenement in Chelsea. The children were often left to fend for themselves, with little supervision or guidance. Albert, like his siblings, quickly became a troublemaker. By the age of 12, he was already in trouble with the law, having been arrested for theft and other minor crimes. He spent time in a reform school, but rather than rehabilitate him, the experience seemed to harden him further.

As a teenager, DeSalvo continued to exhibit troubling behavior. He was known to be manipulative, charming when he wanted something, and prone to outbursts of anger. He dropped out of high school and joined the U.S. Army at the age of 17. During his time in the military, DeSalvo was stationed in Germany, where he met and married Irmgard Beck. Despite his troubled past, DeSalvo managed to maintain a relatively stable life for a few years, working various jobs and raising a family.

However, the seeds of deviance planted in his childhood began to surface in increasingly disturbing ways. DeSalvo developed a compulsion for petty crimes, often involving sexual misconduct. He was arrested multiple times for peeping into windows, breaking and entering, and indecent assault. These early signs of sexual deviancy would later escalate into something far more sinister.

The Boston Strangler: A City in Fear

The Boston Strangler's reign of terror began in 1962, a time when the city was unprepared for the horror that was about to unfold. The first victim, 55-year-old Anna Slesers, was found strangled with the belt of her bathrobe in her apartment on June 14, 1962. Her body was left in a suggestive position, a signature that would become a chilling hallmark of the Strangler's crimes.

In rapid succession, more women were found murdered in their homes, all strangled with articles of their own clothing. The victims ranged in age from 19 to 85, and the attacks took place in various neighborhoods across Boston. Despite the diversity in the victims' ages and locations, the pattern of the killings was unmistakable. Each victim was found in a state of undress, often with a scarf, nylon stocking, or other fabric tied around their necks in a bow.

The sheer brutality of the crimes, combined with the apparent ease with which the killer was able to enter the victims' homes, created an atmosphere of terror in Boston. Women were advised to take extra precautions, and many began living in fear, altering their routines, and becoming suspicious of strangers. The police were inundated with reports of potential suspects, but despite their best efforts, they were unable to catch the killer. The case became a media sensation, with newspapers dubbing the unknown assailant the "Boston Strangler."

Albert DeSalvo's Arrest: From Petty Crime to Murder

Albert DeSalvo was not immediately connected to the Boston Strangler murders. In fact, his arrest in 1964 was for a completely unrelated crime. DeSalvo had developed a disturbing modus operandi that earned him another nickname: "The Measuring Man." Posing as a modeling agent, DeSalvo would approach women in their homes, convincing them to allow him to measure their bodies under the pretense of assessing their suitability for modeling work. During these encounters, DeSalvo would sexually assault the women, though he did not kill them.

DeSalvo was eventually caught and arrested for these assaults, but his name would not be linked to the Boston Strangler until he made a shocking confession while in prison. After being arrested for the "Measuring Man" assaults, DeSalvo was placed in a psychiatric facility where he met fellow inmate George Nassar. It was to Nassar that DeSalvo first confessed to being the Boston Strangler, detailing the murders with chilling precision.

Nassar, sensing an opportunity to reduce his own sentence, relayed DeSalvo's confession to his attorney, F. Lee Bailey. Bailey took on DeSalvo's case, believing that his client was indeed the infamous Strangler. In a highly publicized trial, DeSalvo was not actually tried for the Boston Strangler murders—instead, he was charged with the "Measuring Man" crimes and sentenced to life in prison. However, his confession to the Strangler murders cemented his place in criminal history.

The Confession: Truth or Fabrication?

Albert DeSalvo's confession to being the Boston Strangler has been the subject of intense debate and scrutiny for decades. On one hand, DeSalvo's detailed descriptions of the murders, including specific information that had not been released to the public, seemed to confirm that he was indeed the killer. He was able to describe the crime scenes, the methods he used to gain entry to the victims' homes, and the positions in which the bodies were found. These details appeared to corroborate his claim of being the Strangler.

However, there were also significant inconsistencies in DeSalvo's confession. For instance, he was unable to accurately describe the appearance of some of the victims, and his accounts of certain murders did not match the physical evidence found at the crime scenes. Additionally, there was no physical evidence—such as fingerprints or DNA—that directly linked DeSalvo to the murders.

This lack of concrete evidence led some investigators and experts to question whether DeSalvo was truly the Boston Strangler or if he was taking the blame for someone else's crimes.

One theory suggests that DeSalvo, a known attention-seeker and manipulator, may have confessed to the murders in order to gain notoriety and secure a book deal. DeSalvo had a history of exaggerating and fabricating stories about himself, and some believe that he saw the confession as a way to achieve the fame and recognition he craved, even if it meant being labeled as one of the most notorious serial killers in history.

Others have suggested that DeSalvo may have been coerced into confessing or that he was used as a scapegoat by the authorities who were under immense pressure to solve the case. The possibility that there may have been multiple killers, rather than a single Boston Strangler, has also been considered. This theory posits that DeSalvo may have committed some of the murders but not all of them, with other perpetrators responsible for the remaining killings.

The Trial and Imprisonment: A Life Behind Bars

Despite the controversy surrounding his confession, Albert DeSalvo was sentenced to life in prison in 1967, not for the Strangler murders, but for the sexual assaults and other crimes he had committed as the "Measuring Man" and "Green Man." The latter nickname came from a series of rapes in which DeSalvo posed as a maintenance worker dressed in green overalls. These charges alone were enough to keep DeSalvo behind bars for the rest of his life.

DeSalvo's time in prison was marked by repeated attempts to escape, as well as continued efforts to gain attention and notoriety. He frequently communicated with his lawyer, F. Lee Bailey, and other individuals, hoping to leverage his story for financial gain. However, these efforts were largely unsuccessful, and DeSalvo spent his final years in the maximum-security Walpole State Prison in Massachusetts.

On November 25, 1973, DeSalvo was found stabbed to death in his cell. His murder remains unsolved, though it is widely believed that he was killed by fellow inmates, possibly due to debts or grudges he had accrued during his time in prison. The violent end to DeSalvo's life added another layer of mystery to his already enigmatic story, leaving behind more questions than answers.

DNA Evidence: Revisiting the Case Decades Later

For many years, the question of whether Albert DeSalvo was truly the Boston Strangler remained unresolved. However, advances in DNA technology provided an opportunity to reexamine the evidence in the case. In 2013, more than 50 years after the last Strangler murder, Boston authorities announced that they had found a definitive link between DeSalvo and one of the victims, Mary Sullivan, who was murdered in 1964.

Using modern DNA analysis techniques, investigators were able to match a sample of DeSalvo's DNA to evidence found on Sullivan's body. This breakthrough provided the first concrete evidence linking DeSalvo to one of the Strangler murders, lending significant credence to his confession. While this finding did not definitively prove that DeSalvo was responsible for all 13 murders attributed to the Boston Strangler, it did strongly suggest that he was involved in at least one of the crimes.

The DNA evidence has been a crucial development in the case, helping to bring some measure of closure to the families of the victims. However, it has not entirely dispelled the doubts and questions that have surrounded the case for decades. The possibility that DeSalvo was not the sole perpetrator, or that he may have exaggerated his involvement, continues to be a topic of debate among criminologists, historians, and those with a vested interest in the case.

Legacy: The Boston Strangler in Popular Culture and Criminal Psychology

The story of Albert DeSalvo and the Boston Strangler has had a lasting impact on popular culture and the field of criminal psychology. The case has been the subject of numerous books, films, and television shows, each exploring different aspects of the mystery and the psychology behind the murders. The 1968 film *The Boston Strangler*, starring Tony Curtis as DeSalvo, is perhaps the most famous portrayal of the case, dramatizing the events and bringing the story to a wide audience.

In the field of criminal psychology, the Boston Strangler case has been studied as an example of how serial killers can evade capture by exploiting weaknesses in the criminal justice system. The case also highlights the challenges of dealing with confessions from individuals with personality disorders, who may fabricate or exaggerate their involvement in crimes. DeSalvo's ability to manipulate those around him, combined with the lack of physical evidence, made the case particularly difficult to solve and has provided valuable lessons for law enforcement and forensic investigators.

The Boston Strangler case also had a profound impact on the city of Boston and its residents. The fear and anxiety that gripped the city during the early 1960s are still remembered by those who lived through it, and the case remains one of the most infamous chapters in Boston's history. The murders, and the questions that still linger about them, serve as a reminder of the dangers that can lurk behind the façade of normalcy and the complexities of human psychology.

Chapter 26: Richard Angelo

Richard Angelo, a nameless infamous than others, but equally chilling, was a nurse whose crimes horrified the nation when they came to light in the late 1980s. Dubbed the "Angel of Death," Angelo exploited his position as a caregiver to carry out a series of deadly acts under the guise of medical assistance. Unlike other serial killers who operated in the shadows, Angelo committed his heinous crimes in the very place where people felt safest—in a hospital. His story is a stark reminder of how those entrusted with the care and well-being of others can sometimes turn into their worst nightmare.

Richard Angelo's case is unique in the annals of criminal history, not only because of the method of his killings but also because of the complex psychological motives behind his actions. His desire for recognition and a twisted sense of heroism led him down a dark path, one that ended with the deaths of several vulnerable patients. Angelo's story is a disturbing exploration of the potential for evil within those who appear to be the most trustworthy.

Early Life: The Formation of a Dark Mind

Richard Angelo was born on August 29, 1962, in Long Island, New York. His early life was relatively unremarkable, growing up in a middle-class family with loving parents who had high expectations for their son. Angelo's father was a retired police officer, and his mother worked as a homemaker. From a young age, Angelo was described as intelligent and polite, with a strong interest in helping others. This interest would later manifest in his decision to pursue a career in nursing.

As a child, Angelo was known to be somewhat introverted, preferring to spend time alone or with a small circle of friends. He excelled in school, particularly in science, and was known for his meticulous attention to detail. However, beneath this quiet exterior, there were signs of a developing obsession with control and a need for recognition. Angelo harbored a deep-seated desire to be seen as a hero, someone who could save lives and be admired for his bravery and skill.

This desire was evident even in his childhood games, where he often played the role of a rescuer, saving others from imagined dangers. Angelo's fascination with heroism was further fueled by his father's career as a police officer, which Angelo admired and aspired to emulate. However, unlike his father, who upheld the law, Angelo's interpretation of heroism would take a darker turn.

The Path to Nursing: A Desire to Be a Hero

After graduating from high school, Richard Angelo pursued his dream of helping others by enrolling in a nursing program at Farmingdale State College in New York. He excelled in his studies, demonstrating a strong aptitude for the medical field. His instructors and peers noted his dedication to his work and his eagerness to learn. Angelo's passion for nursing seemed genuine, and he quickly became known as a competent and caring professional.

Angelo's choice to become a nurse was influenced by his desire to be in a position where he could directly impact people's lives. He was drawn to the idea of being a hero, of being the one to step in during moments of crisis and save the day. However, this desire was not purely altruistic. Angelo wanted to be recognized for his efforts, to be seen as a savior in the eyes of others. This need for validation and recognition would become a driving force behind his later actions.

After completing his nursing program, Angelo began working at several hospitals in the Long Island area. He gained experience in various departments, but it was in the intensive care unit (ICU) where he found his true calling. The ICU was a high-stakes environment where life and death were daily occurrences, and Angelo thrived in this setting. He enjoyed the challenge and the opportunity to make a difference in the lives of critically ill patients.

However, despite his apparent success, Angelo felt unfulfilled. He believed that his efforts were going unnoticed, that he was not receiving the recognition he deserved. This sense of inadequacy began to fester, leading Angelo to develop a dangerous plan to fulfill his desire for heroism. He would create emergencies in the hospital by deliberately putting patients in critical condition, only to step in and save them, thereby earning the admiration and praise he craved. This twisted plan would soon result in tragic consequences.

The Murders: A Deadly Quest for Recognition

Richard Angelo's descent into murder began in the mid-1980s while he was working as a nurse at Good Samaritan Hospital in West Islip, New York. It was here that he started implementing his deadly plan, targeting patients who were already vulnerable due to their critical conditions. Angelo's method was both cunning and cruel: he would inject his victims with a lethal combination of drugs, including Pavulon and Anectine, both of which are muscle relaxants that can cause respiratory failure if administered in high doses.

Angelo's goal was not to kill his patients outright but to bring them to the brink of death. He wanted to create a medical emergency that would allow him to step in as the hero, performing life-saving measures and, in his mind, earning the recognition he felt he deserved. However, this twisted plan often went awry, and many of Angelo's victims did not survive the ordeal.

Between 1987 and 1989, Angelo is believed to have been responsible for the deaths of at least 25 patients at Good Samaritan Hospital. His victims were mostly elderly or critically ill, people who were already in a fragile state. This made it difficult for authorities to detect a pattern in the deaths, as they were often attributed to the patients' underlying health conditions. Angelo's actions went unnoticed for a time, allowing him to continue his deadly game.

However, as the number of unexplained deaths began to rise, hospital staff started to suspect that something was amiss. Angelo's colleagues noticed that many of the patients who died had been under his care shortly before their deaths. This raised red flags, and an internal investigation was launched. Despite this, Angelo remained undeterred, confident in his ability to manipulate the situation and continue his quest for recognition.

The Arrest: The Fall of the Angel of Death

Richard Angelo's downfall began on October 11, 1987, when one of his victims, 73-year-old Gerolamo Kucich, survived Angelo's deadly injection. Kucich, who had been admitted to the hospital with a heart condition, suddenly became critically ill after receiving an injection from Angelo. However, unlike Angelo's previous victims, Kucich managed to survive the ordeal, although he suffered significant distress.

Kucich later described his experience to the medical staff, detailing how Angelo had administered an injection just before he began to feel his chest tighten and his breathing become labored. This account was enough to raise suspicions, and the hospital decided to contact the authorities. The police began an investigation, closely monitoring Angelo's activities and reviewing the medical records of the patients who had died under his care.

The investigation revealed a disturbing pattern: many of the patients who had died during Angelo's shifts had been administered drugs that were not prescribed or medically necessary. Further examination of the patients' records showed that the drugs used were consistent with those that could induce respiratory failure, leading to cardiac arrest. The evidence against Angelo began to mount, and it became clear that he was not the hero he claimed to be, but rather a cold-blooded killer.

On November 15, 1987, Richard Angelo was arrested and charged with multiple counts of murder, attempted murder, and assault. During his interrogation, Angelo confessed to his crimes, admitting that he had injected his victims with lethal drugs in an attempt to create life-threatening situations that he could then "save" them from. He expressed a deep need for recognition and validation, stating that he wanted to be seen as a hero, someone who could be counted on in times of crisis.

Angelo's confession shocked the nation, as it revealed the extent of his deception and the calculated nature of his crimes. The image of a trusted nurse, someone who was supposed to care for and protect the vulnerable, had been shattered, replaced by the chilling reality of a man who saw his patients as mere tools in his quest for self-aggrandizement.

The Trial: Justice for the Victims

Richard Angelo's trial began in February 1989, and it quickly became a media sensation. The public was both horrified and fascinated by the details of the case, and the courtroom was packed with spectators eager to witness the proceedings. Angelo was charged with multiple counts of second-degree murder, manslaughter, and assault, as the prosecution sought to bring justice for the victims and their families.

During the trial, the prosecution presented a compelling case against Angelo, using his own confession as a key piece of evidence. They also called numerous witnesses, including medical experts who testified about the effects of the drugs Angelo had used, as well as the nurses and doctors who had worked alongside him. The prosecution painted a picture of a man who was deeply disturbed, driven by a pathological need for attention and recognition.

Angelo's defense team, meanwhile, argued that he was mentally ill and should not be held fully responsible for his actions. They claimed that Angelo suffered from a personality disorder that caused him to act out his fantasies of heroism in a dangerous and misguided manner. The defense also suggested that Angelo had not intended to kill his victims but had instead been attempting to create situations where he could save them, albeit with tragic consequences.

Despite the defense's arguments, the jury was not swayed. After several weeks of testimony and deliberation, Richard Angelo was found guilty on multiple counts of second-degree murder and manslaughter. On February 20, 1989, he was sentenced to 61 years to life in prison, effectively ensuring that he would spend the rest of his life behind bars.

The verdict brought some measure of closure to the families of Angelo's victims, although the pain of their loss would never fully heal. The case also had a profound impact on the medical community, prompting hospitals to implement stricter oversight and monitoring of their staff to prevent similar tragedies from occurring in the future.

Psychological Analysis: The Mind of a Killer

Richard Angelo's case has been the subject of much psychological analysis, as experts have sought to understand the factors that drove him to commit such heinous acts. One of the most striking aspects of Angelo's behavior was his need for recognition and validation, which was rooted in a deep sense of inadequacy and low self-esteem. Despite his outward success as a nurse, Angelo felt that he was not appreciated or valued for his work, leading him to seek out more extreme methods of gaining attention.

This need for recognition is a common trait among individuals with narcissistic personality disorder, a condition characterized by an inflated sense of self-importance and a constant need for admiration. However, Angelo's case also exhibited elements of Munchausen syndrome by proxy, a disorder in which a caregiver deliberately causes harm to those in their care in order to gain attention and sympathy. While Munchausen syndrome by proxy typically involves a parent harming their child, Angelo's actions fit the broader pattern of this disorder, as he sought to create medical emergencies to fulfill his desire for heroism.

Angelo's actions also reflect a profound lack of empathy, as he was willing to put his patients' lives at risk to achieve his goals. This lack of empathy is a hallmark of psychopathy, a personality disorder characterized by a lack of remorse, manipulativeness, and a tendency to engage in antisocial behavior. While Angelo may not have been a classic psychopath, his actions demonstrate a disturbing willingness to use others as tools in his pursuit of recognition.

The combination of these psychological factors created a dangerous mix, leading Angelo to commit a series of murders that shocked the nation. His case serves as a reminder of the importance of psychological screening and monitoring in the medical field, particularly in positions where individuals have control over the lives of others.

Legacy: The Impact of Angelo's Crimes

The case of Richard Angelo had a lasting impact on the medical community and the public at large. The revelation that a trusted nurse could turn into a cold-blooded killer sent shockwaves through the healthcare industry, leading to a reevaluation of how hospitals monitor and supervise their staff. In the wake of Angelo's crimes, hospitals across the country implemented stricter protocols for administering medications and keeping detailed records of patient care.

Angelo's case also highlighted the importance of psychological evaluations for healthcare professionals. While the vast majority of nurses and doctors are dedicated and compassionate caregivers, Angelo's actions showed that there can be exceptions. Hospitals and medical schools began placing a greater emphasis on psychological assessments to identify individuals who may pose a risk to patients, with the goal of preventing similar tragedies from occurring in the future.

The story of Richard Angelo also became a cautionary tale in popular culture, serving as a stark reminder of the potential for evil within those who are supposed to protect and care for others. His case was featured in numerous true crime documentaries and books, which explored the psychological factors that drove him to commit his crimes. Angelo's actions continue to be studied by criminologists and psychologists, who seek to understand the complex interplay of personality disorders, environmental factors, and individual choices that can lead to such horrific outcomes.

Chapter 27: John Haigh (the Acid Bath Murderer)

John George Haigh, infamously known as "The Acid Bath Murderer," is a figure who embodies the chilling reality that the most terrifying monsters often come in unassuming guises. Haigh's life and crimes are a study in contrasts—he was outwardly charming, intelligent, and well-dressed, yet beneath this veneer lay a cold-blooded murderer who dissolved his victims in acid to cover his tracks. His case shocked Britain in the 1940s, not only because of the brutality of his crimes but also because of the meticulous and calculating manner in which he carried them out. Haigh's story is a dark chapter in the annals of British crime, revealing the depths of human depravity and the dangers of unchecked ambition.

Early Life: The Making of a Murderer

John George Haigh was born on July 24, 1909, in Stamford, Lincolnshire, England, into a strict religious family. His parents, John Robert Haigh and Emily, were devout members of the Plymouth Brethren, a conservative Christian sect that preached a rigid and literal interpretation of the Bible. Haigh's upbringing was marked by an intense focus on sin, guilt, and the fear of divine retribution. His father, in particular, was a domineering figure who believed that the world outside their home was full of sin and corruption.

As a child, Haigh was isolated from his peers and discouraged from forming friendships outside the family. His parents imposed strict rules on him, and he was often punished for minor infractions. This oppressive environment fostered in Haigh a deep sense of inadequacy and a desire to escape the confines of his upbringing. He developed a keen sense of deception, learning to lie and manipulate to avoid punishment and gain his parents' approval.

Haigh's early life was also marked by a series of vivid and disturbing dreams, which he later claimed were prophetic. These dreams often involved blood, violence, and religious imagery, themes that would later surface in his criminal activities. As he grew older, Haigh began to rebel against his parents' strictures, developing a taste for luxury and the finer things in life. He became increasingly obsessed with money and status, believing that wealth was the key to escaping the limitations of his upbringing.

After finishing school, Haigh briefly worked as a clerk, but he quickly grew dissatisfied with the mundane nature of the job. He longed for excitement and easy money, leading him to embark on a career of petty crime. Haigh's early criminal activities included fraud, theft, and embezzlement, and he was frequently in trouble with the law. Despite his criminal tendencies, Haigh maintained a respectable appearance, presenting himself as a suave and sophisticated gentleman.

The Descent into Murder: A Calculated Plan

By the late 1930s, John Haigh had developed a criminal modus operandi that involved befriending wealthy individuals, forging their signatures on documents, and then stealing their money. However, Haigh soon realized that his schemes were risky and often led to his arrest and imprisonment. He began to search for a way to eliminate the primary witnesses to his crimes—his victims—while leaving no trace of their existence. It was during this period that Haigh became fascinated with the concept of "getting away with murder."

In 1944, Haigh began experimenting with sulfuric acid, discovering that it could completely dissolve organic material, leaving behind no recognizable remains. He believed that by using acid to dispose of his victims' bodies, he could commit the perfect crime—one in which there would be no body, no evidence, and therefore no case. This belief marked the beginning of Haigh's transformation from a petty criminal to a serial killer.

Haigh's first known murder occurred in 1944 when he targeted a man named William McSwan, who had been his employer and business partner. McSwan was a successful entrepreneur who owned a chain of amusement arcades, and Haigh saw him as the perfect victim—wealthy, trusting, and easily accessible. Haigh lured McSwan to his basement in London, where he struck him over the head with a blunt object, killing him instantly. He then placed McSwan's body in a 40-gallon drum and filled it with sulfuric acid, leaving it to dissolve over the next two days.

When Haigh returned to the drum, he found that McSwan's body had been reduced to a thick sludge. He carefully poured the remains down a drain, effectively erasing any physical evidence of the murder. Haigh then assumed control of McSwan's finances, forging documents to transfer the deceased man's assets into his own name. To McSwan's family and friends, Haigh claimed that McSwan had fled to Scotland to avoid conscription into the army during World War II.

Flush with his newfound wealth, Haigh continued his lavish lifestyle, frequenting high-end hotels, restaurants, and casinos. However, his appetite for money and power was insatiable, and he soon set his sights on his next victims.

The Killing Spree: A Trail of Death

After successfully murdering and disposing of William McSwan, John Haigh embarked on a killing spree that spanned the next four years. His next victims were McSwan's parents, Donald and Amy. In 1945, Haigh lured the elderly couple to his basement under the pretense of a surprise reunion with their son, William. Once there, Haigh murdered them in the same manner as their son, dissolving their bodies in acid and disposing of the remains. He then took control of their financial assets, selling their properties and collecting their life savings.

Haigh's ability to charm and manipulate his victims allowed him to continue his murderous activities without arousing suspicion. He carefully selected his targets, focusing on wealthy individuals who had few close relatives or friends. His next victim, in 1947, was a woman named Dr. Archibald Henderson, whom he met through a mutual acquaintance. Haigh befriended Dr. Henderson and his wife, Rose, ingratiating himself into their lives by feigning interest in purchasing one of their properties.

Haigh convinced the Hendersons to visit his workshop under the guise of discussing the property sale. Once there, he shot Dr. Henderson in the head, killing him instantly. He then lured Rose into the workshop and murdered her in the same manner. As with his previous victims, Haigh placed their bodies in a drum of sulfuric acid and disposed of the remains. He forged documents to transfer the Hendersons' assets to himself, once again living off the wealth of his victims.

Haigh's final known victims were a wealthy widow named Olive Durand-Deacon and her friend Margaret Lofty. Haigh met Durand-Deacon at the Onslow Court Hotel in Kensington, where they both resided. He learned that she was interested in investing in new business ventures, and he used this opportunity to lure her to his workshop under the pretense of discussing a potential investment in an artificial fingernail company.

In February 1949, Haigh murdered Olive Durand-Deacon in his workshop, shooting her in the head before placing her body in a drum of acid. However, Haigh's meticulous plan began to unravel when Durand-Deacon's disappearance was reported to the police by her friend. The authorities launched an investigation, and their inquiries led them to Haigh.

The Investigation and Arrest: The Acid Bath Murderer Unmasked

The disappearance of Olive Durand-Deacon marked the beginning of the end for John Haigh. The police quickly discovered that Haigh had been the last person to see Durand-Deacon alive, and they began to investigate his background. As they dug deeper, they uncovered Haigh's long history of fraud and deception, leading them to suspect that he was involved in Durand-Deacon's disappearance.

The police obtained a search warrant for Haigh's workshop, where they made a gruesome discovery. Inside the workshop, they found a 40-gallon drum containing the remains of Durand-Deacon, partially dissolved in sulfuric acid. They also discovered several personal items belonging to Haigh's other victims, including jewelry, documents, and clothing. This evidence provided a clear link between Haigh and the murders, and he was arrested on suspicion of murder.

During his interrogation, Haigh confessed to the murders in chilling detail, describing how he had killed his victims, dissolved their bodies in acid, and disposed of the remains. He claimed that he had been driven by a need for money and that he believed he could get away with the murders by eliminating all physical evidence. Haigh's confession was particularly shocking because of his apparent lack of remorse and his matter-of-fact attitude toward the killings.

Haigh also made a bizarre claim during his confession, stating that he had drunk the blood of his victims as part of a ritualistic practice. This statement led the media to label him a "vampire," further sensationalizing the case. However, there was no evidence to support Haigh's claim, and it is widely believed that he fabricated this story to bolster an insanity defense.

The Trial: A Case That Gripped the Nation

John Haigh's trial began in July 1949, and it quickly became one of the most sensational cases in British legal history. The public was both horrified and fascinated by the details of Haigh's crimes, and the trial attracted widespread media coverage. The prosecution presented a compelling case, using Haigh's own confession and the physical evidence found in his workshop to establish his guilt.

Haigh's defense team attempted to argue that he was insane at the time of the murders, citing his claims of drinking blood and his long history of disturbing dreams and religious obsessions. They called several psychiatric experts to testify that Haigh suffered from paranoid schizophrenia and was unable to distinguish right from wrong. However, the defense's attempt to paint John Haigh as a mentally disturbed individual who was not fully responsible for his actions ultimately failed. The prosecution countered by arguing that Haigh was a highly calculating and methodical killer who was fully aware of the criminal nature of his actions. They pointed to the meticulous planning and execution of the murders, as well as his attempts to profit from his victims' assets, as evidence of his rational state of mind.

The court was also unconvinced by Haigh's bizarre claims of drinking his victims' blood, viewing these statements as a deliberate ploy to support his insanity defense. The media's portrayal of Haigh as a "vampire" added a sensationalist element to the trial, but it did little to sway the jury. The evidence against Haigh was overwhelming, and his demeanor in court—calm, composed, and lacking in remorse—further solidified the image of a cold-blooded, calculating killer.

After a brief deliberation, the jury found John Haigh guilty of murder. The judge, Mr. Justice Humphreys, sentenced him to death, stating that Haigh's crimes were "among the most wicked that have ever been heard in this country." The trial had gripped the nation, and the public's fascination with the case was reflected in the extensive newspaper coverage and the large crowds that gathered outside the courtroom each day.

Execution: The End of the Acid Bath Murderer

John Haigh was sentenced to death by hanging, and his execution was scheduled to take place at Wandsworth Prison. In the days leading up to his execution, Haigh reportedly remained calm and showed little sign of fear or regret. He continued to maintain his innocence, claiming that he had only killed in self-defense and that the acid baths were a necessary measure to protect himself from his victims.

On August 10, 1949, Haigh was hanged by Albert Pierrepoint, one of Britain's most famous executioners. Haigh's execution marked the end of the Acid Bath Murderer's reign of terror, but the public's fascination with his crimes continued for years to come. His case became a symbol of the potential for evil that can lurk beneath a charming and respectable exterior, and it served as a reminder of the dangers posed by individuals who are willing to go to extreme lengths to achieve their goals.

Psychological Analysis: Understanding Haigh's Mind

John Haigh's case has been the subject of extensive psychological analysis, as experts have sought to understand the factors that drove him to commit such horrific crimes. One of the most striking aspects of Haigh's personality was his ability to compartmentalize his life, presenting himself as a respectable and charming gentleman while secretly engaging in brutal acts of murder. This duality suggests that Haigh may have had psychopathic tendencies, characterized by a lack of empathy, a propensity for manipulation, and a desire for control.

Haigh's upbringing in a strict religious household likely played a significant role in shaping his personality. The oppressive environment in which he was raised may have contributed to his deep-seated feelings of inadequacy and his desire to rebel against authority. His obsession with wealth and status can be seen as an attempt to compensate for the lack of emotional support and validation he received as a child.

Moreover, Haigh's fascination with blood and violence, as evidenced by his claims of drinking his victims' blood, has led some experts to speculate that he may have suffered from a form of paraphilia, a condition in which individuals derive sexual gratification from unusual or extreme activities. While there is no concrete evidence to support this theory, it adds another layer of complexity to Haigh's already disturbing psychological profile.

Ultimately, Haigh's case highlights the dangerous combination of narcissism, greed, and a lack of moral restraint. His ability to rationalize his actions and his belief that he could commit the "perfect crime" demonstrate a profound detachment from reality and a complete disregard for the lives of others. Haigh's crimes were not motivated by passion or anger but by a cold and calculated desire for personal gain, making him one of the most chilling figures in the history of British crime.

Legacy: The Lasting Impact of Haigh's Crimes

The story of John Haigh, the Acid Bath Murderer, continues to capture the public's imagination more than seven decades after his execution. His case has been the subject of numerous books, documentaries, and television programs, each exploring the dark and twisted mind of a man who believed he could dissolve his way to freedom. Haigh's crimes also had a significant impact on British criminal law, particularly in the way that evidence was collected and presented in court.

Haigh's method of disposing of his victims' bodies presented a unique challenge to the police and forensic experts of the time. The lack of physical remains made it difficult to prove that a murder had occurred, leading to changes in the way that circumstantial evidence was treated in court. Haigh's case demonstrated the importance of forensic science in solving crimes and highlighted the need for advancements in techniques for detecting and preserving evidence.

In popular culture, Haigh's story has become synonymous with the idea of the "perfect crime," a concept that has fascinated writers and filmmakers for generations. His ability to elude capture for so long, coupled with the gruesome nature of his crimes, has made him a legendary figure in the annals of true crime. However, Haigh's legacy is also a cautionary tale about the dangers of unchecked ambition and the lengths to which some individuals will go to achieve their goals.

Chapter 28: Ed Kemper

Edmund Emil Kemper III, more commonly known as Ed Kemper, is one of the most notorious and chilling figures in the annals of criminal history. Born on December 18, 1948, in Burbank, California, Kemper's early life was marked by a series of traumatic experiences that would lay the foundation for his later atrocities. Standing at 6 feet 9 inches and possessing a high IQ of 145, Kemper was an imposing and highly intelligent individual. However, beneath this outward appearance lurked a deeply disturbed mind, shaped by a turbulent childhood, a dysfunctional family, and a growing resentment towards women, particularly his mother.

Early Life: Seeds of Destruction

Kemper's childhood was far from idyllic. His parents, Edmund Emil Kemper II and Clarnell Stage, had a tumultuous relationship characterized by frequent arguments and emotional distance. After their divorce, young Ed was left in the custody of his mother, Clarnell, a domineering and abusive woman who openly expressed her disdain for him. She often belittled him, comparing him unfavorably to his father, and forced him to sleep in a dark, cold basement out of fear that he might harm his sisters.

This harsh treatment had a profound impact on Kemper's psyche. He grew increasingly withdrawn, developing violent fantasies that centered around power and control. These fantasies began to manifest in disturbing behaviors, such as decapitating his sisters' dolls and killing small animals. At the age of 10, Kemper ran away from home to find his father, only to be rejected and sent back to his mother. This rejection deepened his feelings of abandonment and rage, further warping his developing mind.

First Murders: The Unseen Killer

Kemper's descent into violence began at the tender age of 15 when he committed his first murders. On August 27, 1964, after an argument with his grandmother, he shot her in the head, then stabbed her repeatedly. When his grandfather returned home, Kemper killed him as well, claiming that he did not want his grandfather to find out what he had done to his grandmother. Afterward, he called his mother, who instructed him to turn himself in to the police.

Kemper was subsequently arrested and sent to Atascadero State Hospital, a maximum-security facility for mentally ill convicts. There, he was diagnosed with paranoid schizophrenia, though some experts have since questioned this diagnosis, suggesting that he may have been more accurately described as a sociopath. Despite his diagnosis, Kemper was considered a model prisoner. His intelligence and charm allowed him to manipulate the staff into believing that he was rehabilitated. In 1969, at the age of 21, he was released on parole and sent to live with his mother in Santa Cruz, California—a decision that would have tragic consequences.

The Co-ed Killer: A Reign of Terror

Upon his release, Kemper initially attempted to lead a normal life. He attended community college and aspired to become a state trooper, but his application was rejected due to his imposing size. Unable to find a stable career, he worked a series of menial jobs and continued to live with his mother, whose constant belittling and criticism reignited the rage that had simmered during his time in prison.

Between May 1972 and April 1973, Kemper embarked on a killing spree that would earn him the moniker "The Co-ed Killer." His modus operandi involved picking up young female hitchhikers, whom he would then take to secluded areas. There, he would kill them through strangulation, stabbing, or shooting, and then engage in acts of necrophilia with their corpses. Afterward, he would dismember their bodies, often keeping their heads as trophies, before disposing of the remains in various locations.

Kemper's ability to blend into society allowed him to evade detection for months. He was polite, articulate, and seemed harmless—traits that made him an unlikely suspect. He even frequented a local bar where off-duty police officers gathered, earning their trust and gathering information about the ongoing investigation into the murders.

The Final Murders: Matricide and Confession

Despite the horrific nature of his crimes, it was the murder of his mother that would ultimately bring Kemper's killing spree to an end. On April 20, 1973, after a particularly bitter argument, Kemper bludgeoned his mother to death with a claw hammer while she slept. He then decapitated her, engaged in acts of necrophilia with her severed head, and used it as a dartboard. To further humiliate her, he cut out her vocal cords and placed them in the garbage disposal.

Afterward, Kemper invited his mother's friend, Sally Hallett, over to the house and killed her as well. He later explained that he murdered Hallett to create a cover story, making it appear as though his mother and her friend had gone away on a trip together. However, instead of continuing his killing spree, Kemper drove to Pueblo, Colorado, where he called the police and confessed to his crimes. He waited for the authorities to arrive and surrendered without resistance.

Trial and Incarceration: The End of the Road

During his trial, Kemper was surprisingly candid about his actions, providing detailed confessions and expressing a desire to be executed. However, the jury found him guilty of eight counts of first-degree murder, and he was sentenced to life imprisonment without the possibility of parole. Kemper was sent to the California Medical Facility in Vacaville, where he remains to this day.

In prison, Kemper has continued to demonstrate his intelligence and manipulative abilities. He has become a model inmate, assisting in the recording of audiobooks for the blind, and has even been interviewed by psychiatrists and criminologists seeking to understand the mind of a serial killer. Despite his cooperation and seemingly remorseful demeanor, Kemper has never been granted parole, as authorities believe that he remains a threat to society.

Psychological Profile: The Anatomy of a Killer

Ed Kemper's psychological profile is a complex web of trauma, intelligence, and a profound sense of powerlessness that fueled his violent tendencies. His troubled relationship with his mother played a significant role in shaping his homicidal urges. Clarnell's constant emasculation and psychological abuse instilled in Kemper a deep-seated hatred for women, which he acted out in his brutal killings. His high intelligence allowed him to carefully plan and execute his crimes, while his ability to appear normal made him a master manipulator, both during his killing spree and later in prison.

Some experts have argued that Kemper's crimes were a desperate attempt to assert control over his life, which had been dominated by his mother's oppressive presence. His choice to target young women, and eventually his own mother, reflects his desire to reclaim the power he felt had been stolen from him. The gruesome nature of his crimes, particularly the acts of necrophilia and mutilation, suggests a deep psychological need to degrade and dehumanize his victims, reducing them to mere objects that he could dominate completely.

Legacy: A Case Study in Evil

Ed Kemper's story continues to captivate and horrify people to this day. His case has been the subject of numerous books, documentaries, and films, as well as academic studies seeking to unravel the mind of a serial killer. Kemper himself has expressed regret for his actions, claiming that he wishes to help prevent others from following in his footsteps. However, his willingness to discuss his crimes in such graphic detail has led some to question the sincerity of his remorse.

Kemper's life and crimes serve as a chilling reminder of the potential for evil that can exist within even the most seemingly ordinary individuals. His story underscores the importance of understanding the psychological factors that can contribute to such extreme behavior, as well as the need for early intervention in cases of childhood trauma and mental illness. While Kemper remains behind bars, the legacy of his crimes continues to resonate, offering a stark warning of the dangers that can arise when deep-seated rage and resentment are left unchecked.

Chapter 29: Richard Cottingham (the Torso Killer)

Richard Cottingham, notoriously known as "The Torso Killer," is one of the most horrifying figures in the history of American serial killers. Born on November 25, 1946, in the Bronx, New York City, Cottingham's name became synonymous with some of the most gruesome crimes in the late 20th century. His moniker, "The Torso Killer," is derived from his macabre practice of dismembering his victims, often decapitating them and leaving behind only their torsos, an act that shocked and horrified both law enforcement and the public. Over a span of more than a decade, Cottingham embarked on a chilling killing spree that left an indelible mark on the history of crime in America.

Early Life: The Unseen Darkness

Richard Cottingham's early life seemed unremarkable on the surface, yet beneath the facade of normalcy, there were signs of a disturbed psyche. Raised in a middle-class family, Cottingham moved with his family to New Jersey during his adolescence. His upbringing was not marked by the extreme abuse or neglect often seen in the backgrounds of other serial killers, but he was described as a loner who struggled to form meaningful relationships. As a child, Cottingham developed an obsession with pornography and sadomasochism, which would later play a significant role in his violent crimes.

Cottingham's behavior as a teenager was concerning but not overtly alarming. He exhibited signs of antisocial tendencies, such as stealing and bullying, yet these actions were often dismissed as typical adolescent rebellion. He managed to graduate from high school and secured a job as a computer operator at Blue Cross Blue Shield in

Manhattan, a position that afforded him the opportunity to lead a double life—one as a seemingly responsible employee and the other as a sadistic killer.

The First Murders: A Killer Begins His Reign

Cottingham's descent into murder began in the late 1960s, although his first known killing did not occur until 1967. This initial murder, which went unsolved for years, involved the brutal slaying of Nancy Schiava Vogel, a 29-year-old mother of two. Vogel was found strangled in her car; her body positioned in a manner that suggested a deep level of depravity. At the time, the police had little evidence linking Cottingham to the crime, and it wasn't until decades later that he would confess to her murder.

Following this first kill, Cottingham continued to live a seemingly ordinary life, even getting married and fathering three children. His outward appearance as a family man concealed the dark urges that were brewing beneath the surface. Over the next several years, Cottingham honed his skills as a predator, learning to lure women into his grasp through manipulation and deceit. He often targeted prostitutes, believing that their marginalized status would make them less likely to be missed, and that the police would not prioritize their cases.

The Torso Murders: A Reign of Terror in New York

The late 1970s and early 1980s marked the height of Cottingham's killing spree, earning him the nickname "The Torso Killer." His method of operation during this period became increasingly gruesome and methodical. Cottingham would lure his victims, often young women or prostitutes, to secluded locations, such as cheap motels, where he would subject them to unimaginable torture. His preferred methods included strangulation, stabbing, and sexual assault. However, it was his post-mortem mutilations that truly set him apart from other killers.

Cottingham would often dismember his victims, severing their heads and limbs, and leaving behind only their torsos. These grisly scenes were intended to shock and confuse investigators, making identification of the victims and the determination of the cause of death more difficult. The first known torso murder occurred in December 1979, when the bodies of two women, identified as Deedeh Goodarzi and an unidentified Jane Doe, were found in a Times Square motel room. Their heads and hands had been severed, and the room had been set on fire in an attempt to destroy evidence. This brutal crime sent shockwaves through New York City and initiated a massive manhunt for the killer.

Escalation and Capture: The Downfall of a Sadist

Despite the brutality of his crimes, Richard Cottingham managed to evade capture for years, in part due to the chaotic nature of his crime scenes and the lack of a clear pattern in his killings. However, his reign of terror came to an end in May 1980, when he was apprehended while attempting to kidnap and murder 18-year-old Leslie Ann O'Dell at a Quality Inn in Hasbrouck Heights, New Jersey.

O'Dell, who had been lured to the motel under the guise of a paid sexual encounter, was subjected to hours of torture by Cottingham. However, she managed to survive by convincing him that she wouldn't report the crime, all the while secretly planning her escape. Her eventual screams for help alerted motel staff, who called the police. When officers arrived, they found Cottingham covered in O'Dell's blood, attempting to flee the scene. His arrest marked the end of one of New York's most notorious killing sprees.

The Trial and Convictions: Justice Served

Richard Cottingham's trial was a sensational affair, marked by graphic testimonies and the public's horrified fascination with the details of his crimes. He was charged with multiple counts of murder, attempted murder, sexual assault, and kidnapping. Despite his initial pleas of innocence, the overwhelming evidence, including O'Dell's testimony and forensic evidence from the crime scenes, led to his conviction.

In 1981, Cottingham was convicted of the murders of three women in New York and New Jersey and was sentenced to multiple life terms in prison. However, his legal battles did not end there. In the years that followed, he was linked to additional murders and was eventually convicted of a total of six homicides. Cottingham himself has since confessed to at least 11 murders, though it is widely believed that the true number of his victims could be much higher.

Psychological Profile: Understanding the Mind of the Torso Killer

Richard Cottingham's psychological profile is that of a deeply disturbed individual driven by sadistic urges and a need for control. Unlike some serial killers who are motivated by financial gain or personal vendettas, Cottingham's crimes were purely acts of violence for the sake of violence. His obsession with torture and mutilation reflects a profound need to exert power over his victims, reducing them to mere objects for his sadistic pleasure.

Cottingham's double life as a family man and a serial killer is a classic example of compartmentalization, a psychological defense mechanism that allowed him to separate his monstrous deeds from his everyday life. This duality enabled him to maintain relationships and hold down a job while committing heinous crimes. His ability to blend into society, coupled with his knowledge of police procedures, which he acquired through his job at Blue Cross Blue Shield, made him a particularly elusive and dangerous predator.

The Confessions: A Killer Speaks

In the years following his conviction, Richard Cottingham has become more forthcoming about his crimes, offering detailed confessions to law enforcement officials and journalists. These confessions have provided invaluable insights into his methods and motivations, though they have also raised new questions about the true extent of his crimes.

Cottingham has admitted to targeting vulnerable women, particularly those involved in the sex trade, whom he viewed as easy prey. His confessions also revealed his meticulous planning and his awareness of the difficulties that dismembered bodies would pose to investigators. Despite these admissions, Cottingham has shown little remorse for his actions, often describing his crimes in a detached and clinical manner that underscores the depth of his psychopathy.

Legacy: The Impact of the Torso Killer

Richard Cottingham's crimes left a lasting impact on both the victims' families and the broader public consciousness. The brutality of his murders, particularly the dismemberments, challenged law enforcement agencies to improve their investigative techniques and led to changes in how such cases were handled. His case also highlighted the vulnerability of marginalized groups, particularly sex workers, and the need for greater protection and support for these communities.

Cottingham's story has been the subject of numerous books, documentaries, and true crime television shows, each attempting to unravel the mystery of how an ordinary-looking man could commit such extraordinary acts of evil. His case has also been studied by criminologists and psychologists seeking to understand the nature of sadistic killers and the factors that contribute to their development.

Chapter 30: Robert Yates

Robert Lee Yates Jr., often referred to as the "Spokane Serial Killer," is one of the most notorious American serial killers of the late 20th century. Born on May 27, 1952, in Oak Harbor, Washington, Yates led a double life that allowed him to evade detection for years. A decorated Army National Guard helicopter pilot with a seemingly normal family life, Yates harbored a dark secret—he was a prolific killer who preyed on vulnerable women, particularly sex workers, in the Spokane area. His crimes, which spanned from the late 1970s until his arrest in 2000, shocked the nation and left a trail of devastation in their wake.

Early Life: The Formation of a Killer

Robert Yates was born into a middle-class family and raised in a relatively stable environment. His early life was marked by a strong religious influence, as his family was deeply involved in the local Seventh-day Adventist Church. Despite this religious upbringing, Yates displayed troubling behaviors from a young age. He was known to be a quiet, introverted child who struggled with forming relationships, a pattern that would persist throughout his life.

As a teenager, Yates began to exhibit signs of a disturbed psyche. He developed an obsession with violence and death, which he later claimed was rooted in a fascination with the Bible's depiction of the apocalypse and judgment. Despite these early warning signs, Yates managed to graduate from Oak Harbor High School in 1970 and went on to attend college briefly before enlisting in the U.S. Army in 1975. His military career would play a significant role in shaping both his public persona and his methods as a serial killer.

Military Career: The Perfect Cover

Yates' military career was marked by distinction and success. He served as a helicopter pilot, flying medevac missions in Germany, and later participated in operations in Somalia, Haiti, and the Balkans. Yates was awarded numerous commendations, including the Army Commendation Medal, the Humanitarian Service Medal, and several others. His time in the military allowed him to develop skills that would later aid him in his crimes, such as knowledge of forensic techniques, firearms proficiency, and the ability to navigate complex terrain.

The discipline and structure of military life also provided Yates with a perfect cover for his secret life as a serial killer. His military service allowed him to travel frequently, providing opportunities to commit murders in different locations without arousing suspicion. His status as a respected soldier and family man made it difficult for authorities to believe that he could be responsible for the heinous crimes that were occurring in and around Spokane.

The First Murders: A Killer Begins His Spree

Yates' first known murders occurred in the late 1970s, although he would not be connected to these crimes until years later. On July 13, 1975, Yates shot and killed Susan Savage and Patrick Oliver, a young couple who were camping near Walla Walla, Washington. Their bodies were discovered with multiple gunshot wounds, but the case quickly went cold due to a lack of evidence and suspects.

It wasn't until the mid-1990s that Yates began his most notorious killing spree, targeting sex workers in the Spokane area. His method was chillingly methodical: he would cruise the streets of Spokane's red-light district in his white Corvette, luring women into his car with the promise of money for sex. Once they were in his vehicle, Yates would drive them to a secluded location where he would shoot them in the head with a .25-caliber handgun. After killing his victims, Yates would dump their bodies in rural areas, often covering them with plastic bags or leaves to delay their discovery.

The Spokane Murders: A Reign of Terror

Between 1996 and 1998, Yates is believed to have killed at least 13 women, although the true number of his victims may be higher. The murders sent shockwaves through Spokane; a city unaccustomed to such violent crimes. The victims were all women, most of whom were struggling with addiction and involved in sex work. This made them particularly vulnerable to Yates, who exploited their desperation to satisfy his sadistic urges.

The discovery of the bodies in various locations around Spokane and neighboring counties led to a massive manhunt. The police were initially stymied by the lack of physical evidence linking the crimes to a single suspect. Yates was meticulous in covering his tracks, ensuring that he left behind minimal forensic evidence. However, the investigation eventually began to close in on him due to a combination of witness testimonies, behavioral profiling, and advances in forensic science.

The Arrest: The End of the Killing Spree

Robert Yates' reign of terror came to an end on April 18, 2000, when he was arrested by Spokane police after a routine traffic stop. The arresting officers noted the suspicious behavior of Yates, who was driving a white Corvette that matched the description of a vehicle seen near several of the crime scenes. A search of his vehicle revealed bloodstains and other forensic evidence linking him to the murders.

Following his arrest, Yates initially denied any involvement in the crimes. However, faced with overwhelming evidence, including DNA matches to the victims, Yates eventually confessed to the murders as part of a plea deal to avoid the death penalty. In exchange for his confession and cooperation in locating the bodies of some of his victims, Yates was sentenced to 408 years in prison without the possibility of parole.

Psychological Profile: The Mind of Robert Yates

Understanding the psychology of Robert Yates is crucial to comprehending the motivations behind his heinous crimes. Yates' psychological profile reveals a man who was able to compartmentalize his violent impulses from his everyday life. On the surface, Yates appeared to be a devoted family man and a respected soldier, yet beneath this facade lay a deeply disturbed individual driven by a need for control and dominance over his victims.

Yates exhibited traits commonly associated with psychopathy, including a lack of empathy, a superficial charm, and a tendency to manipulate those around him. His choice of victims—vulnerable women involved in sex work—suggests a deep-seated misogyny and a desire to assert power over those he perceived as weak or disposable. Yates' military training likely played a role in shaping his methodical approach to murder, as he was able to remain calm and calculated under pressure, minimizing the risk of detection.

The Trial and Sentencing: Justice Served

Robert Yates' trial was a highly publicized event, drawing widespread media attention due to the shocking nature of his crimes and his status as a former military hero. During the trial, Yates admitted to killing 13 women in Spokane but was also linked to several other unsolved murders in Washington state. His confession and the plea deal that followed were controversial, as many felt that Yates should have faced the death penalty for his crimes.

In 2002, Yates was sentenced to death by lethal injection for two murders committed in Pierce County, Washington, in addition to the 408-year sentence he received for the Spokane murders. However, in 2018, the Washington State Supreme Court declared the death penalty unconstitutional, and Yates' death sentence was commuted to life in prison without the possibility of parole. He is currently serving his sentence at the Washington State Penitentiary in Walla Walla.

The Aftermath: The Impact on the Community

The crimes of Robert Yates had a profound impact on the Spokane community and the families of his victims. The brutal nature of his killings and the fact that he managed to evade capture for so long left many feeling angry and betrayed. The case also highlighted the vulnerability of sex workers and the need for better protection and support for marginalized groups.

The Yates case led to significant changes in how law enforcement agencies in Washington state approached investigations involving serial killers. Advances in forensic science, particularly in the use of DNA evidence, played a crucial role in solving the case and have since become standard practice in homicide investigations. The case also underscored the importance of interagency cooperation, as multiple law enforcement agencies worked together to bring Yates to justice.

Legacy: A Dark Chapter in Criminal History

The legacy of Robert Yates is one of horror and tragedy. His crimes serve as a grim reminder of the potential for evil that can exist within even the most seemingly ordinary individuals. Yates' ability to lead a double life for so many years, committing brutal murders while maintaining the appearance of a devoted family man and respected soldier, has made him one of the most chilling figures in American criminal history.

Yates' story has been the subject of numerous books, documentaries, and true crime television shows, each attempting to unravel the mystery of how a man with such a distinguished military career and a seemingly normal family life could commit such horrific acts. His case continues to be studied by criminologists and psychologists seeking to understand the factors that drive individuals to become serial killers.

Chapter 31: Gary Ridgway (Green River Killer)

Gary Leon Ridgway, notoriously known as the "Green River Killer," is one of the most prolific serial killers in American history. His reign of terror spanned nearly two decades, during which he confessed to murdering 71 women, though the actual number may be higher. Ridgway primarily targeted vulnerable young women and girls, many of whom were runaways or sex workers, in the Seattle and Tacoma areas of Washington state. His nickname, the "Green River Killer," originated from the early discovery of several of his victims near the Green River in King County, Washington. Ridgway's ability to evade capture for so long, despite being one of the most hunted criminals in U.S. history, is a chilling testament to his cunning and the flaws in the investigative processes of the time.

Early Life: The Making of a Monster

Gary Ridgway was born on February 18, 1949, in Salt Lake City, Utah. He was the second of three sons born to Mary and Thomas Ridgway. His upbringing was marred by dysfunction and emotional abuse. Ridgway's mother was described as domineering and controlling, often humiliating him and his brothers. His father, on the other hand, was a bus driver who frequently spoke of his disdain for sex workers, a sentiment that may have influenced Ridgway's later choice of victims.

Ridgway's childhood was also marked by disturbing behavior. From a young age, he exhibited signs of a troubled mind. He was known to have a bedwetting problem that persisted into his teenage years—a behavior often associated with serial killers in psychological profiles. Ridgway's mother would reportedly berate him for his bedwetting and then clean him in a manner that Ridgway later described as sexually arousing and confusing. This complex relationship with his mother, marked by both arousal and anger, is believed to have contributed to his violent impulses and his later actions.

As a teenager, Ridgway exhibited more troubling behavior. At the age of 16, he lured a six-year-old boy into the woods and stabbed him in the liver, leaving the boy for dead. Miraculously, the boy survived, but the incident was a clear indication of Ridgway's capacity for violence. Despite this early act of violence, Ridgway graduated from Tyee High School in 1969 and soon after joined the U.S. Navy. His time in the Navy was relatively uneventful, though he did contract gonorrhea, which reportedly angered him as it interrupted his frequent visits to sex workers during his service in the Philippines.

The Path to Murder: Ridgway's Early Crimes

After his discharge from the Navy, Ridgway returned to the Seattle area, where he began working as a truck painter, a job he would hold for 30 years. His return to civilian life did little to quell the violent impulses that had plagued him since childhood. In fact, it was during this time that Ridgway began to act on his murderous urges.

Ridgway's first confirmed murder occurred in 1982, though it is believed that he may have killed earlier. His modus operandi was chillingly consistent: Ridgway would cruise the Pacific Highway South, an area known for its high concentration of sex workers. He would lure women into his truck with the promise of money for sex, drive them to a secluded location, and then strangle them—often with his bare hands or a ligature. After killing his victims, Ridgway would sometimes engage in necrophilia before disposing of their bodies in wooded areas, ravines, or the Green River.

The Green River Murders: A Reign of Terror

The Green River Killer's reign of terror officially began in the summer of 1982, when the bodies of five women were discovered in or near the Green River in King County, Washington. These initial victims, Wendy Coffield, Debra Bonner, Marcia Chapman, Cynthia Hinds, and Opal Mills, were all young women involved in sex work. The discovery of their bodies sent shockwaves through the community and marked the beginning of one of the largest and most complex serial murder investigations in U.S. history.

The King County Sheriff's Office quickly formed the Green River Task Force to investigate the murders. Despite the massive resources dedicated to the case, including the involvement of famed FBI profiler John E. Douglas, the task force struggled to find leads. The lack of physical evidence, combined with the transient nature of many of the victims, made it difficult to track the killer. Ridgway was methodical in his approach, leaving little evidence behind and spreading out his crimes over a wide geographic area, which further complicated the investigation.

As the years went on, the bodies continued to pile up. Ridgway's victims were typically found in clusters, often in remote, wooded areas. He would revisit the dump sites to engage in necrophilia with the decomposing bodies, a fact that only came to light after his arrest. This gruesome practice was a reflection of Ridgway's deep-seated need for control and domination over his victims, even in death.

The Investigation: Near Misses and Missed Opportunities

Gary Ridgway's ability to evade capture for so long is a story of near misses and missed opportunities. Despite being a prime suspect early in the investigation, Ridgway managed to stay one step ahead of law enforcement for nearly two decades.

In 1983, Ridgway was first questioned by police after he was seen with one of the victims, Marie Malvar, shortly before her disappearance. Ridgway denied any involvement, and without sufficient evidence to hold him, the police let him go. This would not be the last time Ridgway slipped through the cracks. In 1984, he passed a polygraph test, further convincing investigators that he was not the killer.

One of the most significant missed opportunities came in 1987 when police obtained a warrant to search Ridgway's home and vehicles. Despite finding evidence that could have linked him to the murders, such as trace elements of paint consistent with the paint used in his job and small amounts of blood, the technology at the time was not advanced enough to conclusively connect Ridgway to the murders. As a result, Ridgway remained free to continue his killing spree.

Arrest and Confession: The End of the Green River Killer

Gary Ridgway's reign of terror finally came to an end in 2001, nearly 20 years after his first known murder. The breakthrough in the case came with the advent of DNA technology, which had advanced significantly since the initial investigation. In 1987, police had taken a saliva sample from Ridgway, but it wasn't until 2001 that DNA testing could definitively link Ridgway to the semen found on three of the victims: Marcia Chapman, Opal Mills, and Carol Christensen. The DNA match was the evidence investigators needed to finally arrest Ridgway.

Following his arrest, Ridgway initially denied involvement in the murders. However, faced with overwhelming evidence, including DNA matches and other forensic evidence, he eventually confessed to killing 71 women as part of a plea deal to avoid the death penalty. During his confessions, Ridgway displayed a chilling lack of remorse, describing the murders in a matter-of-fact manner. He explained that he targeted sex workers because he believed they were less likely to be reported missing and because he thought he was "helping" society by getting rid of them.

Ridgway's confessions provided investigators with details about the murders that had previously been unknown, including the locations of undiscovered bodies. Over the course of several months, Ridgway led investigators to the remains of several of his victims, providing some measure of closure for the families who had spent years searching for answers.

Psychological Profile: Inside the Mind of Gary Ridgway

Understanding the psychology of Gary Ridgway is key to understanding his motivations as a serial killer. Ridgway fits the profile of a psychopathic killer—someone who is devoid of empathy, highly manipulative, and driven by a need for control and dominance. However, there are other elements of his psychological makeup that provide further insight into his actions.

Ridgway's childhood experiences, particularly his troubled relationship with his mother, played a significant role in shaping his later behavior. The combination of sexual arousal and humiliation he experienced as a child may have contributed to his later need to assert control over women, particularly those he perceived as "dirty" or "immoral," such as sex workers. His anger towards his mother and other women in his life likely fueled his desire to dominate and kill his victims.

Ridgway's ability to maintain a facade of normalcy—holding down a steady job, getting married multiple times, and even fathering a son—while committing such heinous acts is a testament to his psychopathic nature. He was able to compartmentalize his life, keeping his violent impulses hidden from those around him. This duality is a common trait among serial killers, who often present a charming and unassuming exterior to the world while harboring dark and violent fantasies.

The Trial and Sentencing: Justice for the Victims

Gary Ridgway's trial was one of the most highly publicized in American history, drawing widespread media attention due to the shocking nature of his crimes and the sheer number of his victims. In 2003, as part of a plea bargain to avoid the death penalty, Ridgway pleaded guilty to 48 counts of aggravated first-degree murder. In exchange for his guilty plea and his cooperation in locating the remains of his victims, Ridgway was sentenced to life in prison without the possibility of parole.

During the sentencing phase of the trial, Ridgway sat emotionless as the families of his victims delivered impact statements, describing the pain and suffering he had caused. Ridgway's lack of emotion during this time was consistent with his psychopathic tendencies, as he appeared indifferent to the suffering of others.

Despite Ridgway's guilty plea, the case did not end with his sentencing. In the years following his conviction, law enforcement agencies across the country have continued to investigate other cold cases, seeking to determine if Ridgway was responsible for additional murders. The true number of his victims may never be known, but Ridgway's legacy as one of the most prolific serial killers in history is secure.

Aftermath: The Impact of the Green River Killer

The case of Gary Ridgway had a profound impact on law enforcement, forensic science, and society as a whole. The Green River murders highlighted the vulnerabilities of certain populations, particularly sex workers, and the challenges faced by law enforcement in protecting them. The case also underscored the importance of advancements in forensic technology, particularly DNA testing, in solving complex criminal cases.

For the families of Ridgway's victims, the end of the Green River Killer's reign of terror brought a bittersweet sense of closure. While Ridgway's arrest and conviction provided some measure of justice, the pain of losing a loved one to such a brutal killer remains a lifelong burden. The families of the victims have worked to ensure that their loved ones are remembered not just as victims of a serial killer, but as individuals who lived and were loved.

The Green River Killer case also serves as a stark reminder of the capacity for evil that can exist within seemingly ordinary individuals. Ridgway was a man who, on the surface, appeared to lead a normal life—holding down a steady job, maintaining relationships, and raising a family. Yet beneath this facade lay a man capable of unspeakable violence and cruelty. His ability to hide in plain sight for so long raises important questions about the nature of evil and the complexities of the human psyche.

Chapter 32: Robert Hansen (the Butcher Baker)

Robert Christian Hansen, notoriously dubbed the "Butcher Baker," stands as one of the most chilling and methodical serial killers in American history. Between 1971 and 1983, Hansen embarked on a killing spree that claimed the lives of at least 17 women, though the true number of his victims may never be known. Hansen's crimes are particularly horrifying not just because of their brutality, but because of the meticulous and calculated manner in which he carried them out. Operating primarily in the remote wilderness of Alaska, Hansen abducted, raped, and murdered women, often releasing them into the wild and hunting them down like animals. His story is one of a seemingly ordinary man with deep-seated insecurities who hid a monstrous double life behind the facade of a quiet baker and family man.

Early Life: A Childhood of Isolation and Abuse

Robert Hansen was born on February 15, 1939, in Estherville, Iowa. He was the son of a Danish immigrant father who was a strict disciplinarian and ran a bakery. Hansen's childhood was marked by a sense of isolation and inadequacy, largely stemming from his strained relationship with his father and his peers. From an early age, Hansen struggled with a severe stutter and was afflicted with acne so severe that it left his face permanently scarred. These physical ailments made him a target of relentless bullying at school, where he was often teased and ostracized by his classmates. The humiliation and rejection he experienced during his formative years sowed the seeds of the deep-seated anger and resentment that would later fuel his violent tendencies.

Hansen's relationship with his father was fraught with tension and harsh discipline. His father was a domineering figure who expected perfection and demanded hard work, often forcing Hansen to spend long hours in the family bakery. The lack of affection and support from his father compounded Hansen's feelings of worthlessness and inadequacy, leading him to retreat further into himself. He developed an intense hatred for those who bullied him, particularly women who rejected his advances, and began to fantasize about enacting revenge on those who wronged him.

In his teenage years, Hansen found a solitary refuge in hunting, a hobby introduced to him by his father. He spent countless hours in the woods, honing his skills with a rifle and bow, finding a sense of control and power that eluded him in his social life. Hunting became an obsession for Hansen, not just as a means of survival, but as a way to exert dominance over the helpless creatures he preyed upon. This need for control and power would later manifest in his gruesome crimes.

The Evolution of a Predator: From Petty Crime to Serial Murder

Robert Hansen's transition from a troubled youth to a cold-blooded killer was a gradual process, marked by escalating criminal behavior and increasing violence. In his early 20s, Hansen began to engage in petty crimes, such as arson and theft, which served as outlets for his pent-up anger and frustrations. In 1960, at the age of 21, Hansen was arrested for burning down a school bus garage as an act of revenge against the local high school, where he had been relentlessly bullied. He was sentenced to three years in prison, but served only 20 months. This stint in prison did little to rehabilitate him; instead, it deepened his resentment and further isolated him from society.

After his release, Hansen moved to Alaska in 1967, hoping to start anew. He settled in Anchorage, where he opened a small bakery and became known as a quiet, hardworking man who was well-liked by his neighbors. Hansen married and started a family, further cementing his image as a respectable member of the community. However, beneath this facade, Hansen's darker impulses continued to fester.

By the early 1970s, Hansen began frequenting Anchorage's red-light district, where he developed a fascination with sex workers and dancers. These women, who were often marginalized and living on the fringes of society, became the targets of his escalating violence. Hansen initially began by soliciting these women for sex, only to later escalate to rape. He used threats and intimidation to keep his victims silent, and when the authorities did become involved, the transient nature of his victims made it difficult to build a case against him. This lack of consequences only emboldened Hansen, leading him down the path to serial murder.

The Murders: A Calculated and Methodical Killing Spree

Robert Hansen's method of killing was as horrifying as it was methodical. Unlike many serial killers who act impulsively, Hansen meticulously planned each of his murders, using the skills he had honed as a hunter. His victims were typically young women, often sex workers or dancers, whom he would abduct under the pretense of paying for their services. Hansen's physical appearance—unassuming, average, and somewhat meek—made it easy for him to lure his victims into a false sense of security.

After abducting his victims, Hansen would drive them to his home in Muldoon, a quiet neighborhood in Anchorage, where he had constructed a soundproof basement. Here, he would sexually assault and torture them, taking pleasure in their terror and helplessness.

But Hansen's sadistic nature didn't end with mere torture. He would often fly his victims in his private plane to the remote Knik River, a desolate area surrounded by dense wilderness. It was here that Hansen's twisted hunting fantasies came to life.

Once in the wilderness, Hansen would release his victims, giving them a fleeting hope of escape. However, this was merely part of his sadistic game. Armed with a hunting rifle or bow, Hansen would stalk his victims through the woods, hunting them down like prey. The wilderness, which had once been a place of solace for Hansen, now became the setting for his most horrific crimes. The terror of being hunted, combined with the isolation of the Alaskan wilderness, made escape virtually impossible for his victims. After killing them, Hansen would sometimes return to the bodies to mutilate them further, before burying them in shallow graves or leaving them to be devoured by animals.

The number of women Hansen killed during his spree is still uncertain, but it is believed that he murdered at least 17 women, though some estimates suggest the number could be as high as 30 or more. The remains of some of his victims were never recovered, lost forever in the vast Alaskan wilderness.

The Investigation: The Fall of the Butcher Baker

For years, Robert Hansen's crimes went undetected, as he carefully selected victims who were less likely to be reported missing or whose disappearances would attract little attention. The transient nature of the sex workers and dancers he preyed upon, combined with his unassuming appearance and careful planning, allowed Hansen to operate with impunity. However, in 1983, a series of events would lead to his eventual downfall.

The break in the case came when one of Hansen's intended victims, a 17-year-old sex worker named Cindy Paulson, managed to escape from his clutches. In June 1983, Paulson was abducted by Hansen and taken to his home, where she was handcuffed, assaulted, and threatened with death. Hansen then attempted to transport her to his plane at Merrill Field, intending to fly her to the wilderness for his usual hunting game. However, as Hansen was preparing the plane, Paulson seized the opportunity to escape. Still handcuffed, she ran barefoot to a nearby road and flagged down a passing truck. The truck driver, seeing the terrified and disheveled girl, immediately took her to the police.

Paulson's account of her abduction and the detailed description she provided of Hansen, his plane, and his home, finally gave law enforcement the evidence they needed to act. Despite Hansen's initial attempts to dismiss Paulson's accusations, claiming she was trying to extort him, the Anchorage Police Department, in collaboration with the Alaska State Troopers and the FBI, began to take the case seriously. With the assistance of FBI profiler John Douglas, who helped establish a psychological profile of the killer, the authorities were able to obtain a search warrant for Hansen's property.

On October 27, 1983, police searched Hansen's home and discovered a trove of incriminating evidence, including jewelry belonging to some of the missing women, an aviation map with marked locations that corresponded to where bodies were later found, and firearms that matched the ballistics from the murder scenes. Faced with overwhelming evidence, Hansen eventually confessed to the murders, though he attempted to minimize his culpability by claiming that many of the women had consented to being flown to the wilderness and that some had been killed in self-defense.

The Psychological Profile: Understanding the Butcher Baker

Robert Hansen's psychological makeup is a complex tapestry of deep-seated insecurities, compulsive behaviors, and a profound need for control and domination. His childhood experiences, marked by bullying, rejection, and a lack of parental affection, played a significant role in shaping his violent tendencies. Hansen's sense of inadequacy, particularly in his relationships with women, fueled a deep-seated hatred and desire for revenge against those who he perceived as having wronged him.

Hansen's stutter and severe acne left him feeling emasculated and powerless, which left him feeling emasculated and powerless, which drove him to develop a need for control and dominance that he lacked in his everyday life. His obsession with hunting provided an outlet where he could exert power over living beings, transforming what began as a recreational activity into a grotesque ritual of human predation.

Hansen's psychological profile is characteristic of a sexually sadistic serial killer, a category of offenders who derive pleasure from the suffering and terror of their victims. These individuals often have deep-seated feelings of inadequacy and low self-esteem, which they attempt to counteract through acts of extreme violence and domination. In Hansen's case, his crimes were not merely about the act of killing; they were about asserting his dominance and control over his victims, reducing them to prey in a twisted game where he held all the power.

Hansen's meticulous planning and methodical approach to his murders also suggest a high level of organization and psychopathy. Unlike impulsive killers who act on sudden urges, Hansen carefully selected his victims, planned their abductions, and carried out his crimes in a controlled and calculated manner. His ability to maintain a façade of normalcy—operating a successful bakery, being a family man, and integrating into the community—further highlights the chilling duality of his personality. Hansen was able to compartmentalize his violent impulses, allowing him to lead a seemingly ordinary life while committing horrific crimes.

The Aftermath: The Legacy of Robert Hansen

Robert Hansen was convicted of four murders in 1984 and sentenced to 461 years in prison without the possibility of parole. While he admitted to killing 17 women, he is suspected of having many more victims, some of whom may never be identified. Hansen's case is particularly notable not just for the sheer number of his victims, but for the unique and horrifying method he employed in his killings.

The discovery of Hansen's crimes sent shockwaves through the community of Anchorage and the state of Alaska. The revelation that a seemingly mild-mannered baker was responsible for such heinous acts of violence shattered the community's sense of safety and trust. It also raised important questions about the treatment of sex workers and marginalized women, who were often overlooked by law enforcement and the public, making them vulnerable to predators like Hansen.

The legacy of Robert Hansen continues to resonate in discussions of criminal justice and forensic investigation. His case is often cited in studies of serial killers and sexual sadists, providing insight into the mind of a predator who carefully planned and executed his crimes over more than a decade. The psychological, social, and forensic aspects of Hansen's case have been the subject of numerous books, documentaries, and academic papers, all attempting to understand the complex factors that led to his transformation from a troubled youth to one of the most notorious serial killers in American history.

Chapter 33: Donald Harvey (the Angel of Death)

Donald Harvey, infamously known as the "Angel of Death," is one of the most notorious serial killers in American history, with a death toll that far exceeds many other well-known murderers. Over the course of nearly two decades, from the mid-1970s to the late 1980s, Harvey is believed to have killed at least 37 people, although some estimates suggest the number could be as high as 87. Unlike many serial killers who operate outside the law, Harvey's killing spree took place within the confines of the healthcare system, where he used his position as a nurse's aide to carry out his lethal activities. His victims were patients entrusted to his care, making his crimes not only deeply disturbing but also a profound betrayal of trust. Harvey's case sheds light on the vulnerabilities within the healthcare system, the psyche of a medical professional turned killer, and the ease with which a predator can hide behind the guise of a caregiver.

Early Life: A Troubled Beginning

Donald Harvey was born on April 15, 1952, in Butler County, Ohio. He grew up in a small, rural community, where his early life was marked by instability and hardship. Raised in a family that struggled with financial difficulties, Harvey's childhood was far from idyllic. His father was an alcoholic who was often absent from the home, leaving his mother to raise him and his siblings with little support. The lack of a stable family environment, coupled with the emotional and psychological trauma he experienced at a young age, had a profound impact on Harvey's development.

As a child, Harvey was described as quiet and introverted, often keeping to himself and displaying little interest in social activities. He was also known to have a fascination with death, a trait that would later manifest in his gruesome crimes. Despite his troubled upbringing, Harvey managed to perform reasonably well in school, although he struggled with forming close relationships with his peers. This sense of isolation and detachment from others became a defining characteristic of his personality.

One of the most significant events in Harvey's early life was the sexual abuse he suffered at the hands of a male neighbor when he was a young boy. This traumatic experience had a lasting impact on Harvey, contributing to his feelings of powerlessness and anger. The abuse he endured, coupled with the emotional neglect he experienced at home, created a toxic cocktail of psychological issues that would later drive him to commit his horrific crimes.

The Path to Murder: From Caregiver to Killer

Donald Harvey's journey from a troubled youth to a serial killer began in his late teens when he took a job as a nurse's aide at the Marymount Hospital in London, Kentucky. It was here, at the age of 18, that Harvey claimed his first victim. In 1970, while caring for a stroke patient who was in extreme pain and suffering, Harvey decided to end the man's life by disconnecting his oxygen supply. This act of mercy killing, as Harvey initially rationalized it, marked the beginning of his deadly career.

Harvey quickly realized that he derived a sense of power and control from taking the lives of others. What began as an isolated incident soon escalated into a pattern of killing, as Harvey continued to work in various healthcare facilities over the years. His methods of murder were varied and often subtle, making it difficult for authorities to detect his crimes. Harvey used a variety of means to kill his victims, including suffocation, poisoning with arsenic or cyanide, administering lethal doses of insulin, and even tampering with patients' IVs and ventilators.

Despite the increasing number of deaths that occurred under his care, Harvey managed to evade detection for years. His ability to blend in and maintain the appearance of a diligent and caring healthcare worker allowed him to continue his killing spree with little suspicion. Harvey's manipulative nature and understanding of the medical field enabled him to exploit the weaknesses in the healthcare system, using his position to target the most vulnerable patients—those who were elderly, terminally ill, or suffering from severe illnesses.

The Killings: A Methodical and Deceptive Murderer

Donald Harvey's killing spree spanned multiple healthcare facilities in Ohio and Kentucky, where he worked as a nurse's aide, orderly, and morgue attendant. His victims were often patients who were in critical condition or nearing the end of their lives, making it easier for Harvey to justify his actions as "mercy killings." However, as his crimes continued, it became clear that Harvey was not motivated by compassion, but by a twisted desire for control and the thrill of killing.

Harvey's methods of murder were chillingly methodical and deceptive. He would often choose victims who were already gravely ill, ensuring that their deaths would not raise immediate suspicion. One of his preferred methods was to administer lethal doses of drugs that would go undetected or be mistaken for a natural cause of death. For example, Harvey frequently used cyanide or arsenic to poison his victims, substances that were difficult to trace and would often go unnoticed during routine autopsies.

In some cases, Harvey would tamper with patients' medical equipment, such as turning off ventilators or injecting air into IV lines, causing a fatal air embolism. These methods were particularly insidious, as they could easily be attributed to equipment malfunction or a sudden decline in the patient's condition. Harvey's intimate knowledge of hospital procedures and his access to medications and equipment made him a highly effective and elusive killer.

One of the most disturbing aspects of Harvey's crimes was his apparent lack of remorse. He often described his killings in a cold and detached manner, showing little empathy for his victims. In interviews and confessions, Harvey admitted to feeling a sense of satisfaction and empowerment from his actions, particularly when he believed he was "putting someone out of their misery." This rationalization of his crimes as acts of mercy masked the true nature of his sadistic impulses and the pleasure he derived from exerting control over life and death.

The Investigation: The Angel of Death Unmasked

Donald Harvey's reign of terror came to an end in 1987, when a series of suspicious deaths at the Drake Memorial Hospital in Cincinnati, Ohio, finally caught the attention of authorities. Harvey had been working at the hospital as a nurse's aide, and during his tenure, a number of patients had died under mysterious circumstances. Hospital staff began to notice a pattern of deaths occurring shortly after Harvey had been in the patients' rooms, raising alarm bells among his colleagues.

The investigation into Harvey's activities was initially slow, as many of the deaths he was suspected of causing had been attributed to natural causes. However, suspicions grew when toxicology reports from several deceased patients revealed the presence of cyanide and other toxins in their systems. The discovery of these toxic substances, combined with Harvey's access to medications and his proximity to the victims, led authorities to focus their investigation on him.

In April 1987, after several days of questioning, Harvey confessed to killing at least 37 people over the course of 17 years. His confession was shocking in both its scope and detail, as Harvey calmly described how he had killed his victims and the methods he had used. He admitted to committing the murders not out of mercy, but because he enjoyed the power and control it gave him. Harvey's confession also revealed the extent to which he had been able to manipulate those around him, using his knowledge of the healthcare system to avoid detection and continue his killing spree.

Following his confession, Harvey was charged with multiple counts of murder and was sentenced to several consecutive life terms in prison. Despite the magnitude of his crimes, Harvey's case did not receive the same level of public attention as other serial killers, perhaps due to the nature of his victims and the setting in which the murders occurred. However, his actions have left a lasting impact on the healthcare community, highlighting the need for greater oversight and accountability in medical settings to prevent similar tragedies from occurring in the future.

Psychological Profile: The Mind of the Angel of Death

Donald Harvey's psychological profile is that of a classic Angel of Death—a healthcare professional who kills patients under the guise of providing care or mercy. Unlike many serial killers who kill for sexual gratification or out of a compulsion to inflict pain, Angel of Death killers often rationalize their actions as benevolent, even as they commit acts of murder. However, beneath this facade of compassion lies a deep-seated need for control, power, and dominance.

Harvey's early life experiences, particularly the trauma and abuse he endured, likely played a significant role in shaping his personality and motivations. His feelings of powerlessness and inadequacy, compounded by his isolation and lack of meaningful relationships, may have driven him to seek control in the one area where he could exert influence—over the lives of his patients. By positioning himself as a caregiver, Harvey was able to wield life-and-death power over vulnerable individuals, fulfilling his need for control and alleviating his feelings of helplessness.

Harvey's methodical approach to killing, his ability to maintain a double life as a caring nurse's aide, and his lack of remorse or empathy for his victims suggest that he possessed a high degree of psychopathy. Psychopaths are characterized by a lack of conscience, an inability to form emotional attachments, and a propensity for manipulative and deceitful behavior. Harvey's actions align with these traits, as he was able to carry out his murders with cold precision while maintaining the trust of his colleagues and patients.

The Aftermath: The Impact of Donald Harvey's Crimes

The case of Donald Harvey has had a profound impact on the healthcare community and the field of forensic investigation. His ability to operate undetected for so long highlighted significant gaps in the oversight of healthcare professionals and the need for more stringent monitoring of patient care. In the wake of Harvey's crimes, hospitals and medical facilities have implemented stricter protocols for the administration of medications, the monitoring of patient deaths, and the background checks of healthcare workers.

Harvey's case also raised important ethical questions about the role of healthcare professionals in end-of-life care. While some of Harvey's early victims were terminally ill or suffering from severe pain, his actions were not motivated by compassion but by a desire for control. The distinction between euthanasia, or mercy killing, and the actions of an Angel of Death like Harvey is a critical one, as it underscores the importance of ethical guidelines and safeguards in medical practice.

In the years since Harvey's conviction, his case has been the subject of numerous studies, documentaries, and books, all seeking to understand the mind of a healthcare professional turned serial killer. His story serves as a cautionary tale about the dangers of unchecked power in the medical field and the importance of vigilance in protecting vulnerable patients from those who may seek to do them harm.

Chapter 34: Paul Bernardo and Karla Homolka

Paul Bernardo and Karla Homolka, often referred to as the "Ken and Barbie killers" due to their outwardly attractive appearances, stand out as one of the most notorious and chilling criminal duos in Canadian history. Their crimes, marked by extreme brutality and manipulation, have shocked the public and left an indelible scar on the collective memory. This infamous couple committed a series of heinous acts that revealed a dark underbelly of sadism, deception, and an unsettling dynamic between two individuals who, together, created a lethal force.

Paul Bernardo: The Early Years and Formation of a Predator

Born on August 27, 1964, in Scarborough, Ontario, Paul Bernardo's early life was marked by apparent normalcy. However, beneath the surface, his childhood was marred by dysfunction and abuse. His father, Kenneth Bernardo, was later revealed to be a child molester, and his mother, Marilyn, withdrew emotionally, retreating into the basement of their home. These early experiences of neglect and exposure to perversion arguably played a role in shaping Paul's twisted psyche.

As a young man, Bernardo exhibited an outwardly charming and charismatic personality. He was good-looking, articulate, and seemed to have a bright future ahead of him. However, by his late teens and early twenties, he began to exhibit disturbing behaviors. He developed a fixation on dominance and control, particularly over women. This manifested in his early crimes as the "Scarborough Rapist," where he terrorized the Toronto suburb of Scarborough between 1987 and 1990, committing a series of violent sexual assaults. Despite a police investigation, he managed to elude capture for years, honing his skills as a predator.

Karla Homolka: A Complicit Partner or a Victim?

Karla Homolka was born on May 4, 1970, in Port Credit, Ontario. Like Bernardo, she had a seemingly normal upbringing in a middle-class family. However, those who knew her described her as a person with a strong need for control and a willingness to manipulate those around her to get what she wanted. Her early life, unlike Bernardo's, did not show overt signs of deviant behavior, making her later actions even more shocking.

Karla met Paul Bernardo in 1987, when she was just 17 years old, and the two quickly became inseparable. Their relationship was intense and quickly became toxic, with Karla willingly becoming a participant in Paul's sadistic fantasies. Their dynamic was one of mutual reinforcement, with Karla enabling Paul's violent tendencies and, in some cases, even encouraging them.

While some argue that Karla was a victim of Paul's manipulation, evidence suggests that she was an active participant in their crimes, deriving a twisted pleasure from the acts they committed together. This complicity raises important questions about the nature of their relationship: Was Karla merely a pawn in Paul's sadistic games, or was she an equal partner in the crimes that followed?

The Crimes: A Tale of Torture, Murder, and Betrayal

The crimes of Paul Bernardo and Karla Homolka are marked by their brutality and the shocking nature of the couple's partnership. Together, they committed a series of rapes and murders that have become synonymous with horror and depravity.

- **The Tammy Homolka Incident**

One of the most disturbing aspects of their crimes is the involvement of Karla's younger sister, Tammy Homolka. In December 1990, Paul expressed a desire to have sex with Tammy, who was only 15 years old at the time. Shockingly, Karla not only agreed but also actively facilitated the crime. On Christmas Eve, they drugged Tammy with halothane, a powerful anesthetic stolen by Karla from the veterinary clinic where she worked. Paul raped Tammy while Karla watched and assisted.

During the assault, Tammy choked on her own vomit and died. The couple tried to cover up their crime by cleaning the evidence and making it appear as though Tammy had died of natural causes. The police, unaware of the true circumstances, ruled Tammy's death as accidental, allowing Paul and Karla to evade justice for the time being.

- **The Abduction, Rape, and Murder of Leslie Mahaffy**

In June 1991, the couple escalated their crimes by kidnapping Leslie Mahaffy, a 14-year-old girl from Burlington, Ontario. After luring her into their car, Paul and Karla brought Leslie back to their home, where they subjected her to a nightmarish ordeal of rape and torture over the course of several days. They filmed the assaults, creating gruesome evidence of their crimes.

Leslie's ordeal ended when Paul strangled her to death, and the couple dismembered her body, encasing the remains in concrete blocks. These blocks were later discovered in Lake Gibson, which led to a widespread investigation. The discovery of Leslie's remains was a turning point in the case, bringing the couple's heinous acts closer to public scrutiny.

- **The Abduction, Rape, and Murder of Kristen French**

The couple's next victim, Kristen French, was abducted in April 1992 while walking home from school in St. Catharines, Ontario. Much like Leslie Mahaffy, Kristen was held captive for several days, during which she was repeatedly raped and tortured by the couple. They again filmed their acts, adding to their collection of grotesque trophies.

After three days of unimaginable suffering, Kristen was murdered, and her body was dumped in a ditch. Unlike Leslie Mahaffy's case, Kristen's body was not dismembered, which led to a quicker discovery by the authorities. The brutality of the crime and the fact that it happened in broad daylight sent shockwaves through the community and beyond.

The Downfall: Arrest, Trials, and Controversy

The arrest of Paul Bernardo and Karla Homolka marked the end of their reign of terror, but it also led to a highly controversial and widely publicized legal saga.

- **Paul's Arrest and Conviction**

Paul Bernardo was arrested in February 1993 after DNA evidence linked him to the Scarborough rapes and the murders of Leslie Mahaffy and Kristen French. His trial in 1995 was one of the most sensational in Canadian history. The prosecution presented the videotapes that Paul and Karla had made of their crimes, which were so graphic that they were not shown to the public. The jury found Paul guilty on all charges, and he was sentenced to life in prison without the possibility of parole.

- **Karla's Plea Bargain: The "Deal with the Devil"**

Karla Homolka's role in the crimes became a subject of intense debate and controversy. In exchange for her testimony against Paul, Karla was offered a plea bargain, which allowed her to plead guilty to manslaughter rather than murder. She was sentenced to just 12 years in prison, a sentence many viewed as shockingly lenient given her active participation in the crimes.

The full extent of Karla's involvement was not known at the time of the plea bargain, as the videotapes had not yet been recovered. When the tapes were later found, they revealed Karla's enthusiastic participation in the assaults, leading to public outrage over what was perceived as a gross miscarriage of justice. The media and the public dubbed it a "deal with the devil," and the case continues to be a source of controversy in Canada.

Aftermath and Legacy: The Lingering Horror

The legacy of Paul Bernardo and Karla Homolka is one of horror, legal controversy, and ongoing public fascination. Their crimes have been the subject of numerous books, documentaries, and discussions, each attempting to make sense of the senseless.

- **Paul's Continued Incarceration**

Paul Bernardo remains incarcerated in a maximum-security prison, where he has been denied parole multiple times. His case continues to evoke strong emotions, with many advocating for him to remain imprisoned for life. Despite his efforts to appeal his sentence, there is little sympathy for him, and he is widely regarded as one of Canada's most dangerous criminals.

- **Karla's Life After Prison**

Karla Homolka was released from prison in 2005, having served her full 12-year sentence. Her release sparked outrage and fear, as many believed she had not been adequately punished for her role in the murders. Karla has since attempted to live a low-profile life, changing her name and moving to different locations. However, she remains a figure of public interest and scorn, with many questioning whether she has truly reformed.

- **Cultural Impact and Public Perception**

The case of Paul Bernardo and Karla Homolka has had a profound impact on Canadian society and the criminal justice system. It has sparked debates about the nature of evil, the psychology of criminal partnerships, and the ethics of plea bargains. The case also highlighted the importance of DNA evidence in solving crimes and the potential pitfalls of the legal system when dealing with complex cases of shared criminal responsibility.

Public perception of Karla Homolka remains deeply divided. While some view her as a victim of Bernardo's manipulation, others see her as an equal participant in the crimes, deserving of far harsher punishment. The controversy surrounding her plea bargain has led to calls for reform in how such deals are handled, particularly in cases involving severe crimes.

Media and Pop Culture Representation

The story of Paul Bernardo and Karla Homolka has permeated popular culture, with numerous books, films, and documentaries exploring their crimes. These representations often grapple with the same questions that have haunted the public: How could two seemingly ordinary people commit such horrific acts? What was the true nature of their relationship? And can justice ever be fully served in cases like this?

Chapter 35: Gary Heidnik

Gary Heidnik, often referred to as the "House of Horrors Killer," is a name that strikes fear and revulsion in those familiar with his crimes. His story is one of the most disturbing and grotesque in the annals of American criminal history. Operating in Philadelphia in the late 1980s, Heidnik held six women captive in a basement, torturing and abusing them in unspeakable ways. His actions not only horrified the public but also exposed deep flaws in the mental health and social services systems that failed to intervene before his crimes escalated. Heidnik's case stands out for its sheer brutality, the calculated cruelty he inflicted on his victims, and the chilling psychological profile of a man who saw himself as a godlike figure with absolute power over life and death.

Early Life: A Foundation of Abuse and Neglect

Gary Heidnik was born on November 22, 1943, in Eastlake, Ohio, to a dysfunctional family. His parents' marriage was fraught with tension, and they eventually divorced when Gary was just three years old. Following the divorce, Gary and his younger brother, Terry, were raised by their mother, who struggled with alcoholism. Eventually, the boys were sent to live with their father and stepmother, where they experienced further abuse and neglect.

Gary's childhood was marked by extreme emotional and physical abuse. His father, who was described as strict and authoritarian, would often ridicule and humiliate Gary, contributing to his already fragile self-esteem. One of the most traumatic experiences of Gary's childhood was when his father forced him to wear a soiled diaper on his head as punishment for wetting the bed. This incident, along with other forms of abuse, left deep psychological scars on Gary, contributing to the development of his disturbed personality.

Despite his troubled home life, Gary Heidnik was an intelligent child with a reported IQ of 130. He excelled in school, particularly in subjects like mathematics and science. However, his social skills were severely lacking, and he struggled to form relationships with his peers. Gary was often bullied and ostracized by other children, further isolating him and exacerbating his feelings of anger and resentment. By the time he reached adolescence, Gary had become increasingly withdrawn and disconnected from the world around him.

Military Service: A Brief Respite

In 1961, at the age of 18, Gary Heidnik enlisted in the U.S. Army, hoping to escape his abusive home life and find a sense of purpose. Initially, his military career showed promise. He scored high on intelligence tests and was trained as a medic. However, after just 13 months of service, Gary began to exhibit signs of mental instability. He complained of severe headaches, dizziness, and blurred vision, which led to a diagnosis of schizoid personality disorder. In 1962, he was honorably discharged from the Army due to his mental health issues.

The time Gary spent in the military provided him with valuable medical knowledge, which he would later use in his criminal activities. However, it also marked the beginning of his descent into madness. Following his discharge, Gary's mental health continued to deteriorate, and he was in and out of psychiatric hospitals for several years. His mental illness, combined with his deep-seated anger and resentment, set the stage for the horrific crimes he would eventually commit.

Descent into Madness: A Life of Crime

After his discharge from the Army, Gary Heidnik's life took a downward spiral. He struggled to hold down a job and was plagued by financial difficulties. Despite his intelligence, Gary was unable to find a stable career and drifted from one low-paying job to another. In 1970, he moved to Philadelphia, where he began to exhibit increasingly bizarre and erratic behavior.

Gary's mental health issues became more pronounced during this period. He developed a delusional belief that he was a prophet chosen by God to lead a new religion. In 1971, he established the "United Church of the Ministers of God," a self-proclaimed religious organization that he used as a front for his criminal activities. Gary opened a bank account in the church's name and began soliciting donations from unsuspecting followers. Over time, he amassed a small fortune, which he used to fund his twisted desires.

In addition to his financial schemes, Gary Heidnik's behavior became increasingly violent and predatory. He was arrested several times for various offenses, including the abduction and rape of a mentally disabled woman in 1976. The victim, who was unable to consent due to her intellectual disability, was taken to Gary's home, where she was subjected to sexual abuse. For this crime, Gary was sentenced to several years in a mental institution but was released after serving only a portion of his sentence.

The House of Horrors: A Nightmare Unleashed

Gary Heidnik's most infamous crimes began in 1986, when he started abducting women and holding them captive in the basement of his home at 3520 North Marshall Street in Philadelphia. Over the course of several months, Heidnik abducted six women, all of whom were African American and came from vulnerable backgrounds. Many of the women were mentally disabled or struggling with substance abuse issues, making them easy targets for Heidnik's depraved schemes.

The conditions in which Heidnik kept his victims were nothing short of nightmarish. The basement where the women were held was dark, filthy, and squalid. Heidnik chained his victims to pipes and shackles, often keeping them bound for days at a time. The women were subjected to severe physical and psychological abuse, including beatings, starvation, and sexual assault. Heidnik would often force the women to fight each other for food, further degrading them and exerting his control.

One of the most horrific aspects of Heidnik's crimes was his use of psychological torture. Heidnik would manipulate his victims by pitting them against each other, promising rewards or better treatment to those who complied with his demands. He would also play mind games, such as pretending to show kindness by giving them food or blankets, only to snatch them away as a form of punishment. This constant cycle of cruelty and manipulation kept the women in a state of fear and confusion, making it nearly impossible for them to resist or escape.

The true extent of Heidnik's depravity was revealed when he began to experiment with cannibalism. After one of his victims, Sandra Lindsay, died as a result of the torture she endured, Heidnik dismembered her body and attempted to cook her flesh. He fed parts of her remains to the other captives, further traumatizing them and solidifying his control. Heidnik's descent into cannibalism and his use of human remains in this way is one of the most disturbing elements of his crimes, highlighting the depths of his sadism.

The Capture: A Tale of Survival and Justice

Gary Heidnik's reign of terror came to an end in March 1987, when one of his captives, Josefina Rivera, managed to escape. Rivera had been held captive for four months and had endured unimaginable abuse at Heidnik's hands. However, she managed to earn his trust by pretending to cooperate with him and even helping him with the other captives. Heidnik, believing he had successfully broken Rivera's spirit, allowed her more freedom than the other captives.

On March 24, 1987, Heidnik took Rivera with him on an errand, allowing her to leave the house with him. Rivera seized the opportunity and convinced Heidnik to let her visit her family. Once out of Heidnik's sight, Rivera immediately sought help and contacted the police. She led authorities to Heidnik's house, where they discovered the remaining captives in the basement, along with the remains of Sandra Lindsay.

The police were horrified by the scene they encountered. The basement was filled with evidence of the abuse and torture the women had suffered, including chains, shackles, and makeshift weapons. Heidnik was arrested on the spot and charged with multiple counts of kidnapping, rape, aggravated assault, and murder. The surviving captives were taken to the hospital, where they received medical treatment for their injuries and psychological counseling to help them cope with the trauma they had endured.

The Trial: The Angel of Death's Day in Court

Gary Heidnik's trial began in June 1988, and it quickly became one of the most sensational and widely covered cases in the United States. The public was captivated by the shocking details of the case, and the media dubbed Heidnik the "House of Horrors Killer." The trial revealed the full extent of Heidnik's depravity, as the survivors testified about the abuse they had suffered and the horrific conditions in which they were kept.

Heidnik's defense team attempted to argue that he was not guilty by reason of insanity, citing his long history of mental illness and bizarre behavior. They pointed to his delusions of grandeur, his belief that he was a prophet, and his history of psychiatric treatment as evidence that he was not in control of his actions. However, the prosecution argued that Heidnik was fully aware of the nature of his crimes and that his actions were premeditated and calculated. They pointed to the meticulous planning that went into the abductions, the lengths Heidnik went to in order to avoid detection, and the cruel and sadistic nature of the torture he inflicted on his victims.

The jury ultimately rejected the insanity defense, and on July 1, 1988, Gary Heidnik was found guilty of two counts of first-degree murder, six counts of kidnapping, five counts of rape, and multiple counts of assault and false imprisonment. He was sentenced to death for his crimes, and his execution was scheduled for a later date. The verdict was met with a sense of relief and closure for the survivors and the families of the victims. The conviction of Gary Heidnik brought an end to one of the most horrific crime sprees in American history, but the scars left by his actions would remain with those affected for the rest of their lives.

Aftermath: A Legacy of Trauma and Horror

Gary Heidnik's case left a deep and lasting impact on the community, the criminal justice system, and the field of forensic psychology. The survivors of his crimes faced an uphill battle in the years following his conviction, as they struggled to rebuild their lives and come to terms with the trauma they had endured. The psychological damage inflicted by Heidnik's torture was profound, with many of the survivors suffering from severe PTSD, depression, and anxiety. Their stories became a powerful testament to the resilience of the human spirit, but they also highlighted the long-term effects of such extreme abuse.

The case also prompted widespread outrage and fear, leading to increased scrutiny of how such crimes could occur undetected for so long. The failures of the social services and mental health systems in monitoring Heidnik's behavior and intervening earlier were criticized, and reforms were called for to prevent similar cases in the future. This led to a greater emphasis on the need for better mental health care, more rigorous background checks for those in positions of trust, and improved coordination between law enforcement and social services.

In the field of forensic psychology, Gary Heidnik's case became a subject of intense study and analysis. Psychologists and criminologists sought to understand the underlying factors that led to his extreme behavior, including his troubled childhood, mental illness, and the role of environmental influences. Heidnik's actions were often compared to other notorious serial killers, but his unique combination of delusional thinking, sadistic cruelty, and desire for control set him apart as a particularly dangerous and complex individual.

Execution: The End of a Monster

Gary Heidnik spent over a decade on death row, during which time he continued to appeal his conviction. His defense attorneys argued that he was mentally incompetent to be executed, citing his ongoing delusions and deteriorating mental state. However, these appeals were ultimately unsuccessful, and the courts upheld his death sentence.

On July 6, 1999, Gary Heidnik was executed by lethal injection at the State Correctional Institution in Rockview, Pennsylvania. His execution marked the first in Pennsylvania since 1962, and it was met with mixed reactions. Some saw it as a necessary and just end for a man who had committed unspeakable atrocities, while others questioned the ethics of executing someone with a long history of mental illness.

Chapter 36: Nikolai Dzhumagaliev (the Metal Fang)

Nikolai Dzhumagaliev, known as "Metal Fang" due to the metal teeth he had installed after an accident, is one of the most notorious and horrifying serial killers in Soviet history. His reign of terror in the late 1970s and early 1980s left a trail of fear and horror across the Kazakh SSR (now Kazakhstan). Dzhumagaliev's crimes were not only brutal but also profoundly disturbing, as he targeted women, murdered them with unimaginable cruelty, and even cannibalized his victims. The story of Nikolai Dzhumagaliev is a chilling account of a man whose outward appearance and charisma masked a mind consumed by violent and sadistic fantasies. His case highlights the extreme dangers posed by individuals who harbor deep-seated psychological issues and the challenges law enforcement faces in dealing with such predators.

Early Life: The Making of a Monster

Nikolai Dzhumagaliev was born on November 15, 1952, in the small village of Uzun-Agach in the Kazakh SSR. His early life was relatively unremarkable, growing up in a rural environment with his parents and siblings. Despite the simplicity of his upbringing, Dzhumagaliev exhibited troubling signs from a young age. He was described as an intelligent but introverted child who preferred solitude over social interaction. His relationship with his family was strained, particularly with his father, who was reportedly strict and emotionally distant.

During his childhood, Dzhumagaliev developed a fascination with knives and other sharp objects, a fixation that would later play a significant role in his crimes. He was also known to be an avid reader, often immersing himself in books about war and violence, which fueled his already growing fascination with death and destruction. These early signs of a disturbed mind went largely unnoticed by those around him, as Dzhumagaliev was able to maintain a facade of normalcy.

After completing his basic education, Dzhumagaliev was drafted into the Soviet Army, where he served for a brief period. His time in the military did little to curb his violent tendencies. In fact, it may have exacerbated them, as he was exposed to the harsh realities of life and death on a daily basis. Following his discharge, Dzhumagaliev returned to civilian life, where he worked various jobs, including as a sailor and a driver. However, he struggled to find stability and frequently changed jobs, moving from one place to another.

The Descent into Madness: A Mind Consumed by Delusion

As Dzhumagaliev entered adulthood, his mental state began to deteriorate rapidly. He became increasingly obsessed with his violent fantasies, which centered around the idea of purging the world of "impure" women. Dzhumagaliev developed a delusional belief that it was his divine mission to rid society of women he considered immoral, a belief that drove him to commit his heinous crimes. His misogynistic views were deeply rooted in his psyche, and he saw his actions as a form of twisted justice.

Dzhumagaliev's delusions were further exacerbated by his heavy drinking, which became a regular part of his life. Alcohol served as a catalyst for his violent tendencies, lowering his inhibitions and allowing him to act on his darkest impulses. He also suffered from severe paranoia, believing that he was being watched and followed by mysterious forces. This paranoia contributed to his sense of isolation and further detached him from reality.

In addition to his delusions and paranoia, Dzhumagaliev developed a deep-seated hatred for women, whom he blamed for many of his perceived problems. He viewed them as temptresses who lured men into sin and believed that by killing them, he was performing a service to society. This warped ideology provided him with the justification he needed to carry out his brutal crimes, and he began to actively seek out victims who fit his criteria of "impurity."

The Murders: A Reign of Terror

Nikolai Dzhumagaliev's killing spree began in 1979 when he committed his first known murder. His modus operandi was as brutal as it was methodical. Dzhumagaliev would lure his victims, usually young women, into isolated areas under various pretexts, such as offering them a ride or inviting them to a party. Once they were in his grasp, he would attack them with a knife, slashing and stabbing them with frenzied violence. Dzhumagaliev's strength and savagery made it nearly impossible for his victims to escape.

After killing his victims, Dzhumagaliev's crimes took an even darker turn. He would dismember the bodies and cannibalize their flesh, often cooking and eating parts of them over several days. This gruesome act was not only a way for him to satisfy his twisted desires but also a means of symbolically absorbing their "purity" into himself. In his mind, this cannibalism was a form of ritualistic purification, furthering his delusional belief that he was on a divine mission.

Dzhumagaliev's metal teeth, which he had installed after an accident, became a gruesome symbol of his brutality. The sight of his sharp, metallic fangs was enough to strike fear into the hearts of his victims, adding a terrifying dimension to his already monstrous persona. The fact that he had chosen to replace his natural teeth with metal ones also indicated a deeper psychological disturbance, as he seemed to embrace the image of a predatory creature.

Over the course of a year, Dzhumagaliev killed at least seven women, though the actual number of his victims may be higher. His ability to evade capture for so long was partly due to the remote and rural nature of the areas where he committed his crimes. The Soviet Union at the time also had a deeply flawed and under-resourced criminal justice system, making it difficult for law enforcement to track down a serial killer operating in isolated regions. Moreover, the fear and stigma associated with reporting such crimes meant that some of Dzhumagaliev's victims' disappearances went unnoticed or were not fully investigated.

The Capture: The Fall of the Metal Fang

Nikolai Dzhumagaliev's reign of terror came to an abrupt end in 1980, under circumstances that were both unexpected and dramatic. On one fateful night, Dzhumagaliev invited several acquaintances to his home for a party. After plying them with alcohol, he attacked one of the female guests in front of the others, revealing his true nature in a moment of unbridled violence. The shocked guests managed to overpower him, subduing him until the authorities arrived.

When the police searched Dzhumagaliev's home, they were horrified by what they found. The evidence of his crimes was everywhere: bloodstains, human remains, and various tools and implements used in the dismemberment of his victims. The gruesome discovery confirmed their worst fears—that they had finally caught the serial killer who had been terrorizing the region. Dzhumagaliev was immediately arrested and taken into custody.

The arrest of Nikolai Dzhumagaliev sent shockwaves through the community and the country at large. The Soviet authorities, who had been reluctant to acknowledge the existence of serial killers within their borders, were forced to confront the reality of his crimes. The media coverage of the case was extensive, though heavily censored, as the government sought to control the narrative and prevent widespread panic. Despite these efforts, the details of Dzhumagaliev's crimes leaked out, fueling public fear and outrage.

The Trial and Imprisonment: Justice Served?

Following his arrest, Nikolai Dzhumagaliev was subjected to a psychiatric evaluation, which confirmed that he was suffering from severe mental illness. His delusions, paranoia, and obsession with violence were diagnosed as symptoms of schizophrenia, a condition that had gone untreated for most of his life. The court ultimately declared him criminally insane and unfit to stand trial. As a result, he was committed to a high-security psychiatric hospital rather than being sentenced to prison.

Dzhumagaliev's confinement in a psychiatric institution sparked controversy and debate. Many believed that he deserved the death penalty for his heinous crimes, while others argued that his mental illness meant that he could not be held fully responsible for his actions. The decision to commit him to a psychiatric hospital was seen by some as a lenient and insufficient response to the magnitude of his crimes.

In the years following his commitment, Dzhumagaliev remained a highly dangerous individual. His violent tendencies did not abate, and he was involved in several incidents of aggression towards staff and other patients. His continued presence in the psychiatric hospital posed a significant risk, and he was closely monitored to prevent any further acts of violence.

The Escape: A Second Reign of Terror?

In 1989, nearly a decade after his initial capture, Nikolai Dzhumagaliev managed to escape from the psychiatric hospital where he was being held. The circumstances of his escape remain unclear, but it is believed that he took advantage of lax security measures and the complacency of the staff. His escape caused widespread panic, as authorities feared that he would resume his killing spree.

The search for Dzhumagaliev was extensive and involved law enforcement agencies from across the Soviet Union. His escape became a top priority, with the government offering a substantial reward for information leading to his capture. The public was urged to be vigilant, and his description was widely circulated in an effort to prevent him from disappearing into the vast expanse of the Soviet Union.

Despite the extensive manhunt, Dzhumagaliev managed to evade capture for several years. Rumors and sightings of him surfaced periodically, but none were confirmed. His ability to remain at large for so long only added to his notoriety, and he became something of a boogeyman figure in the popular imagination. Parents would warn their children about the "Metal Fang," and his name became synonymous with fear and horror.

Dzhumagaliev was eventually recaptured in 1991, following a tip-off from a member of the public who recognized him. He was returned to the psychiatric hospital, where he was once again placed under heavy security. His recapture brought an end to the fear and uncertainty that had plagued the region during his years on the run, but the damage he had caused to the community's sense of safety was irreparable.

Legacy: The Horror Endures

Nikolai Dzhumagaliev's story remains one of the most disturbing and macabre in the annals of criminal history. His brutal crimes, coupled with his metal teeth and his delusional belief in his divine mission, have ensured that he will be remembered as one of the most infamous serial killers in Soviet history. The fear and terror he instilled in his victims and the community at large continue to resonate, making him a figure of morbid fascination and revulsion.

Dzhumagaliev's case has also served as a grim reminder of the dangers posed by untreated mental illness and the importance of early intervention. His descent into madness was marked by numerous warning signs, many of which were ignored or overlooked by those around him. Had he received proper psychiatric care earlier in life, it is possible that his crimes could have been prevented. This has led to calls for greater awareness of mental health issues and the need for comprehensive support systems to identify and treat individuals at risk of committing violent acts.

In popular culture, Dzhumagaliev has been the subject of numerous books, documentaries, and films, all of which explore the dark and twisted mind of the Metal Fang. His story continues to captivate and horrify audiences, serving as a chilling example of the depths of human depravity and the horrors that can arise when violent impulses go unchecked.

Chapter 37: Keith Jesperson (the Happy Face Killer)

Keith Hunter Jesperson, infamously known as the "Happy Face Killer," is one of the most chilling serial killers in American history. His moniker comes from the smiley faces he would draw on letters sent to the media and law enforcement, taunting them with details of his crimes. Jesperson's killing spree, which spanned from 1990 to 1995, claimed the lives of at least eight women, although he claimed to have murdered more. Unlike many serial killers who seek to avoid detection, Jesperson reveled in the attention his crimes brought him, flaunting his gruesome acts and goading investigators. The story of Keith Jesperson is not just one of brutal murders but also of a deeply disturbed mind that thrived on power, control, and the twisted satisfaction of outsmarting those trying to catch him.

Early Life: The Seeds of Violence

Keith Jesperson was born on April 6, 1955, in British Columbia, Canada, into a troubled and abusive family. He was the middle child of five, with two brothers and two sisters. Jesperson's father, a domineering and often violent man, played a significant role in shaping his son's future path. The young Jesperson was subjected to physical and emotional abuse, which left deep psychological scars. His father was a strict disciplinarian who imposed harsh punishments, often using violence as a means of control. Jesperson's mother, while less overtly abusive, was emotionally distant and failed to provide the nurturing environment he needed.

From a young age, Jesperson exhibited troubling behavior. He was known to be a loner, struggling to make friends and often resorting to violence when he felt slighted or provoked. His social isolation was compounded by his large size; by the time he was in his teens,

Jesperson was already physically imposing, standing over six feet tall. His size made him a target for bullying, but it also gave him the means to defend himself—often with excessive force. Jesperson's early years were marked by feelings of inadequacy, rejection, and a growing sense of anger that he would carry into adulthood.

One of the most disturbing aspects of Jesperson's childhood was his fascination with hurting animals. He engaged in acts of cruelty, such as torturing and killing small animals, which is often a precursor to more violent behavior in later life. These early acts of violence were a clear indication of Jesperson's emerging psychopathy, but they were largely ignored or dismissed by those around him. Instead of receiving help or intervention, Jesperson was left to grapple with his dark impulses on his own, setting the stage for the horrific crimes he would later commit.

Adulthood: A Life of Frustration and Anger

As Keith Jesperson transitioned into adulthood, his life continued to be marked by frustration, disappointment, and a simmering anger that never fully abated. Despite his size and physical strength, Jesperson struggled to find his place in the world. He held various jobs, including working as a truck driver, which allowed him to travel across the United States and Canada. However, he never found stability or satisfaction in his work, often feeling underappreciated and disrespected by his employers and peers.

Jesperson's personal life was equally troubled. He married Rose Hucke in 1975, and the couple had three children together. However, the marriage was far from happy. Jesperson's violent tendencies and inability to control his temper made him a volatile and abusive partner. His wife and children lived in fear of his sudden outbursts, and the marriage eventually ended in divorce in 1990. The dissolution of his marriage only served to deepen Jesperson's sense of failure and resentment, fueling the anger that had been building within him for years.

In the years following his divorce, Jesperson's behavior became increasingly erratic. He began to frequent bars and pick up women, often using his charm and size to intimidate and manipulate them. While he had always harbored violent fantasies, it was during this period that he began to act on them. The combination of his deteriorating mental state, lack of emotional support, and access to potential victims as a long-haul truck driver created the perfect conditions for his transition from fantasizing about violence to committing murder.

The Killing Spree: A Trail of Death Across the Country

Keith Jesperson's killing spree began in January 1990, when he murdered his first known victim, Taunja Bennett. Bennett, a 23-year-old woman with a developmental disability, was lured by Jesperson into his car with the promise of a ride and a good time. Instead, she met a brutal and senseless death at the hands of a man who had long fantasized about killing. Jesperson beat and strangled Bennett, leaving her body in a remote location in Oregon. After the murder, Jesperson returned home, where he watched news reports about the discovery of Bennett's body with a sense of satisfaction and pride in his ability to evade detection.

However, Jesperson's ego soon led him to make a critical mistake. He wanted recognition for his crime, and when the media failed to link him to Bennett's murder, he grew frustrated. In an attempt to draw attention to himself, Jesperson wrote an anonymous letter to a local newspaper, detailing the murder and signing it with a smiley face—a symbol that would become his trademark. This letter, which provided details only the killer would know, caught the attention of law enforcement and the media, but it also inadvertently led to the wrongful conviction of two innocent people, Laverne Pavlinac and John Sosnovske, who falsely confessed to the crime under pressure from the police.

Jesperson's frustration with not being acknowledged as the true killer only deepened his resolve to continue killing. Over the next five years, he would go on to murder at least seven more women, though he later claimed the number was much higher. His victims were typically women he encountered while on the road, often vulnerable individuals such as sex workers or runaways. Jesperson would lure them into his truck or motel rooms, where he would assault, torture, and eventually kill them, usually by strangulation—a method he preferred because it allowed him to feel a sense of power and control over his victims.

After each murder, Jesperson would dispose of the bodies in remote locations, making it difficult for authorities to link the crimes together. Despite the brutality of his actions, Jesperson continued to evade capture, in part due to his transient lifestyle as a truck driver, which allowed him to commit murders in different states without drawing attention to himself. The lack of a clear pattern or geographic focus made it challenging for law enforcement to recognize that they were dealing with a serial killer.

The Happy Face Letters: A Killer's Taunting Game

One of the most disturbing aspects of Keith Jesperson's criminal behavior was his desire for attention and recognition. Unlike many serial killers who go to great lengths to conceal their crimes, Jesperson actively sought out the spotlight, taunting authorities and the media with his "Happy Face" letters. These letters, which he sent to newspapers and law enforcement agencies, were filled with graphic details of his murders, as well as boasts about his ability to evade capture. Each letter was signed with a smiley face, a chilling symbol of the pleasure Jesperson derived from his crimes and the mockery he made of the justice system.

The Happy Face letters were not only a means for Jesperson to brag about his crimes but also a way for him to assert his dominance over his victims, the authorities, and society as a whole. In his twisted mind, the letters were proof of his superiority, as he believed he was smarter than the police and could continue killing without consequence. The smiley face signature became a macabre calling card, a reminder that the man responsible for these heinous acts was still out there, free to strike again.

Jesperson's need for recognition was so strong that he even confessed to murders he did not commit, simply to maintain the attention of the media and law enforcement. In one of his letters, he claimed responsibility for a murder that had been committed by another serial killer, which further complicated the investigation and added to the confusion surrounding his case. This behavior was indicative of Jesperson's deep-seated need for validation and his desire to be seen as a figure of fear and power.

The Downfall: A Slip-Up Leads to Capture

Despite his meticulous efforts to avoid capture, Keith Jesperson's downfall ultimately came about due to a combination of his arrogance and a critical mistake. In March 1995, he murdered his final known victim, 41-year-old Julie Winningham, in Washington state. Winningham was a woman Jesperson had been dating, and unlike his previous victims, she was someone with whom he had developed a personal relationship. After killing her, Jesperson made a fatal error: he left too many clues behind, including a direct link to himself.

Following Winningham's murder, Jesperson was arrested on suspicion of her death. Faced with mounting evidence and the realization that his time was running out, Jesperson began to confess to his other murders. During his interrogation, he provided chilling details about the murders, including the methods he used, the locations of the bodies, and his motivations. Jesperson's confessions were as much about relieving his burden of guilt as they were about continuing to assert control over the narrative of his crimes.

In October 1995, Jesperson pleaded guilty to the murders of Julie Winningham and two other women. He was sentenced to life in prison without the possibility of parole. Over time, Jesperson continued to confess to additional murders, though the exact number of his victims remains unclear. Some believe that there may be more victims who were never identified or linked to him, lost in the vast network of highways and truck stops that he traveled during his killing spree.

Prison Life: The Happy Face Killer Behind Bars

Keith Jesperson's life in prison has been characterized by a mix of notoriety and isolation. Due to the nature of his crimes and the media attention surrounding his case, Jesperson became a well-known figure within the prison system, though he has largely remained solitary, keeping his distance from other inmates. His life behind bars has been marked by the same need for control and attention that defined his life as a free man.

In interviews and letters from prison, Jesperson has continued to exhibit a lack of remorse for his actions, often speaking about his murders with a disturbing detachment. He has shown little regard for the pain and suffering he caused his victims and their families, instead focusing on his own experiences and how he views himself as a misunderstood figure. Jesperson's attempts to portray himself as a victim of circumstances, rather than a cold-blooded killer, have been met with skepticism and revulsion by the public.

Despite his incarceration, Jesperson has not been entirely forgotten by the media and true crime enthusiasts. His case has been the subject of books, documentaries, and television shows, all of which have explored the dark and twisted mind of the Happy Face Killer. Jesperson himself has been known to cooperate with these projects, providing interviews and insights into his life and crimes, further cementing his place in the annals of criminal history.

Legacy: A Name That Lives in Infamy

Keith Jesperson's legacy as the Happy Face Killer is one of horror, fascination, and a reminder of the darkest aspects of human nature. His crimes, characterized by their brutality and the calculated way in which he carried them out, have left an indelible mark on the collective consciousness. The smiley faces he used to sign his letters have become a symbol of the cold, remorseless nature of his killings, and the twisted pleasure he derived from them.

The story of Keith Jesperson is also a cautionary tale about the dangers of ignoring the warning signs of a deeply disturbed individual. From his early acts of animal cruelty to his escalating violence against women, Jesperson exhibited many of the classic indicators of a potential serial killer. Yet, these signs were largely overlooked, allowing him to carry out his murderous rampage unchecked for years. His case highlights the importance of early intervention, mental health support, and the need for society to take seriously the red flags that often precede such horrific acts.

In the end, Keith Jesperson's name will forever be associated with the terror he inflicted on his victims and the families they left behind. His story serves as a grim reminder of the evil that can lurk behind a seemingly ordinary exterior, and the lengths to which some individuals will go to satisfy their darkest desires. The Happy Face Killer may be behind bars, but the fear and fascination he inspired continue to linger, ensuring that his legacy will endure for years to come.

Chapter 38: Dennis Nilsen

Dennis Nilsen, one of Britain's most notorious serial killers, presents a complex and disturbing case that continues to intrigue and horrify the public. Often referred to as the "Kindly Killer" due to his calm demeanor and the apparent care he took in the aftermath of his crimes, Nilsen's actions reveal a deeply troubled individual whose internal struggles manifested in a series of gruesome murders. His case is not only one of the most horrifying in British criminal history but also one of the most psychologically complex, raising questions about the nature of identity, loneliness, and the capacity for evil.

Early Life: Roots of a Troubled Mind

Dennis Andrew Nilsen was born on November 23, 1945, in Fraserburgh, a small fishing town in Scotland. His early life was marked by significant emotional upheaval, which many believe laid the groundwork for his later actions. Nilsen was the middle child in a dysfunctional family. His parents' marriage was fraught with tension, and they divorced when he was just four years old. This separation had a profound impact on Nilsen, leading to a sense of abandonment and a deep-seated fear of rejection.

A key event in Nilsen's early life was the death of his grandfather, Andrew Whyte, who had been a significant figure in his life. Nilsen adored his grandfather, seeing him as a protector and a source of stability in his otherwise chaotic world. When his grandfather died in 1951, Nilsen was devastated. His mother took him to see the body, an experience that had a lasting effect on him. The sight of his grandfather's corpse left Nilsen with a morbid fascination with death, a theme that would later define his criminal behavior.

Nilsen's adolescent years were marked by confusion and internal conflict. He realized that he was homosexual, a fact that caused him considerable distress, particularly given the social attitudes of the time. He struggled with feelings of shame and isolation, which were compounded by his inability to form meaningful relationships. These early experiences of loneliness and rejection would later play a crucial role in his development as a serial killer.

The Army Years: A Mask of Normalcy

In 1961, at the age of 16, Nilsen joined the British Army, where he trained as a cook. The military provided him with a sense of structure and purpose, allowing him to mask the turmoil that was brewing beneath the surface. Nilsen excelled in his role, and his colleagues described him as a competent and reliable soldier. During this time, Nilsen's fascination with death and the macabre continued to grow. He would often dissect animals and experiment with preserving their remains, foreshadowing the gruesome rituals he would later perform on his human victims.

Despite his outward success in the military, Nilsen's internal struggles persisted. He continued to grapple with his sexuality and his inability to connect with others on an emotional level. His relationships with fellow soldiers were marked by a tension between camaraderie and an unfulfilled desire for intimacy. This period of Nilsen's life highlights the duality that would later characterize his criminal behavior: a respectable exterior hiding a deeply disturbed inner world.

Life in London: The Descent into Darkness

After leaving the army in 1972, Nilsen moved to London, where he worked as a police officer for a brief period before taking up a series of civil service jobs. It was during this time that Nilsen's dark impulses began to surface. He frequented gay bars and developed a pattern of bringing men back to his flat, where he would engage in sexual activity with them. However, these encounters left him feeling empty and unfulfilled, exacerbating his sense of loneliness.

Nilsen's descent into murder began in December 1978, when he encountered Stephen Holmes, a 14-year-old boy, at a pub in London. Nilsen invited Holmes back to his flat with the promise of alcohol. The night passed uneventfully, but when morning came, Nilsen was gripped by an overwhelming fear of being abandoned. In a desperate attempt to prevent Holmes from leaving, Nilsen strangled him with a necktie and then drowned him in a bucket of water. This was the beginning of a horrific pattern of behavior that would continue for the next five years.

The Murders: A Gruesome Routine

Nilsen's murders followed a chillingly consistent pattern. He would typically meet his victims in bars or on the street, often targeting vulnerable young men who were down on their luck or struggling with homelessness. After luring them back to his flat, Nilsen would offer them food and alcohol. Once they were unconscious or asleep, he would strangle them, often using a necktie or a piece of rope, and then drown them in a bathtub or sink.

What set Nilsen apart from other serial killers was the macabre ritual he performed after his victims were dead. Nilsen would wash and dress the bodies, sometimes keeping them in his bed for days or even weeks, as if they were his companions. He would engage in conversations with the corpses and perform acts of necrophilia, driven by a twisted need for companionship and control.

As the bodies began to decompose, Nilsen would dismember them and attempt to dispose of the remains in various ways. In his first flat at 195 Melrose Avenue, he would boil the flesh off the bones and flush the remains down the toilet or bury them in his garden. However, when he moved to a second-floor flat at 23 Cranley Gardens in 1981, his options for disposal were limited. He resorted to storing the bodies under the floorboards, a decision that would ultimately lead to his downfall.

The Arrest: The Smell of Death

Nilsen's killing spree came to an end in February 1983, when his attempts to dispose of body parts by flushing them down the toilet led to a blocked drain. Residents of the building at Cranley Gardens complained of the foul smell emanating from the drains, prompting a plumber to investigate. When the plumber discovered what appeared to be flesh and bone fragments, he alerted the police.

The investigation led to Nilsen's arrest on February 9, 1983. When confronted by police at his flat, Nilsen immediately confessed to the murders, stating calmly, "It's a long story, but essentially, I killed them. I have about 15 or 16, take your pick." This chilling admission marked the beginning of a detailed and disturbing confession that would shock the nation.

The Trial: A Portrait of Madness

Nilsen's trial began in October 1983, and it quickly became one of the most sensational legal cases in British history. The prosecution presented overwhelming evidence of Nilsen's guilt, including the grisly remains found in his flat and his own detailed confessions. The defense argued that Nilsen was insane, suffering from a personality disorder that impaired his ability to control his actions.

Psychiatrists offered conflicting opinions on Nilsen's mental state, with some diagnosing him with a form of schizophrenia or borderline personality disorder, while others argued that he was fully aware of his actions and their consequences. Nilsen himself seemed to vacillate between regret and detachment, at times expressing remorse for his crimes, while at other times appearing disturbingly indifferent.

In the end, the jury found Nilsen guilty of six counts of murder and two counts of attempted murder. He was sentenced to life imprisonment, with the judge recommending that he never be released. The case left a lasting impact on the British public, raising difficult questions about the nature of evil and the potential for darkness within the human soul.

Life in Prison: Reflections of a Killer

Dennis Nilsen spent the remainder of his life in prison, where he continued to be a figure of both fascination and revulsion. He maintained a sense of detachment from his crimes, often referring to his victims as "shadows" or "specters" rather than real people. Nilsen spent much of his time writing, producing a lengthy autobiography titled "The History of a Drowning Boy," which provides a chilling insight into his twisted mind.

Nilsen's writings reveal a man who was deeply conflicted, struggling to understand his own actions and the impulses that drove him to kill. He described his murders as acts of "compassion" and "love," claiming that he was attempting to preserve the lives of his victims by keeping them with him in death. This disturbing rationale highlights the profound psychological disturbances that characterized Nilsen's personality.

Despite his attempts to rationalize his actions, Nilsen remained an isolated figure in prison. He had few visitors and was largely shunned by other inmates. In 2018, Nilsen died in prison from natural causes at the age of 72, bringing an end to one of the most horrifying chapters in British criminal history.

The Legacy: A Case that Haunts the Nation

The case of Dennis Nilsen continues to haunt the collective memory of Britain, serving as a stark reminder of the potential for evil that can lurk beneath a seemingly ordinary exterior. Nilsen's crimes were not only shocking in their brutality but also in the methodical and detached manner in which they were carried out.

Nilsen's legacy is one of horror and revulsion, but it also raises important questions about the nature of criminal behavior and the factors that can drive an individual to commit such heinous acts. His case has been the subject of numerous books, documentaries, and television dramas, each attempting to make sense of the senseless and to understand the mind of a killer who defied all conventional understanding of morality and humanity.

The Psychological Profile: Understanding Nilsen's Mind

Dennis Nilsen's psychological profile is one of the most complex and disturbing in the annals of criminal history. His actions suggest a deep-seated need for control, intimacy, and a pathological fear of abandonment. These needs were so powerful that they drove him to commit acts of unspeakable horror in a twisted attempt to fulfill them.

Nilsen's fascination with death and his need to preserve his victims' bodies reveal a profound inability to form healthy relationships. His murders were not driven by a desire for power in the traditional sense but by a desperate need to keep his victims close, even after death. This desire manifested in his ritualistic behavior, such as bathing and dressing the bodies, which can be seen as an attempt to create a perverse form of companionship.

Psychiatrists who studied Nilsen's case have suggested that he may have suffered from several psychological disorders, including borderline personality disorder and schizoid personality disorder. These conditions are characterized by a lack of empathy, emotional detachment, and a distorted sense of reality. Nilsen's actions, including his necrophilic tendencies, indicate a profound disconnection from societal norms and a disturbed understanding of life and death.

Moreover, Nilsen's deep-seated fear of abandonment and his inability to cope with rejection played a critical role in his crimes. His killings were not impulsive but carefully planned and executed, reflecting a cold and calculating mind. This combination of emotional neediness and calculated brutality made Nilsen a particularly dangerous and unpredictable individual.

The Aftermath: Impact on Society and Law Enforcement

The discovery of Dennis Nilsen's crimes had a significant impact on British society and law enforcement. The case exposed vulnerabilities in how the police handled missing persons cases, particularly among marginalized communities such as homeless individuals and the LGBTQ+ community. Nilsen's victims were often young men who had fallen through the cracks of society, and the lack of urgency in investigating their disappearances highlighted systemic issues within the police force.

In response to the public outcry following Nilsen's arrest, there were calls for reforms in how police handle cases involving vulnerable individuals. This included the need for better communication between different police departments and a more proactive approach to investigating disappearances, especially when the missing person was known to be living on the fringes of society.

The case also prompted discussions about mental health and the treatment of individuals exhibiting disturbing behavior. While Nilsen's actions were extreme, they highlighted the importance of recognizing and addressing mental health issues before they escalate into violence. The case served as a grim reminder of the potential consequences of untreated psychological disorders and the need for a more compassionate and effective mental health care system.

Cultural Representations: Nilsen in Media and Popular Culture

The story of Dennis Nilsen has been retold in various forms of media, from documentaries to dramatizations, each attempting to delve into the mind of one of Britain's most infamous killers. One of the most notable portrayals was the 2020 television series "Des," starring David Tennant as Nilsen. The series focused on Nilsen's arrest and the subsequent police investigation, offering a chilling insight into his character and the horrifying nature of his crimes.

Books and documentaries about Nilsen often explore not just the gruesome details of his murders, but also the psychological factors that drove him to kill. These works aim to provide a deeper understanding of the man behind the crimes, exploring themes of loneliness, identity, and the dark side of human nature.

Nilsen's case has also been a subject of academic study, with criminologists and psychologists analyzing his behavior to better understand the motivations of serial killers. His methodical approach, combined with his apparent lack of remorse, makes him a particularly intriguing case for those studying criminal psychology.

Chapter 39: William Bonin (the Freeway Killer)

William George Bonin, infamously known as the "Freeway Killer," was a notorious American serial killer and sex offender whose brutal crimes shocked the nation in the late 1970s and early 1980s. Bonin was responsible for the abduction, rape, torture, and murder of at least 21 young boys and men across Southern California, though the actual number of his victims could be higher. His moniker, the "Freeway Killer," was derived from his method of disposing of his victims' bodies along freeways, making his crimes particularly difficult to trace. Bonin's reign of terror not only highlighted the dangers lurking in seemingly mundane places but also exposed the systemic failures of law enforcement and the criminal justice system in preventing the recurrence of such horrific acts. His case remains one of the most chilling examples of a sadistic serial killer whose monstrous actions left an indelible scar on the collective memory of the public.

Early Life: The Birth of a Monster

William Bonin was born on January 8, 1947, in Willimantic, Connecticut. His childhood was marked by extreme dysfunction and abuse, factors that would later contribute to the formation of his sadistic tendencies. Bonin was the second of three brothers, and the family environment was one of neglect, violence, and substance abuse. His father, Robert Bonin, was a compulsive gambler and alcoholic, often physically abusive towards his wife, Alice, and their children. His mother, overwhelmed by the chaos and instability in the household, was unable to provide the care and support her children desperately needed.

At a young age, Bonin was placed in the care of his maternal grandfather, a man who would subject him to repeated sexual abuse. This trauma would have a profound impact on Bonin, warping his perception of sex and violence. The abuse he endured in his formative years sowed the seeds of a deep-seated rage and a twisted understanding of power and control, elements that would later manifest in his horrific crimes.

By the time Bonin was a teenager, his behavior had become increasingly erratic and violent. He exhibited signs of early psychopathy, such as cruelty to animals and a lack of empathy towards others. In an attempt to mitigate his troubling behavior, Bonin's mother placed him in a juvenile detention center, where he was further subjected to abuse by older boys. This experience only deepened his anger and resentment, reinforcing his belief that violence was a means to assert dominance and control over others.

Military Service and Early Crimes: The Prelude to Atrocity

In 1965, at the age of 18, William Bonin enlisted in the United States Air Force. His time in the military was relatively uneventful on the surface, but it was during this period that Bonin's dark urges began to take shape. Stationed in Vietnam, Bonin served as an aerial gunner, a role that required him to participate in air raids and combat missions. The exposure to death and destruction in the war zone desensitized him to violence, further eroding any remnants of empathy he might have had.

While in the Air Force, Bonin was also known to engage in deviant sexual behavior, including the sexual assault of fellow servicemen. These incidents were largely covered up or ignored by military authorities, allowing Bonin to continue his predatory behavior unchecked. After being honorably discharged in 1968, Bonin returned to civilian life, but his violent tendencies and sexual sadism had been deeply ingrained.

Upon his return to the United States, Bonin's criminal behavior escalated. He was arrested in 1969 for the sexual assault of five young boys in California. The details of his crimes were horrifying: Bonin would lure his victims into his vehicle, often under the guise of offering them a ride or a gift. Once inside, the boys were bound, gagged, and sexually assaulted. Despite the severity of these offenses, Bonin was sentenced to just four years in prison, a sentence that would prove to be grossly inadequate given the nature of his crimes.

While incarcerated, Bonin underwent a psychiatric evaluation that revealed he had an "undetermined sexual preference" and "antisocial personality disorder." However, these findings did little to prevent his release, and in 1974, Bonin was paroled, having served only half of his sentence. His release marked the beginning of a series of violent assaults that would culminate in a killing spree of unprecedented brutality.

The Killing Spree: A Reign of Terror on California's Freeways

Between 1979 and 1980, William Bonin embarked on a gruesome killing spree that left at least 21 young boys and men dead, although it is believed that the actual number of victims could be higher. Bonin's modus operandi was terrifyingly consistent: he would cruise the highways and freeways of Southern California, searching for hitchhikers, runaways, or boys who were simply walking alone. Once he had selected his victim, Bonin would offer them a ride, often luring them into his van with promises of drugs, alcohol, or money.

Once the victim was inside the van, the true horror began. Bonin, sometimes with the assistance of one of his accomplices, would overpower the victim, binding their hands and feet with cords or rope. The victims were then subjected to prolonged and brutal sexual assaults, often accompanied by torture. Bonin derived pleasure from inflicting pain and suffering, using various methods to humiliate and degrade his victims. He would gag them to muffle their screams and would sometimes insert foreign objects into their bodies as a form of further torment.

The murders themselves were equally brutal. Bonin would strangle his victims with their own t-shirts, ropes, or ligatures, watching as they struggled for breath. In some cases, he would use a tire iron or a blunt object to bludgeon them to death. The final act of violence often involved mutilating the victim's body, either before or after death, as a means of further asserting his dominance. After the murders, Bonin would dispose of the bodies by dumping them along freeways, often in remote or isolated areas where they would not be immediately discovered.

Bonin's killing spree was characterized by a chilling lack of remorse or fear of being caught. He seemed to revel in the media coverage of the "Freeway Killer," even going so far as to boast about his crimes to his accomplices. Bonin's sense of invincibility was fueled by the fact that law enforcement was struggling to connect the murders, which occurred across multiple jurisdictions and involved victims from different backgrounds. The randomness of his attacks and the lack of a clear pattern made it difficult for police to develop a profile or predict his next move.

Accomplices: A Web of Depravity

William Bonin did not act alone in his horrific crimes. Over the course of his killing spree, he enlisted the help of several accomplices, each of whom played a role in the abduction, assault, and murder of his victims. These accomplices included Vernon Butts, a factory worker and part-time magician; Gregory Miley, a teenage drifter;

and James Munro, a young man who Bonin had befriended shortly before his arrest.

Vernon Butts was the most involved of Bonin's accomplices, participating in at least nine of the murders. Butts shared Bonin's sadistic tendencies, and the two would often work together to subdue and torture their victims. Butts would later claim that he was fascinated by death and saw the murders as a way to explore his own morbid curiosities. Gregory Miley, though less involved, also participated in several of the killings, helping Bonin to restrain and assault the victims. Miley later testified that Bonin had a "special way" of killing, describing how Bonin derived pleasure from the act of strangulation.

James Munro was the last of Bonin's accomplices, and his involvement came towards the end of the killing spree. Munro had initially moved in with Bonin as a way to escape his troubled home life, but he soon found himself drawn into the horrific world of Bonin's crimes. Munro would later claim that he was manipulated and coerced by Bonin, who had a dominant and controlling personality. However, Munro's participation in at least one of the murders suggests that he was not entirely a passive bystander.

The presence of accomplices in Bonin's crimes is a chilling reminder of the power of manipulation and the ways in which individuals can be drawn into acts of extreme violence. While Bonin was undoubtedly the mastermind behind the murders, his ability to enlist others in his crimes speaks to his charismatic and persuasive nature. Each of these men played a role in the horrific events that unfolded, and their involvement only adds to the sense of horror surrounding the case.

Capture and Trial: The End of the Freeway Killer

William Bonin's reign of terror came to an end on June 11, 1980, when he was arrested by police in Downey, California. His capture was the result of a combination of luck, persistence by law enforcement, and a tip-off from a former acquaintance. The breakthrough in the case came when police received information that Bonin had been seen driving his van near the location where one of the victims had been abducted. Surveillance was set up, and Bonin was eventually caught in the act of assaulting a young boy in his van, a crime that would have likely ended in murder had the police not intervened.

Upon his arrest, Bonin showed little emotion, offering no resistance as he was taken into custody. The evidence against him was overwhelming: inside his van, police found ropes, knives, and other tools of torture, along with bloodstains and fibers that matched those found on the victims. A search of Bonin's home yielded further damning evidence, including personal items belonging to some of the victims, photographs, and a collection of newspaper clippings about the murders. Bonin's demeanor during his arrest and subsequent interrogation was disturbingly calm and cooperative. He confessed to the murders in great detail, providing investigators with a chilling account of his crimes. Bonin showed no remorse as he described how he had abducted, tortured, and killed his victims, often speaking about the murders as if they were mundane events.

The trial of William Bonin was a sensational event, drawing widespread media attention and public outrage. The gruesome nature of his crimes, combined with the sheer number of victims, made him one of the most reviled figures in the history of American criminal justice. The prosecution presented overwhelming evidence against Bonin, including his confessions, the testimony of his accomplices, and forensic evidence linking him to the murders.

Bonin was charged with 14 counts of murder, along with multiple counts of sexual assault and kidnapping. During the trial, his defense attempted to argue that Bonin was mentally ill and incapable of controlling his actions. However, the jury was not swayed by this argument, given the calculated and methodical nature of his crimes. Bonin's own testimony, in which he coldly recounted the details of the murders, only served to reinforce the image of him as a sadistic and unrepentant killer.

In 1982, William Bonin was convicted of 10 of the murders and sentenced to death. In a separate trial, he was convicted of four additional murders and received a second death sentence. His accomplices, Vernon Butts, Gregory Miley, and James Munro, were also convicted for their roles in the crimes, with Butts committing suicide in his jail cell before he could be sentenced, Miley receiving a sentence of 25 years to life, and Munro receiving a lighter sentence in exchange for testifying against Bonin.

Bonin's time on death row was marked by a series of appeals, but his conviction and sentence were upheld at every level. He remained defiant throughout, never expressing remorse for his actions. Bonin's final appeal was denied in 1996, and he was executed by lethal injection at San Quentin State Prison on February 23, 1996. He was the first person to be executed by lethal injection in California, and his death marked the end of one of the most horrific chapters in the state's history.

Legacy: The Impact of the Freeway Killer

The case of William Bonin, the "Freeway Killer," left a lasting impact on the public, law enforcement, and the criminal justice system. His crimes exposed significant flaws in the way serial killers were tracked and apprehended, particularly in cases where victims were spread across multiple jurisdictions. The randomness of Bonin's attacks, coupled with the lack of communication between different police departments, allowed him to continue his killing spree for an extended period. In the wake of his crimes, there was a greater emphasis on cooperation and information sharing between law enforcement agencies, a practice that has since become standard in the investigation of serial crimes.

Bonin's case also highlighted the dangers faced by vulnerable populations, particularly young boys and teenagers who were often overlooked by society. Many of Bonin's victims were runaways or hitchhikers, individuals who were already at risk due to their precarious living situations. His ability to prey on these young men without detection for so long underscored the need for better protection and support systems for at-risk youth.

The brutality and callousness of Bonin's crimes also sparked a renewed public debate about the death penalty and the appropriate punishment for those who commit heinous acts. Bonin's execution was seen by many as a just and necessary conclusion to his horrific crimes, while others questioned whether the death penalty was the right response to such extreme cases of criminal behavior. The debate over capital punishment continues to this day, with Bonin's case often cited as an example of the kind of offender for whom the death penalty is considered appropriate.

In the broader context of criminal psychology and the study of serial killers, William Bonin's case provides a stark example of how childhood abuse, neglect, and early exposure to violence can contribute to the development of a sadistic personality. Bonin's life and crimes have been the subject of numerous studies, books, and documentaries, all seeking to understand the factors that led him to commit such unimaginable acts of violence. His case remains a cautionary tale about the potential consequences of untreated trauma and the importance of early intervention in the lives of those who exhibit signs of severe psychological disturbance.

Chapter 40: Jack the Ripper

Jack the Ripper remains one of the most infamous and mysterious figures in the annals of criminal history. Operating in the East End of London in 1888, this unidentified serial killer is believed to have been responsible for the brutal murders of at least five women, all of whom were prostitutes. The killer's gruesome methods, his taunting letters to the police, and the inability of law enforcement to capture him have cemented Jack the Ripper as a figure of enduring fascination and terror. Despite numerous investigations, theories, and suspects over the years, the true identity of Jack the Ripper has never been conclusively determined, making this case one of the greatest unsolved mysteries in history.

Historical Context: Victorian London and the East End

To understand the impact and terror that Jack the Ripper's crimes wrought, it's essential to comprehend the social and economic context of London during the late 19th century. Victorian London was a city of stark contrasts. While the West End of London was home to the wealthy and powerful, the East End, where Jack the Ripper committed his murders, was notorious for its poverty, overcrowding, and crime.

The East End was a maze of narrow, dark alleyways and dilapidated housing, where the working class and destitute lived in squalor. The area was rife with unemployment, homelessness, and disease. Many women in the East End turned to prostitution as a means of survival, making them particularly vulnerable to violence and exploitation. The social conditions in the East End created an environment where crime could thrive, and where the lives of its inhabitants were often viewed as expendable by the more affluent parts of the city.

The police force, still in its relative infancy, was overwhelmed by the crime and social unrest in the area. Law enforcement was not equipped to handle the complex and brutal nature of Jack the Ripper's crimes, which were unlike anything the city had seen before. The newspapers of the time, which were growing in influence, sensationalized the murders, feeding public fear and fascination. This combination of poverty, crime, and media attention created a perfect storm in which the legend of Jack the Ripper could take hold.

The Canonical Five: Victims of Jack the Ripper

The five victims most commonly attributed to Jack the Ripper are Mary Ann Nichols, Annie Chapman, Elizabeth Stride, Catherine Eddowes, and Mary Jane Kelly. These women, known as the "Canonical Five," were all murdered within a three-month period in 1888, and their deaths share several similarities that have led investigators to believe they were all killed by the same person. However, it is worth noting that some experts believe Jack the Ripper may have had additional victims, or that not all of the Canonical Five were necessarily killed by the same individual.

- **Mary Ann Nichols**

The first of the Canonical Five, Mary Ann "Polly" Nichols, was discovered in the early hours of August 31, 1888, in Buck's Row, Whitechapel. Nichols was a 43-year-old prostitute who had fallen on hard times. Her body was found with her throat slashed deeply from left to right, and she had multiple stab wounds to her abdomen. The brutality of the attack shocked the local community, but it was only the beginning of a series of murders that would escalate in savagery.

- **Annie Chapman**

Annie Chapman, the second victim, was found on September 8, 1888, in the backyard of 29 Hanbury Street, Spitalfields. Like Nichols, Chapman was a middle-aged woman who struggled with poverty and alcoholism, and she also resorted to prostitution. Her throat had been slashed, and her abdomen had been cut open, with several internal organs removed. The level of precision and mutilation suggested that the killer had some anatomical knowledge, leading some to speculate that Jack the Ripper might have been a doctor or butcher. The ferocity of the attack and the removal of organs marked a significant escalation in the killer's methods.

- **Elizabeth Stride**

Elizabeth Stride, the third victim, was found on the night of September 30, 1888, in Dutfield's Yard, off Berner Street. Unlike the other victims, Stride's body had only one significant wound: her throat had been cut. There were no abdominal mutilations, leading some to believe that the killer may have been interrupted before he could complete his work. Stride's death is sometimes debated among Ripperologists (those who study Jack the Ripper), with some arguing that her murder may not have been committed by the same person who killed the other women. However, the timing and location of her death place her squarely within the sequence of Ripper killings.

- **Catherine Eddowes**

On the same night as Elizabeth Stride's murder, just a short distance away in Mitre Square, the body of Catherine Eddowes was discovered. Eddowes' murder is considered one of the most brutal of the Ripper's crimes. Her throat had been slashed, and her abdomen was extensively mutilated, with her intestines pulled out and draped over her shoulder. Several of her internal organs, including her kidney and part of her uterus, were removed and taken by the killer.

Eddowes' face was also mutilated, with cuts and slashes that disfigured her features. The precision and ferocity of the attack further fueled speculation that the killer had medical knowledge.

- **Mary Jane Kelly**

The final and most gruesome murder attributed to Jack the Ripper was that of Mary Jane Kelly, a 25-year-old prostitute. Kelly was found on November 9, 1888, in her small room at Miller's Court. Unlike the other victims, who were all killed outdoors, Kelly was murdered in the privacy of her own room, which allowed the killer to take his time and inflict horrific injuries. Kelly's body was mutilated beyond recognition; her throat was cut down to the spine, and her abdomen was eviscerated, with many of her organs removed and placed around the room. Her face was so severely mutilated that it was almost unrecognizable. The level of violence and the complete destruction of Kelly's body suggested that the killer was escalating in his brutality, perhaps driven by a deepening psychosis.

The Investigation: A Desperate Hunt for a Phantom

The investigation into the murders attributed to Jack the Ripper was one of the most extensive and high-profile manhunts in British history. The Metropolitan Police, led by Inspector Frederick Abberline, faced immense pressure from both the public and the media to catch the killer. The East End was gripped by fear, and the failure to apprehend the murderer led to widespread criticism of the police.

One of the main challenges facing the investigators was the lack of forensic technology available at the time. Fingerprinting had not yet been introduced, and DNA analysis was over a century away. The police relied on witness statements, physical evidence at the crime scenes, and what little they could infer from the nature of the injuries. The chaotic and crowded environment of Whitechapel made it difficult to gather reliable evidence, and the transient population meant that witnesses were often hard to track down.

The police received numerous letters from individuals claiming to be the killer, but most of these were dismissed as hoaxes. However, a few letters stood out, particularly the one signed "Jack the Ripper," which gave the killer his infamous name. This letter, along with the "From Hell" letter received by George Lusk, the head of the Whitechapel Vigilance Committee, suggested a taunting, almost playful relationship between the killer and the authorities. The "From Hell" letter was accompanied by a small box containing half of a human kidney, which some believed was taken from Catherine Eddowes.

The lack of progress in the investigation led to growing frustration and desperation. Various suspects were considered, from local butchers and doctors to members of the aristocracy. Among the most famous suspects were Montague John Druitt, a barrister and teacher; Aaron Kosminski, a Polish-born barber-surgeon; and Prince Albert Victor, Duke of Clarence and Avondale, the grandson of Queen Victoria. Despite the scrutiny of these and other suspects, no conclusive evidence was ever found to definitively identify Jack the Ripper.

Theories and Suspects: The Endless Search for the Ripper's Identity

Over the years, countless theories have been proposed regarding the identity of Jack the Ripper, ranging from the plausible to the fantastical. The most enduring theories focus on individuals who had the means, motive, and opportunity to commit the murders, but none have been conclusively proven.

- **Montague John Druitt**

Montague John Druitt was a barrister and schoolteacher who was considered a suspect largely because of his sudden death shortly after the final Ripper murder. Druitt's body was found in the River Thames in December 1888, and it was determined that he had committed suicide. Some theorists suggest that Druitt's suicide was driven by guilt over the murders, but there is little evidence to support this claim. Druitt came from a respectable family, and his mental health had reportedly been deteriorating before his death, leading some to believe that he may have been suffering from a severe psychological disorder that could have driven him to commit the crimes.

- **Aaron Kosminski**

Aaron Kosminski, a Polish immigrant who worked as a barber in Whitechapel, is another frequently mentioned suspect. Kosminski was known to have a history of mental illness and was committed to an asylum in 1891. He reportedly had a deep-seated hatred of women, particularly prostitutes, which some theorists believe could have motivated the Ripper murders. Kosminski's proximity to the crime scenes and his erratic behavior have led some to argue that he is a likely candidate, but like Druitt, there is no definitive evidence linking him to the murders.

- **Prince Albert Victor**

Prince Albert Victor, Duke of Clarence and Avondale, was the grandson of Queen Victoria and second in line to the British throne. The theory that Prince Albert Victor, also known as "Eddy," was Jack the Ripper is one of the more sensational and controversial hypotheses. Some theorists have suggested that the prince was either directly involved in the murders or that he was implicated in a cover-up orchestrated by the British royal family and government to protect the monarchy from scandal. This theory often involves elaborate conspiracies, including Freemasons and government officials, but it is widely regarded as speculative and lacking credible evidence. Historians have pointed out that Prince Albert Victor was not in London during some of the murders, further casting doubt on this theory.

- **Dr. Thomas Neill Cream**

Dr. Thomas Neill Cream was a Canadian-born doctor and serial killer known as the "Lambeth Poisoner." He was convicted and executed in 1892 for poisoning several people in London. Some theorists have linked Cream to the Ripper murders, suggesting that he might have been responsible for the killings before switching to poison as his method of murder. However, Cream was imprisoned in the United States during the time of the Ripper murders, making it highly unlikely that he was the killer. Some have speculated that Cream may have committed the murders after his release or that he had an accomplice, but these ideas remain unsubstantiated.

- **Walter Sickert**

Walter Sickert, a well-known British artist, has also been proposed as a suspect in the Ripper case. The theory gained popularity largely due to the work of crime novelist Patricia Cornwell, who argued that Sickert's paintings contained hidden clues linking him to the murders. Cornwell even went so far as to purchase Sickert's paintings and conduct DNA tests on letters purportedly written by the Ripper, claiming to find evidence that linked him to the crimes. However, most experts dismiss this theory, noting that Sickert was not in London during some of the murders and that the supposed clues in his paintings are more likely coincidences or artistic expressions rather than confessions.

- **Francis Tumblety**

Francis Tumblety was an American quack doctor who was in London at the time of the Ripper murders. He was arrested on unrelated charges shortly after the last of the Canonical Five murders and fled to the United States. Some Ripperologists have suggested that Tumblety, who was known for his misogynistic views and his collection of female body parts, could be a viable suspect. However, there is little direct evidence linking him to the murders, and he was never charged with any crime related to the Ripper case.

The Ripper Letters: Taunts and Mysteries

One of the most intriguing aspects of the Jack the Ripper case is the series of letters purportedly sent by the killer to the police and the press. The most famous of these is the "Dear Boss" letter, which was signed "Jack the Ripper" and is believed to be the origin of the name by which the killer is known. In the letter, the writer mockingly describes the murders and hints at future killings. The letter was accompanied by a small box containing part of a human kidney, which some believe was taken from Catherine Eddowes, one of the Ripper's victims.

The authenticity of the Ripper letters has been the subject of much debate. Some experts believe that the letters were hoaxes, written by journalists or pranksters seeking to sensationalize the case. Others argue that the letters contain details that only the killer could have known, making them a possible communication from Jack the Ripper himself. The "From Hell" letter, in particular, has attracted significant attention due to its macabre tone and the accompanying kidney. However, without definitive proof, the true authorship of these letters remains another unsolved aspect of the case.

Cultural Impact: The Legend of Jack the Ripper

Jack the Ripper has transcended his status as a historical criminal to become a cultural icon, representing the embodiment of fear and mystery. His crimes have inspired countless books, films, television shows, and works of art. The Ripper's identity and the nature of his crimes continue to captivate the public imagination, making him a symbol of the unknown and the unknowable.

The Ripper's influence extends beyond entertainment, as his case has also had a lasting impact on criminal psychology and the study of serial killers. Jack the Ripper is often cited as the first modern serial killer, and his crimes have been analyzed by criminologists, psychologists, and historians seeking to understand the motivations and methods of such offenders. The case has contributed to the development of criminal profiling and the study of psychopathology, as experts attempt to piece together the psychological makeup of the Ripper based on his actions.

The enduring fascination with Jack the Ripper has also led to the emergence of "Ripperology," a field of study dedicated to investigating the case and uncovering the identity of the killer. Ripperologists have spent decades poring over evidence, examining old police files, and proposing new suspects. Despite the lack of definitive answers, the quest to solve the mystery of Jack the Ripper continues to this day, with new theories and discoveries keeping the case alive in the public consciousness.

The Legacy of Jack the Ripper: Fear, Fascination, and the Search for Answers

The legacy of Jack the Ripper is a complex and multifaceted one. On one hand, he is a symbol of the darkest aspects of human nature, a figure who embodies the fear of the unknown and the terror of random, senseless violence. The Ripper's crimes were brutal and horrifying, leaving a lasting impact on the victims' families, the community of Whitechapel, and the city of London as a whole.

On the other hand, the Ripper has become a figure of enduring fascination, a puzzle that has captivated generations of investigators, historians, and the general public. The mystery of his identity, the grisly nature of his crimes, and the failure of the authorities to catch him have all contributed to the Ripper's status as a legend. His story serves as a reminder of the limitations of law enforcement, the fragility of human life, and the ways in which society reacts to violence and fear.

Jack the Ripper's place in history is unique, as he remains one of the few serial killers whose identity has never been definitively established. This uncertainty has allowed his story to evolve over time, with each new theory and piece of evidence adding to the mythos surrounding the Ripper. The case continues to be a source of speculation, debate, and intrigue, ensuring that Jack the Ripper will remain an enduring figure in the annals of criminal history.

Epilogue

As we reach the end of our journey through the macabre corridors of history, we are left with more questions than answers. The stories of these infamous psycho killers challenge our understanding of humanity, pushing us to grapple with the uncomfortable truth that such evil can, and has, existed in the world. These are not mere characters from a horror story; they were real people whose actions left indelible marks on society, and whose names have become synonymous with terror.

In exploring the lives and crimes of these individuals, we have ventured into the darkest depths of the human psyche. We have seen how ordinary men and women—neighbors, co-workers, and even loved ones—could hide unimaginable horrors behind a façade of normalcy. Their stories are chilling reminders that the potential for evil exists within us all, and that under certain circumstances, it can manifest in ways that defy belief.

But what have we learned from this exploration? Perhaps it is the fragility of the human mind that stands out the most. Each of these killers, in their own way, reflects the complexities of mental illness, trauma, and the darker aspects of human nature. While their actions are inexcusable, understanding the factors that contributed to their descent into madness can help us prevent such tragedies in the future. By studying their lives, we hope to gain insights into the warning signs, the triggers, and the circumstances that might drive someone to commit unspeakable acts.

Moreover, these profiles remind us of the resilience of the human spirit. For every killer, there were victims—innocent lives lost to senseless violence. And yet, in the wake of these tragedies, communities have come together, determined to remember the victims, honor their memories, and ensure that their stories are not forgotten. The legacy of these killers is not just one of fear and horror, but also of the strength and courage of those who survived and those who sought justice.

As we close this chapter, we are left with a profound sense of both dread and responsibility. The stories of these killers are cautionary tales, urging us to remain vigilant, to seek understanding, and to never forget the darkness that can lurk within the human soul. But they also challenge us to look beyond the fear and horror, to see the humanity in even the most twisted minds, and to strive for a world where such atrocities are not repeated.

Thank you for embarking on this journey. May these stories serve as a reminder of the fragility of life, the importance of empathy, and the enduring need for vigilance in the face of evil.

The End.